THE SCOTS OVERSEAS

By the same author

THE MAKING OF THE SCOTTISH PRAYER BOOK OF 1637
SHETLAND LIFE UNDER EARL PATRICK
SCOTLAND: CHURCH AND NATION THROUGH SIXTEEN CENTURIES
THE SCOTTISH REFORMATION
SCOTLAND: JAMES V TO JAMES VII

A SOURCE BOOK OF SCOTTISH HISTORY (with W. Croft Dickinson)
A SHORT HISTORY OF SCOTLAND (with R. L. Mackie)

THE SCOTS OVERSEAS

Gordon Donaldson

ILLUSTRATED

GREENWOOD PRESS, PUBLISHERS
WESTPORT, CONNECTICUT

063965 \ 069284

Library of Congress Cataloging in Publication Data

Donaldson, Gordon.
   The Scots overseas.

    Reprint of the ed. published by R. Hale, London.
    Bibliography: p.
    Includes index.
    1. Scotch in foreign countries. 2. Scotland--
Emigration and immigration. I. Title.
DA774.5.D6 1976   325'.2411   75-36360
ISBN 0-8371-8625-0

© Gordon Donaldson 1966

All rights reserved

Originally published in 1966 by Robert Hale, London

Reprinted with the permission of Robert Hale & Company

Reprinted in 1976 by Greenwood Press,
a division of Williamhouse-Regency Inc.

Library of Congress Catalog Card Number 75-36360

ISBN 0-8371-8625-0

Printed in the United States of America

CONTENTS

∪63965 1   069284

ILLUSTRATIONS

PREFACE

THE history of the Scottish nation has for many centuries now been something more than the history of the inhabitants of the geographical bounds of a small, poor and remote country. A study of the spectacular outward movement of people from Scotland is part of Scottish history, in the sense that the vitality which stimulated the expansion of the nation arose from conditions within Scotland itself. It is part of Scottish history, too, in so far as the activities of Scots abroad and their relations with their kinsfolk in Scotland have reacted on the life of the homeland. But the story of the Scots overseas is no less a contribution to the history of the United States, the British Dominions and many other parts of the world. The subject is a vast one, which presents an almost inexhaustible field for investigation, and many specialized studies ought to be undertaken.

In writing on a topic which touches on the history of many different lands over a long period, I owe much to many colleagues and others with whom I have had correspondence and conversations on various aspects of life in Scotland and overseas. I owe a special debt to my colleague Mr. John M. Simpson, who read the whole of this book in typescript and made many valuable suggestions. My thanks are due also to Mr. John Imrie, Curator of Historical Records in the Register House, who put at my disposal the information which I have presented in Appendix B. I am grateful, too, to the Scots Ancestry Research Society, which made available the particulars about its work which appear in the final chapter.

G.D.

1

THE SCOTTISH HOMELAND

SCOTLAND, from which colonists have gone out in such large numbers in recent centuries, was itself heavily colonized in earlier times, and indeed for hundreds of years the history of the country was very largely shaped by immigrants. The original Scots, who in the end gave their name to the entire country, themselves came to Scotland as colonists from Ireland, and settled in Argyll in the sixth century. Not much later, the south-eastern part of modern Scotland was invaded by Angles, who had come across the North Sea to what is now England and had given their name to that country. Central and eastern Scotland was inhabited in those days by the Picts, whose origin is obscure, and south-western Scotland was occupied by a branch of the Britons, the people who had held all of central and southern Britain before Angles and Saxons arrived there. From about the eighth century to the tenth, other invaders came across the North Sea to the shores of Scotland—the Norsemen or Scandinavians. Besides raiding all round the coasts, they settled in strength in the north, where their race and language prevailed in Caithness, Orkney and Shetland, and they left traces of their occupation all down the west coast to the Solway Firth and down the east coast at least as far as the Moray Firth. The next colonists came from the south. The Normans, who had established their rule over England by force under William the Conqueror, infiltrated into Scotland as well. Normans, or Anglo-Normans, were brought in by Scottish kings to fill high offices in Church and State, they received substantial grants of land and they impressed on Scotland the institutions which had already been established in Norman England. Many familiar surnames now thought of as characteristically Scottish, like Bruce, Cumming, Fraser, Hay, Oliphant, Somerville, Stewart, are in fact a legacy of the 'Norman Conquest' of Scotland.

In consequence of these many immigrations over several centuries, there had come to be a variety of races in Scotland. But the manifold differences gradually merged into a twofold division between Celtic and Teutonic. The Celtic peoples were the Scots, the Picts and the Britons, the Teutonic peoples were the Angles, the Scandinavians and the Anglo-Normans. Languages which had been spoken by some of the peoples—the Pictish tongue, the Welsh of the Britons, the French of the Normans and the Norse of the Scandinavians—in time died out, leaving as the only rivals the Gaelic introduced by the Scots and the northern English, introduced by the Angles, which became lowland Scots. The Teutons and their English speech were the more expansive and aggressive, and by the later Middle Ages all the southern and eastern parts of the country had become Teutonic, in language if not in race, while the Gaelic-speaking Celts were confined to the centre and west.

The racial and linguistic division thus came to coincide with the principal geographical division into 'Highlands' and 'Lowlands'. But this division requires definition, for it is less simple than is often believed. The Lowlands are not confined to the south of the country, but extend almost the whole length of the east coast and include the three northern counties of Caithness, Orkney and Shetland. An eastern coastal plain begins in Caithness and stretches down from there along nearly the whole of the east coast, extending various distances inland and finally crossing the full breadth of the country from the Firth of Forth to the Firth of Clyde. The southern uplands, that is the hills between the Forth-Clyde line and the Border, while not 'lowland' in a physical sense, are racially and linguistically part of the Lowlands. Thus the Lowlands, properly understood, include most of Caithness, parts of Easter Ross, the south side of the Moray Firth and the eastern coastal plain from Aberdeenshire south, as well as all the country south of the Forth-Clyde isthmus. The Highlands, which therefore lie to the west, rather than to the north, of the Lowlands, include the mountainous centre of Scotland, the entire west coast down to Kintyre, and also the western isles.

Broadly speaking, these two great divisions of Scotland represented two different ways of life—a mainly pastoral economy, based on herds of cattle, in the more barren Highlands, and a largely arable type of farming in the more fertile Lowlands. Because of this difference, nearly all the medieval burghs, religious houses, royal castles and cathedrals were established in the Lowlands, and later it was in the Lowlands that various industries principally developed. Everything conspired to contribute to the differentiation of Highlander from Lowlander, and the differences in race and language were only two of the many features which helped to keep them apart. Geographical differences were such as to encourage differences of outlook. From the east coast the Lowlander saw an open horizon, beckoning him to maritime enterprise on waters which were Scotland's ready-made highway to continental countries. On the west coast, the sea runs far in among the roots of the mountains, but even on the outer shores of the west mainland the prospect is not of a horizon but of island upon island, and until the very end of the Middle Ages no one was conscious that the western ocean led to faraway lands. The climate is equally contrasted. The eastern and lowland areas are in general fairly dry, with much cool weather and with bracing—or some might call them harsh—winds, fostering a race of men who are, in their own word, somewhat dour, but enterprising and energetic. The centre and west are quite different. Though inland and high-lying areas have severe winters, the west coast has in general mild conditions, usually kinder to both plant life and cattle than those of the east, but western Scotland is one of the world's wet regions, and much of the rain falls in the autumn. In Skye in 1934 the three months of August, September and October together produced only six rainless days, with difficulties in harvesting which may be imagined. The enduring impression made on anyone who has lived in the West Highlands is, however, not so much of mere rain as of furious storms. In almost any month, winds of near hurricane strength can lash the country with torrential rain; and from the coasts they carry over the land salt spray which blasts all plant life and can even kill trees. 'Under such skies,' Dr. Johnson remarked, 'can be expected no great exuberance of vegetation. Their winter overtakes their summer, and their harvest lies upon the ground drenched with rain.' Few activities are more dispiriting than farming under such conditions, and climatic adversity is such that it is apt to breed apathy. Besides, the number of days when the weather makes outdoor work of any kind impossible is so great that the inhabitants have gained a reputation for indolence which is not wholly undeserved.

Conditions all over Scotland were such that a competence could not be gained except by a good deal of hard work, and those who responded to the challenge necessarily became tough and industrious. In the pre-industrial age—until, that is, the eighteenth century—the predominant pattern was of a subsistence agriculture. The overwhelming majority of the people of Scotland worked on the land, from which they obtained their food and drink, wool for their clothing and peat for their fuel. Even the inhabitants of the burghs were themselves smallholders, with their cattle and their strips of arable land. In such an economy, essentially rural, the population was distributed mainly according to the fertility of the soil, and owed little to other natural resources such as minerals. This meant that the inhabitants were spread more evenly than they are in the industrial world of today, and fertile pockets like the Solway shores, the Tweed valley, the 'Laigh' or coastal plain of Moray and the Black Isle in Easter Ross, held far more people, relatively to the whole, than they do now.

Agrarian pursuits, supplemented by a few crafts and a little trade, sufficed to sustain a population which grew only slowly throughout the Middle Ages and was still little more than a million in 1700. Already in the later seventeenth century, however, there were signs that population might press on subsistence, if only because the visitations of the plague, which in earlier times had periodically caused large numbers of deaths, had now ceased. In later generations other scourges were overcome—smallpox at the end of the eighteenth century, 'fevers' in the nineteenth, tuberculosis in the twentieth— with a great reduction in infant mortality and an increased expectation of life. By the second quarter of the twentieth century the population topped the five million mark. As an industrial economy developed, from the eighteenth century onwards, it provided employment for growing numbers of people, but all along there was an excess of population which could not be absorbed in a country with limited resources, and, in a remarkable process of the expansion of a people, hundreds of thousands of Scots left their homeland.

The many people who inhabited early Scotland at first formed distinct political units, but they were gradually brought under the rule of a single king. The Picts and the Scots were united in 844 in the kingdom of Alba, or Scotland north of the Forth and Clyde; and in or about 1018 the kings of Alba established their control over the country between those rivers and the present border, by conquering Lothian and effecting a dynastic union with the British kingdom of the south-west. In 1266 the western isles were ceded by Norway to the king of Scots, and in 1468–9 Orkney and Shetland too came under Scottish rule. Since that time the frontiers of the Scottish state have remained unchanged, but the frontiers of the Scottish nation have expanded to the ends of the earth.

Long after the peoples were united under one sovereign, the geographical configuration of the country still presented so many obstacles to communications that until a relatively late date the central government was weak and administration was not adequate to preserve order and to make unity effective. It was not until the reign of James VI (1567–1625) that control was established over the Borders and the Highlands and criminal justice became generally effective. There were, however, strong local loyalties, arising partly from the fact that even in the Lowlands one fertile and populous area was often separated from another. Thus the Tweed valley was cut off by bleak hills from Edinburgh and its hinterland, Angus and Mearns were almost severed from Aberdeenshire where the mountains thrust eastwards to the sea; on the other hand, when communications were easier by water than by land, the Lothian and Fife shores of the Firth of Forth formed one community and the north and south sides of the Firth of Tay another.

Besides, there were elements in Scottish society which often strengthened local loyalties and which gave cohesion of a kind which the government did not give. Pre-eminent among them was a tie which can broadly be described as one of kinship, though it is not easy to define it with precision. Throughout lowland Scotland, in the later Middle Ages and down to the sixteenth century at least, a great family and its dependents formed a social unit and tended all to move in unison in political activities as well. A noble like the Earl of Arran, shall we say, was head of the house of Hamilton. He was regarded as a leader by his own immediate kinsmen, by collateral branches of the house descended from a common ancestor, by numerous lairds or small landowners bearing the name of Hamilton and by a multitude of men of humble rank who also had the Hamilton surname but whose blood relationship to the Earl of Arran was, at best, not demonstrable. These men all constituted the 'Hamilton name'. But even they did not constitute the whole of the Earl of Arran's following. Other men of middle and low degree, with surnames other than Hamilton, were linked to the Hamilton connection by a tradition of hereditary service to some Hamilton laird, by tenancies on Hamilton estates which might go on from generation to generation, or by 'bonds' whereby they undertook to render service in return for protection. All those persons formed the 'Hamilton interest'. Comparable to the Hamiltons were the Douglases under the Earl of Angus, the Hepburns under the Earl of Bothwell, the Gordons under the Earl of Huntly, the Kennedies under the Earl of Cassillis, and a great many more. Thus most lowland Scots, at least outside the larger burghs, were accustomed to look to a great man for leadership.

By the seventeenth century, these ties were weakening in lowland Scotland and they soon disappeared, partly because of the extension throughout the country of centralized machinery for the maintenance of law and order and partly because of the economic changes which, a little later, led to the movement of so many people from the countryside into the towns. In the Highlands, however, a social structure based on the 'clan' persisted longer than anything of the kind lasted in the Lowlands. No one has yet explained the origin and the precise nature of highland clans. They certainly did not consist, as is so often supposed today, of people all bearing the same surname. And it is impossible that they could have, for the very good reason that until the seventeenth century few Highlanders had surnames at all. A clan consisted of men bearing a great variety of names. But the concept of accepting the leadership of a chief persisted in the Highlands until well into the eighteenth century. It was probably fostered not only by the physical obstacles which prevented the normal system of law and order from spreading through the Highlands, but also by the physical obstacles within the Highlands themselves, especially the mountains which cut off one glen from another and tended to make the people of each glen an exclusive, self-sufficient community.

In view of the deep-rooted differences between Highlands and Lowlands, and, on the other hand, the affinity in race and language between lowland Scots and the people of England, it is remarkable that an independent Scottish state, separate from England and with a frontier at the Tweed and the Solway, ever emerged at all. Lowland Scotland was, indeed, again and again the channel through which English ideas, culture and institutions, penetrated into Scotland, and for a time, in the thirteenth century, it seemed not unlikely that Scotland might lose its identity altogether. Skilful and statesmanlike tactics on the part of English kings might then have brought about a peaceful union. But Edward I's attempt at armed conquest provoked the Scots to resistance, at first unsuccessfully under William Wallace, then successfully under Robert Bruce, and initiated a war which went on intermittently for almost three hundred years. Already before the war had started, the Scots had shown themselves sufficiently conscious of their nationality, and early in the course of the struggle itself they announced that 'As long as a hundred of us remain alive we will never be subject to the English king; because it is not for riches, or honours or glory that we fight, but for liberty alone, which no worthy man loses save with his life'. The independence of the country and the integrity of the nation found expression in loyalty to the monarchy, which symbolized the state and which gave cohesion to the whole country, Highlands and Lowlands alike. During the long war between England and Scotland, the two peoples became conditioned to enmity, the Scots became proud of their distinctive characteristics, and the tendency to assimilate their institutions to those of England was checked.

In the end, English attempts at armed conquest failed, but when the centuries of war ended, the inexorable infiltration of English influence into Scotland was resumed. Union of the two countries at last came about not by war but by the peaceful accession of the Scottish king, James VI, to the throne of England as James I (1603). This was only a personal union, leaving the two countries still with each its own parliament and its own administration, but in 1707 the two kingdoms were formally united into one kingdom of Great Britain and it was arranged that Scotland should send to the parliament at Westminster forty-five members of the House of Commons and sixteen representative peers to sit in the House of Lords. During the generations since, the two countries have in many ways drawn ever closer to each other, but the many centuries of separation and hostility had left a heritage of distinctive characteristics which have not yet been effaced. Scotland, while no longer a state, is still conscious that it possesses a distinct entity as a nation. Besides, according to the treaty of union of 1707, many Scottish institutions, in local government and in the legal system, were expressly preserved, and in recent times Scotland has acquired separate administrative departments, under a Secretary of State for Scotland, to carry out many of the functions of government.

The union of 1707 also provided for the maintenance of a Church of Scotland which is not only independent of the Church of England but has several sharply defined individual characteristics, many of them reflecting the distinctive history of the Scottish people. The Reformation in Scotland took a course different from that in England, because of the political accident that in England the Crown supported the reformers and enabled them to take over most of the existing system of church government without serious dislocation,

2

whereas in Scotland the Crown opposed the reformers and they had to carry through their movement by means of a rebellion and revolution against the government of Mary, Queen of Scots. In time, when Queen Mary was deposed and succeeded by her Protestant son, James VI, the Scottish Church tended to come into line with that of England, but a Presbyterian movement then arose which insisted that all ministers should be of equal rank and that the church should be governed not by bishops but by committees of ministers called presbyteries, under a general assembly composed of ministers and elders. The controversy between the two rival systems of Episcopacy and Presbyterianism went on for over a hundred years (1575–1690), with now one party, now the other, in the ascendant. The Stewart kings supported Episcopacy, and in the course of the struggle against Charles I the National Covenant was adopted (1638) as a manifesto setting forth the nation's grievances. Out of this there developed the concept of a 'covenanted nation', standing in a special relationship to God as a 'chosen people' comparable to the people of Israel, and this concept involved not only the idea of the preeminent merits of the Scottish Presbyterian Church but also its mission to spread its system of church government to England and other countries. In the end it was the Presbyterian system which prevailed in Scotland, when, in 1689, James VII was deposed in favour of William of Orange and his wife Mary.

After the Reformation the Roman Catholic Church dwindled almost to extinction in all parts of Scotland, not so much because of the prevailing attachment to Protestantism as because Roman Catholic effort in Scotland was for a time extremely meagre and there were hardly any priests. From the late seventeenth century, however, there was persistent and sustained Roman Catholic effort in parts of the Outer Islands, the west mainland and the Highlands of Aberdeenshire and Banffshire, and in these areas, as well as in a pocket in Dumfriesshire, the Roman Catholic faith established itself. Even then, its adherents did not exceed in number 30,000 so late as 1800, and it was only in the nineteenth century, when there was a large immigration of Irish to the industrial areas of Scotland, that the Roman Catholic Church attained its present position as the second largest denomination in the country. Roman Catholics seldom suffered serious persecution or prosecution, but they were subjected to a good deal of vexation and they were excluded from political life until the nineteenth century.

The Episcopal Church, which had ceased to be established in

1689, retained a number of adherents, especially in Angus, Kincardineshire, Aberdeenshire and parts of the West Highlands. Their numbers declined, as Jacobitism declined, in the eighteenth century, and have remained small, but the attachment to this church of many of the nobility and gentry and its association with the Church of England have given it an importance greater than its numerical strength warrants.

Scottish Presbyterians were not all satisfied with the Church of Scotland as it had been established in 1690, and for a hundred and fifty years there was a series of secessions from it. At first the trouble was with the rigid covenanters, or Cameronians, who were dismayed that the Church of Scotland was no longer pledged to demand that England also should be Presbyterian. Then disputes arose because the Church of Scotland would not insist on the strictest doctrines of Calvinism; and another issue was the appointment of ministers not by the people or their representatives but by the individual patron of the parish. The 'Original Secession' of 1733 split in the 1740s into 'Burgher' and 'Anti-Burgher' sections, and those in turn divided, about 1800, into 'New Light' and 'Old Light' groups. In 1761 the Second Secession, or Relief Church—ancestor of the United Presbyterian Church—was formed. The disputes among those warring sects seem barren now, but at the time each secession and schism resulted in the formation of a new church, and feeling ran so high that some of those bodies excommunicated each other. The greatest of the secessions was the Disruption of 1843. The fundamental issue which led to this crisis was the belief of a strong party that the affairs of the Church of Scotland should be entirely in the hands of its own ministers and elders, meeting in the general assembly, and that Parliament should have no control over it. The original intention of the party which sought change was to secure a majority in the assembly and thereupon to break the existing connection of the Church with the State. In this they failed, but in 1843 they carried a very large minority out of the Church of Scotland to found the Free Church of Scotland. The Disruption split the country and the people as nothing had done since the seventeenth century. The supporters of the Free Church contributed nobly to provide churches, manses, schools and theological colleges which would vie with those of the despised 'Establishment', and there was only partial truth in the statement that the 'Free Kirk' was 'the wee kirk, the kirk without the steeple', whereas the 'Auld Kirk' was 'the cauld kirk, the kirk without the people'.

The Disruption was the last of the secessions, and since then the tendency has been towards reunion of the various Presbyterian denominations, culminating in 1929, when the United Free Church (in which the greater part of the Free Church, as well as the successors of the Relief Church and of part of the Original Secession, had already been merged) united with the Church of Scotland. Each reunion, however, left behind a dissenting minority, and there are still several very small Presbyterian churches—the United Free Church, the Free Church, the Free Presbyterian Church and the Reformed Presbyterian Church (formed by the Cameronians). The fact of the secessions, and the failure of the reunions to command universal assent, indicate the existence of a critical and independent spirit as an important feature of Scottish church life and indeed of the Scottish character.

Such a critical and independent—and, one may add, argumentative—spirit could not have been fostered without education. From its earliest days, the reformed Church in Scotland had stressed the need to educate the people, partly indeed so that they might be indoctrinated with the Protestant theology but partly in the hope that they would be in no danger of falling under the domination of a new priestly caste. Already in the seventeenth century it was the normal thing for a parish in lowland Scotland to have a school and schoolmaster, although it was much longer before the Highlands were adequately served. The 'ignorant yokel', so familiar a figure in English literature, if not in English life, has no place in Scotland, and for generations Scotland was far ahead of England in its educational standards. Not least important was the fact that there were no class distinctions in the Scottish educational system, and that it was usually possible for anyone desirous of education to have it and for a 'lad o' pairts', however humble his background, to proceed to a university. By the time the great emigrations from Scotland were under way every Scot regarded a school as an essential element in a community, and this concept was one which he carried with him wherever he went.

The whole of Scottish Protestantism was for a long time marked by austerity in church services, a suspicion of the adornment of church buildings and their furnishings and an emphasis on preaching at the expense of other parts of public worship. In the absence of a liturgy, which would have enabled the congregation to participate in the service, the proceedings were dominated by the minister from his lofty pulpit and indeed the minister was held in such awe that if he was so minded he could tyrannize over the community. The only part the congregation took in a service was to join in singing the metrical psalms, which alone were permitted, to the exclusion of hymns composed by mere mortals. Instrumental music in church was abhorred and the singing was led by a precentor. For generations he would read a metrical psalm line by line and the people sing a line at a time after him—a practice needless in Scotland where most people could read, but originally imitated from the Puritans of England, where people were generally illiterate. Scottish Protestantism was also associated with strict oversight of private morals by the ministers and the kirk sessions of elders, often exercised by the public denunciation of delinquents from the pulpit and their exposure to the public gaze on 'stools of repentance'. Certain moral standards were thus constantly held before the eyes of the people, but there is no doubt that there was a great deal of hypocrisy and that the system did little to check certain types of immorality. In present-day discussions, it seems sometimes to be implied that fornication is an invention of the twentieth century, but no such idea could linger in the mind of anyone who has read kirk session records. In the course of the last hundred years or so the ancient system of discipline has been gradually laid aside, but the smaller and stricter sects are still noted for the forthright pronouncements they issue, wholly without fear or favour, on moral issues.

After the covenanting phase in the seventeenth century, when the Scots thought it was their duty to carry Presbyterianism to England, Wales and Ireland, missionary aims outside Scotland were largely lost sight of for a long time, and when foreign missions were first proposed they were regarded with a good deal of hesitation, if not suspicion. But once they were accepted as a proper function of Scottish Churches, they captured the imagination of the Presbyterian bodies—and also of the Episcopalians. During the last century and more, Scotland has had a great record of devoted missionary work in all parts of the world from, quite literally, China to Peru.

This outward-looking characteristic was in some ways in accordance with the earlier traditions of the country. During the long periods of wars with England, Scotland had inevitably become the ally of England's other enemy, France, and the military and political association was accompanied by many cultural contacts. Indeed, one curious result of this situation was that England, although lying nearer the continent of Europe, became more insular than Scotland. She developed a peculiar legal system, divergent from that which prevailed in any continental country, her universities developed along lines not paralleled elsewhere, and her architecture, by the fifteenth and sixteenth centuries, had its own native styles. Scotland, on the other hand, had closer affiliations with the continent. Her legal system was akin to those of France and the Netherlands, her universities and other institutions followed continental models, and her architecture, at the end of the Middle Ages, shows some signs of French, but none of English, influence. Apart from the French connection, Scotland had close ties with the Low Countries, Denmark and the Baltic, so that she was not isolated in a remote northern backwater but was drawing cultural inspiration from the main stream of European development. And, in the days before large ports, with elaborate docks and quays, were thought of, there were all around the shores of Scotland countless little harbours, suitable for the small vessels of the time, from which any adventurous Scot could set out for places on the continent where, as likely as not, he would find kinsfolk ready to welcome him.

2

THE BEGINNINGS OF SCOTTISH EXPANSION

LONG before emigration in anything like the modern sense was thought of, many Scots were wanderers far from their own land, and settlers in other lands. They went in search of education, they went to seek professional advancement, they went in pursuit of a military career, they went to sell their merchandise or to ply their crafts, they went sometimes, so it would appear, out of a mere restlessness which drove them from place to place.

Before the Reformation, churchmen and scholars, bonded together in a community of learning and in a religious communion co-extensive with western Europe, were peculiarly conscious of their ties with the Continent. They could travel freely, to find everywhere much the same conditions and institutions and also the same language—Latin—and they could find employment almost as easily in other lands as in their own. Ambitious clerics, too, learned that one path to advancement lay through the papal court. There, however, they had to lay out money in fees for promotion, and, in order to check the consequent drain of bullion from the country, fifteenth-century Scottish governments found it necessary to impose restrictions on clerical excursions to Rome.

Until the foundation of Scotland's own universities in the fifteenth century, the Scot who wanted advanced education had no choice but to leave home, either for England or the Continent. Scottish students had been going to Oxford in the thirteenth century, and a Scottish lady founded Balliol College there. Once the long wars between Scotland and England began, however, Scots were apt to be less welcome in England, and, to make matters worse, for nearly half a century (1378–1418) England and Scotland were supporting rival popes. Severed from England by political and ecclesiastical hostility, Scottish students went very largely to French universities, especially Paris. Then, at the beginning of the fifteenth century, France abandoned the cause of the pope whom, along with Scotland, she had previously supported, so that the Scots were cut off from France as well; besides, a few years later most of the north of France, including Paris, was for a time occupied by the English. It was in these circumstances of isolation that Scotland's first university, at St. Andrews, began its career (1411–14).

However, even when St. Andrews was followed by Glasgow (1451), Aberdeen (1495) and Edinburgh (1583), Scots continued to go abroad as students. The French universities of Orleans, Avignon and Paris were popular with them, as well as Louvain and Cologne. But they were to be found further afield—in Copenhagen, Tübingen, and Bologna, for instance. Not content with a few years of study, several Scots remained abroad for long periods, teaching as well as studying. John Athilmere, for instance, was twenty years in Cologne, John Major twenty years in Paris, and the blind theologian, Robert Wauchope, is hardly remembered in his native Scotland but was renowned on the Continent, where he did most of his work.

The tradition of the wandering scholar and churchman did not come to an end with the Reformation, for the Reformation was itself an international movement, and did something to stimulate migration. While Scottish reformers were still pressing their cause at home, with little success, against the opposition of the government, they sometimes had to take refuge in foreign countries, and some of them actually settled there, like John Macalpine, who Latinized his name as Machabeus and became a professor at Copenhagen. On the other hand, once the Reformation was successful in Scotland, it was the turn of Roman Catholics to take refuge abroad, and some of them became residents in foreign monasteries.

So far as education was concerned, there was some apprehension after the Reformation lest Scottish boys, following their fathers' footsteps to continental universities, might be 'corrupted by pestilent popery'. But there were, of course, universities where the theological climate was congenial enough to Scottish Protestants—parts of Germany and the Low Countries, and even France, where the Huguenots had five universities. The attraction of France could therefore continue, and many Scots went to those universities either as students or as teachers, some of them to remain for many

069284

years. However, apart from Protestant universities, scholarship did to some extent surmount confessional barriers, and Scots were still, after the Reformation, to be found in Paris, as well as in other Roman Catholic universities on the Continent. The records of the university of Paris contain some 400 Scottish names over the century between 1519 and 1615.

As long as medieval religious thought prevailed, pilgrimage to foreign shrines was another reason, or pretext, for travel abroad. The less adventurous might be content with a visit to the 'Holy Blood' at Hales, in England, or to the shrine of St. Thomas at Canterbury, but Rome attracted many pilgrims and some Scots found their way to the shrine of St. James at Compostella in Spain, from which they brought back cockle shells as a token that they had made the journey. Any pilgrimage was apt to be partly a holiday as well as a religious exercise, and there must have been a special fascination about a trip to Compostella, for it lay on the shore of the Atlantic, near the north-western tip of Spain, which represented something like the edge of the world to the medieval mind.

The Scots who went abroad as fighting men in the fifteenth century went mainly to help their allies, the French, against the English, in the later phases of the Hundred Years' War. In 1418, in response to French appeals, the Duke of Albany, Regent of Scotland, sent a force to France under his second son, the Earl of Buchan, with the Earl of Wigtown and Sir John Stewart of Darnley. Buchan, after a victory against the English at Baugé, in 1421, was appointed constable of France. In 1424 the Earl of Douglas, who had brought further forces from Scotland, was appointed lieutenant general of the French armies and was created Duke of Touraine. But later in the year both Buchan and he were killed at the battle of Verneuil. Soon after this, the French campaigns against the English were headed by Joan of Arc, and many Scots fought under her standard. When the Anglo-French war petered out, the Scots who remained in France were formally organized as the Scots Guard. As such, they and their successors continued to do great service as the personal bodyguard of the king, and were trusted even by that most suspicious of monarchs, Louis XI, as Scott relates in *Quentin Durward*. They also fought with much distinction when the French kings went to war in Italy at the end of the century, and Bernard Stewart of Aubigny twice held Calabria for France. In later generations, however, although the name *Garde Écossais* was maintained, the personnel became mainly French.

Many warriors neither died in France nor returned to Scotland, but settled in France, where some of them were endowed with lands and honours by the French kings and others acquired estates by marrying French heiresses. Thus we find Robert Patillo, lord of Sauveterre, Robert Cunningham, lord of Chevreuse and Villeneuve, William Monypenny, lord of Concressault, Stewart of Darnley, lord of Aubigny and Evreux. There were, indeed, nearly as many names of Scottish origin in France as there were names of Norman-French origin in Scotland, though some of them were transformed almost beyond recognition: thus Quinemont is Kinninmond, Gohory is Gowrie, Dromont is Drummond and D'Oillençon is Williamson. Robert Monteith de Salmonet looks like a genuine French seigneur, but his apparent territorial designation was based on the fact that his father had been a salmon-fisherman in Scotland.

At the other extreme from the Scottish warriors were the peaceful traders and craftsmen who crossed the North Sea to foreign ports and often penetrated far inland as well. Besides Scottish skippers, and traders by sea, the Scottish pedlar was a familiar figure in many European countries. While few of the traders and craftsmen may have settled permanently overseas, many certainly lived there for many years, and one does not go far in Scottish records without coming across such phrases as 'Elizabeth Ra, daughter and heir of the deceased John Ra, formerly indweller in Stra Streit in Brugis',[1] or 'A.B. is brother german of the deceased W.B., indweller in the burgh of M. in the parts of Zealand'.[2] There were, in fact, stable communities of Scots in a number of European towns, especially in the Low Countries. The resident Scots in Bruges had a chapel of St. Ninian; there were always Scots in Veere, through which most of the Scottish trade with the Netherlands passed; and in 1700, it has been estimated, the Scottish community in Rotterdam numbered about 1,000. Commercial ties with Denmark and Sweden explain the ease with which Scots reached those lands, where they sometimes settled to exercise their crafts and to promote enterprises like cloth-manufacture, glove-making and linen weaving.[3] Scottish trade with the Baltic likewise opened up a vast area to adventurous Scots: it is hardly surprising that the Scottish community in Danzig had their own altar in one of the churches, but from the ports the pedlars

---

[1] *Protocol Book of James Young* (Scot. Record Soc.), No. 144.
[2] *St. Andrews Formulare* (Stair Soc.), No. 301. The burgh is undoubtedly Middelburg.
[3] Cf. T. C. Smout, *Scottish Trade on the Eve of Union*.

made their way inland, and in the early seventeenth century the number of Scots in Poland was put—by a wild guess—at no less than 30,000. Equally, it is not surprising that Scots should appear in North German ports like Hamburg or Bremen; but it is startling to find in 1576 that eleven signatories to a letter describe themselves as Scottish citizens of Regensburg (Ratisbon).

Sometimes Scots seemed to be hard put to it to explain exactly why they were wandering on the Continent. Thus, of three who turned up at Breslau in 1479, one was a pedlar who said he had been to Rome on pilgrimage and was now on his way to see his uncle in Danzig; a second—a linen weaver to trade—also alleged that he had been in Rome on a pilgrimage, but he had worked in Lübeck and Hamburg: the third, a tailor, had been out of Scotland for eleven years, apparently exercising his craft and earning a living thereby. Possibly there were sometimes vague speculative hopes of fortunes to be made; but it is hard to exclude an element of a desire to wander for the sake of wandering. Such a *wanderlust* looks like a tendency contrary, or perhaps complementary, to the other pattern of behaviour which exiled Scots already showed in the Middle Ages, namely the tendency to seek the society of their fellow-countrymen in communities overseas.

Scotland's nearest neighbour, England, was an objective of the wandering Scot just as much as continental countries were. The Reformation, which made England and Scotland two Protestant countries joined by a friendly understanding against the papalist powers of the continent, increased the number of Scots who went to England for part of their education, often after taking a first degree at home; the two sons of John Knox were among them. If Scots learned in England, they taught in England, too, as schoolmasters: one of many such was James White, who had such 'great profit' from his school in London that there was thought to be no hope of attracting him back to Edinburgh. Scottish divines discovered that there are good livings to be had south of the Border and their discovery has never since been forgotten. The fact that England came to be predominantly Episcopalian while Scotland was predominantly Presbyterian was so far from being an obstacle to the ambitious that, in the late nineteenth and the early twentieth centuries, out of five successive archbishops of Canterbury three were Scots. Of migrants of less note there was an uncounted multitude, very few of whom are known by name. About 1550 it was said that over 3,000 Scotsmen, with their families, had settled in England within the previous half-country, and both English and Scottish observers pronounced that they were self-effacing and adaptable in their new home and soon shed their Scottish characteristics. It was said in 1705 that there were between 500 and 1,000 Scots hawkers in England.

Clearly, all this considerable, and many-sided, movement of Scots to other countries represented, at least in part, emigration or something very like it. But it did not, of course, in any sense represent colonization. The earliest Scottish ventures in colonization were actually not made abroad at all; they were made within the geographical bounds of Scotland itself.

The northern islands of Orkney and Shetland were dependencies of the united kingdom of Norway and Denmark until 1468, but even before their transference to Scotland there had been a considerable infiltration of lowland Scots to Orkney. The title and authority of Earl of Orkney had passed to a Scottish family in the thirteenth century; in the fourteenth many of the leading ecclesiastical appointments in the islands came to be held by Scotsmen; and Scottish earls and Scottish bishops introduced so many dependents of their own race that by the fifteenth century the lowland Scottish tongue was displacing the old Norse language in Orkney and much of the native legal system was being superseded. In Shetland the Scottish penetration started later than it did in Orkney, but in the second half of the sixteenth century a considerable number of Scots, especially from the Lothians, Fife and Angus, settled in the islands, and by 1600 about 25 per cent of the population had surnames which point to a Scottish origin. The latest document written in the Norse tongue in Shetland belongs to the early seventeenth century. When one looks at the terms on which lands in Shetland were granted to the Scottish incomers, who were expressly authorized to 'ryve out and win'—as we should say, break in—land for cultivation, one can be in no doubt about the existence of a concept of the exploitation by colonists of the natural resources of the islands. Something of the character of the Scottish settler in Shetland is portrayed in Triptolemus Yellowlee, a character in Scott's novel *The Pirate*.

In the northern isles, colonization by lowland Scots was quite spontaneous. In the western isles, by contrast, it was adopted by King James VI as a piece of conscious and deliberate government policy, though with far less success. James regarded the western islanders as 'utterly barbarous', and proposed to civilize them by a policy of the 'plantation' of the islands by 'answerable inlands subjects' (that is, obedient Lowlanders).[1] As one aspect of this policy, the government in 1597 authorized the creation of three burghs in the Highlands, and shortly afterwards, when the large island of Lewis was forfeited by its native proprietor, a number of gentlemen from Fife, 'the lowland adventurers', undertook to 'plant themselffis thairin be force'.[2] The proposed burghs did not materialize, however, and after two attempts to establish themselves in Lewis the Lowlanders had finally, in 1607, to give up their attempt, in the face of native hostility. Further south, however, something was achieved. In 1609 the Earl of Argyll, who had received a charter of lands in Kintyre, set about the erection of the burgh of Lochhead or Campbeltown, which became the centre for a 'plantation' of Lowlanders. Lowlanders were planted by Argyll in the burgh of Inveraray as well. It is not difficult to see in those proceedings an attempt to introduce Lowlanders where they would serve as a wedge between the Celtic peoples of western Scotland and the Celts of Ireland.

A similar strategic concept lay behind what proved to be the first successful Scottish colony of any magnitude, and indeed the most successful Scottish colony of all time, namely the plantation of Ulster. The share of the Scots in that plantation was, indeed, in more ways than one a logical extension of the developments which had already proceeded within Scotland itself. One part of it—the arrival of Scots in County Antrim—was actually in part a secondary migration of Lowlanders who had been planted by the Earl of Argyll in Kintyre and who crossed to Ireland when conditions in Kintyre became disturbed. In County Down, the young O'Neill chieftain was forced by insolvency to part with his lands, and among the purchasers were two enterprising Scotsmen, Hugh Montgomery of Braidstane, who became Viscount of Airds, and James Hamilton, who became Viscount Clandeboye, and Montgomery and Hamilton brought in their fellow-countrymen as settlers from 1606 onwards. The ambitious scheme of the English government for the plantation of the remaining counties of Ulster was the consequence of the flight to the continent of the Earls of Tyrone and Tyrconnel in September 1607 and the forfeiture of their estates. Following on this, in 1609 the government invited 'undertakers' to apply for allocations of land, on which they were to settle English or 'inland' (that is, lowland) Scottish inhabitants. There was so much competition for allocations,

[1] *Basilikon Doron*, i. 70.
[2] *Edinburgh Burgh Records*, 1589–1603, 221.

from a few peers and courtiers and from many lairds in Ayrshire, central Scotland, Fife and East Lothian, as well as burgesses of Edinburgh and Glasgow, most of them asking for the maximum allotment of 2,000 acres, that the total demand exceeded the land available, and ultimately 81,000 acres were distributed among fifty-nine Scottish 'undertakers'. While several of them promptly sold their allotments, others either settled in person or left agents and dependents, and, although progress was slow, the ultimate result was to leave its permanent mark on north-eastern Ireland. The specific scheme of plantation was, however, only one phase in a long-term movement which went on intermittently throughout the seventeenth century. In the middle of that century it was believed that 40,000 or 50,000 Scots were settled in Ulster, and by 1691 the estimate was twice as high. And after that, during the 'ill years' of the 1690s, when Scotland suffered from a series of bad harvests and nothing less than famine conditions prevailed for a time, still more Scots crossed the North Channel.

The first effective colonization, both within Scotland and outside it, therefore came from lowland Scots. But it should be mentioned that Highlanders, too, had been pursuing expansionist and aggressive tactics in the sixteenth century. Shetland, which was to be colonized by Lowlanders, complained again and again of raids by men from Lewis, who seem to have terrorized the islanders. And many Highlanders found their way to Ireland as mercenary troops, usually to fight with the Irish against the English. There were many facets to the expansionist tendencies of the Scottish nation at that time.

However, in spite of the beginnings of colonization, the main outlet for Scottish vitality in the seventeenth century, when increasing stability and order at home left less scope for those whose ambitions ran on warlike lines, was service in continental armies. From the 1560s onwards it had been a common occurrence for the Scottish government to grant licences to individuals for the raising of specific numbers of men for service in Denmark, Sweden and the Low Countries. After 1600 the traffic increased, and the Thirty Years' War, beginning in 1618, heightened the demand and widened the opportunities. In that war, first Christian IV of Denmark, then Gustavus Adolphus of Sweden, kings of countries already accustomed to employ Scots, led the Protestant armies in Germany against the house of Hapsburg. Donald MacKay, the first Lord Reay, raised 3,600 men for Christian IV and subsequently served under

Gustavus, along with many other members of Scottish noble and landed families. Gustavus is said to have had 10,000 Scots at his command, and there is some reason for believing this figure an under-estimate. A list has been compiled of no less than fifty-four Scots who served as colonels under Gustavus, and twenty who served in even higher ranks. When France entered the war, in support of the Protestant powers, a renewed stimulus was given to the tradition of Scottish service in the French forces. A brother of the Earl of Argyll raised 4,500 men for this service, and in all more than twice that number are said to have been enlisted. One of the most noted Scots of the time was John Hepburn, who had commanded the Scots brigade under Gustavus and later, after transferring to the French service, died in 1636 with the rank of marshal of France. Many of the Scots who had served on the Continent returned home to fight when war broke out between the Scots and Charles I after the adoption of the National Covenant, and it was one of them, Alexander Leslie, who led the Scottish forces against the king and became Earl of Leven. A picture of one of those Scottish soldiers of fortune was drawn by Scott in Dugald Dalgetty, in *A Legend of Montrose*.

When neither the Thirty Years' War nor civil strife at home absorbed the military energies of the Scots, those who still sought a soldier's career often entered the employment of the United Provinces of the Netherlands. That state was constantly in danger from greater powers, it was for a time the leading Protestant power on the continent, and it possessed ample wealth to pay mercenaries. Service in the Dutch armies became the main outlet for Scots after 1660. Yet others went further afield and Patrick Gordon (1635–99), for example, had a distinguished career as a commander in Russia under Peter the Great. Nor was the tradition of foreign service extinguished after the Scots embarked seriously on emigration to colonies overseas. Thus James Keith (1696–1758), a brother of the Earl Marischal of Scotland, served in Spain and Russia before becoming a field-marshal under Frederick the Great of Prussia, and Samuel Greig (1735–88) was the creator of the Russian navy, which he manned largely with Scottish officers. 'The most spectacular event of the years 1769–70 was the voyage of the Russian Baltic fleet through the Sound, the English Channel and the Straits of Gibraltar all the way to the Levant, where it met and destroyed a Turkish fleet at the battle of Cheshmé. Many observers believed that the Russians would never have got anywhere near Cheshmé but for

Admiral Greig and Captain Elphinston, two Scots in the empress's service.'[1]

The absence of friends and kinsmen from Scotland for long or short periods, and their settlement in other countries, were so common that they must have been one of the more familiar features in the life of the Scottish people. Many of the notable names of Scots who went abroad have been mentioned, and many more names could easily be assembled, of individuals not only notable but also obscure. Taking at random a volume of Scottish record—the *Register of the Privy Seal* for 1574–80—one finds at once illustrations of the whole range of motives which were leading Scotsmen to many other countries. A son of Sir William Murray of Tullibardine went to France for his education. There were merchants or traders, like Alexander Hepburn, who 'deceissit in the eister seyis' [eastern seas]', and Scots who settled overseas, like Henry Duthie, who was a burgess of Hamburg, and a son of David Bruce of Kinnaird who owned a dwellinghouse in a town in Poland. And there were the soldiers in the service of continental powers: the late John Maxwell, 'sometime captain in Sweden', and David Preston, who 'deceissit under the charge of Colonale Balfour in the service of the estaittis of the Law Cuntreis'.[2]

---

[1] Richard Pares, 'A quarter of a millenium of Anglo-Scottish Union', in *History*, October 1954, p. 244.

[2] The archives of the burgh of Aberdeen contain a great many 'birth-brieves' testifying to the blood relationships between Scots on the Continent and Scots at home (*Spalding Club Miscellany*, v. 325–68).

3

THE SCOTS FIND THE NEW WORLD

ALMOST every country in western Europe had formed a settlement of some kind in America before the middle of the seventeenth century. Spain and Portugal had been first in the field, and between them they had established effective claims to the whole of South and Central America, leaving only North America to be contested by later comers. England, after some earlier pioneering efforts, made her first permanent settlement on the American mainland, in Virginia, in 1607. The French established themselves at Port Royal, in what is now Nova Scotia, in 1604, and at Quebec in 1608. The Dutch began to form settlements at the mouth of the Hudson River in 1609 and formed the 'New Netherlands' in that area in 1613. 'New Sweden' made its appearance around Delaware Bay and New Jersey in 1638, but was conquered by the Dutch and added to their dominions.

There seemed to be no reason why Scotland should not follow the same fashion, especially under the rule of a king—James VI and I—who had given his name to Jamestown, the capital of the English settlement in Virginia, and who was anxious that his Scottish subjects should keep abreast of 'other well governed commonwealths'. In 1620 we hear of 'Scottish undertakers of the plantations in Newfoundland', and this at least indicates that the Scots had in mind a settlement to the north of the area which had hitherto attracted most European interest. It happened that Sir William Alexander, later Earl of Stirling—poet, courtier and secretary of state—met Captain John Mason, the English governor of Newfoundland, in 1621, and this turned his attention to the New World. He soon received a grant from the king of territories designated 'Nova Scotia in

America'. New Scotland was to arise alongside New England, New France and the New Netherlands.

In 1622 a small band of colonists, with a smith and a minister among them to attend to their material and spiritual needs, left Galloway and wintered in Nova Scotia, but both the minister and the smith died, and although another ship went out with a second pioneering party in 1623 nothing was achieved except a certain amount of exploration. Alexander wrote *An Encouragement to Colonies* (1625) and as one element in his plans to attract interest and find the necessary 'undertakers' he obtained the king's consent to confer the title of baronet on any gentleman who would furnish six men and 1,000 merks (£666 13s. 4d.) towards the colony. In order that the baronets should receive formal possession, by delivering of 'earth and stone', of their proposed estates in America without leaving Scotland, part of what is now the esplanade of Edinburgh Castle was declared to be Nova Scotian territory. Many baronets were created, but the obligation to furnish men was later commuted for a further money payment, and the whole scheme began to look like nothing more than a device to sell titles and enrich Alexander.

However, a favourable opportunity soon arose for a determined attempt to settle a Scottish colony in Nova Scotia. War between England and France started in 1627 and David Kirke and his brothers were authorized by the English government to operate against the French in Canada. They captured first Port Royal, and then, in August 1629, Quebec. In July 1629 sixty Scottish colonists had landed at Port Royal, and more came in 1631. But a treaty had been made between England and France in 1629, before Quebec had fallen, and that town had to be restored to France. Port Royal was not covered by the terms of the treaty, but Charles I, in the course of negotiations about financial adjustments, ultimately agreed to its restoration too, and in 1631 he ordered the removal of the Scottish colonists and the abandonment of the colony. The colony was surrendered in 1632, the small band of Scottish settlers was evacuated, and French sovereignty over Nova Scotia was restored, to last until 1713.

At an early stage in the Nova Scotia project, Cape Breton, a subdivision of the territory granted to Alexander, had been allotted to Sir Robert Gordon of Lochinvar. Like Alexander, he produced propaganda, in an *Encouragement for all such as have intention to be undertakers in the new plantation of Cape Breton* (1625), but he died in 1627. His schemes were taken up by Lord Ochiltree, who landed some colonists at the site of the later Louisbourg in 1629. They made an even shorter stay than Alexander's colonists, for they were driven out by the French after only a few months. Cape Breton remained French until 1763.

The whole Nova Scotia venture, therefore, left no Scottish colonists on the other side of the Atlantic, and almost its sole permanent result was the existence in Scotland of 'Nova Scotia baronets', whose descendants still hold the title. Yet the episode has never been forgotten, and its commemoration embodies a consciousness of the historic Scottish connection with Canada. In recent years Menstrie Castle, the birthplace of Sir William Alexander, has been restored and now incorporates a Nova Scotia Commemoration Room. The appeal for funds to endow this room was issued by the Lord Lieutenant of the county of Clackmannan and was endorsed by the Lord Lieutenant and the Premier of Nova Scotia.

The Earl of Stirling himself did not lose all interest in the New World, for in 1635 he had a further scheme, this time for a settlement in Maine, and his fellow countrymen kept the possibility of an American colony before them, for in 1647 we hear of a plan for a Scottish plantation in Virginia.[1] As Maine lay within the English sphere of influence, and as Virginia was unquestionably English, these proposals indicate a new line of thought—the emigration of bodies of Scots into English colonies. The next settlements actually made by Scots were to be of this pattern, for they were in East New Jersey and in South Carolina, but the impetus to their planning arose to some extent from the ecclesiastical troubles of the period. During most of the seventeenth century, when the Church of Scotland was Episcopalian, there were many Presbyterian dissenters. Those Presbyterians who felt disposed to leave their homeland for reasons of conscience tended in the main to seek refuge in the Netherlands rather than across the Atlantic, and they helped to swell the Scottish colony in Holland in the 1670s and 1680s. It is, however, curious that much earlier, in 1622, a minister who had been banished from Scotland for his Presbyterian sympathies craved permission from the king to emigrate to Nova Scotia. Possibly he thought of a Scottish version of the English Pilgrim Fathers, who had crossed the Atlantic in 1620, but nothing came of his suggestion.

The more important of the settlements which were made by ecclesiastical dissidents, that in East New Jersey, was initially prompted not by Presbyterians but by Quakers, who were apt to suffer a good deal of ill-treatment in Scotland, as elsewhere, especi-

---

[1] *Extracts from Records of the Burgh of Edinburgh, 1642-55*, 129.

ally at the hands of local authorities. The initiative was largely that of Robert Barclay of Urie (1648–90), who had from time to time been imprisoned for his religious beliefs. New Jersey, after changing hands more than once, was finally acquired by England from Holland in 1674, and in 1683 East New Jersey came under the control of twenty-four proprietors, sixteen of them English and two of them Irish, but there were also five Scots—Robert Barclay of Urie, his brother David, the Earl of Perth, his brother John Drummond, and Robert Gordon, a merchant—as well as a Dutchman resident in Scotland.[1] Like Sir William Alexander and Gordon of Lochinvar before them, the Scottish proprietors issued literature to encourage settlers:

> The woods and plains are stored with infinite quantities of deer and roe, elks, beaver, hares, conies, wild swine and horses etc., and wild honey in great abundance; the trees abound with several sorts of wine-grapes, peaches, apricots, chestnuts, walnuts, plums, mulberries etc., the sea and rivers with fishes. . . . The soil is excellent and fertile. . . . Wheat, barley, oats, pease and beans etc. when sown yield ordinarily twenty and sometimes thirty fold increase. . . . Sheep never miss to have two lambs at a time and for the most part three.[2]

Emigrants began to reach the colony in 1683, but 1684 was the peak year. One ship went from Leith and Aberdeen with 160 passengers and another from Montrose with 130 (including twenty-seven women). Each took about nine weeks on the open ocean, and the Aberdeen vessel had such a stormy passage that she finished the voyage under jury-rig, but the passengers' chief complaint was that they had 'more stomachs than meat', and later emigrants were advised to carry more ample provisions. The fact that one of the ships touched at Aberdeen no doubt suggests Barclay's influence, but he himself did not go to the colony. Nor was the colony designed entirely, or even mainly, for Quakers, and it is not clear if any Scottish Quakers were among the emigrants. Besides, although the appeal of the colony to Presbyterians was advanced by George Scott of Pitlochie, who had himself suffered as a Covenanter, there is little evidence that even the Presbyterian element was strong. One adventurer did write indignantly in 1685 that all the 'campione ground and river side ar takin up alradie by Quakers, Independents, Presbiterians, Anabaptists, and in a word by all the off scourings of hell',[3] but these settlers of various religious persuasions were not necessarily Scottish, and indeed they had probably arrived from

---

[1] Cf. *New Jersey Hist. Soc. Proc.*, 4th ser., viii, 4–12, xv, 1–39.
[2] *Scottish Colonial Schemes*, 235.
[3] *Historical MSS. Commission Report*, x, 137.

England before Scottish settlement started at all. The names we find among the Scottish emigrants rather suggest that the colonists represented a good cross-section of east-coast Lowlanders, men who were neither religious refugees nor economic failures: for example, George Mackenzie, merchant in Edinburgh, James Johnstone of Spottiswoode, Peter Watson from Selkirk, John Cockburn from Kelso, Robert Hardie, merchant in Aberdeen, Thomas Gordon, brother of the laird of Straloch, Thomas and Robert Fullerton, brothers of the laird of Kinnaber, Charles Gordon and James Mudie from Montrose. The settlers, who wrote home from Elizabeth Town, New Perth or Perth Amboy and Woodbridge among other places, expressed themselves as pleased with the climate and with agricultural conditions: 'The soil of the country is generally a red marle earth with a surface of black mould . . . full freighted with grass, pleasant herbs and flowers . . . I know one planter who hath a hundred of cattle, not above three years settled, and no wonder, for some of the grass is as high as my head.'[1] Encouraged by such news, Scots continued to come out in some numbers, and played an important part in the affairs of New Jersey, which was surrendered by the proprietors, to become a crown colony, in 1702.

The other experiment of this period was more specifically Presbyterian and covenanting in origin than the New Jersey venture, but even it had other elements. In the 1660s and 1670s, English thought was in favour particularly of the development of the southern colonies, which produced luxuries for which there was a demand in England and which in their turn imported more English goods than the northern colonies did; besides, in the southern colonies wealth could be produced easily by coloured labour and there was less need for industry by white immigrants. It is not surprising, therefore, that some Scots began to think at this time of a settlement in Florida or South Carolina.[2] The latter territory was debatable between England and Spain, but English colonists had gone there in 1670, and Scottish Covenanters realized its possibilities as a place of refuge as early as 1672. The Scots revived their interest ten years later, and the English proprietors of the colony granted 12,000 acres to Sir John Cochran of Ochiltree and Sir George Campbell of Cessnock. A party of emigrants went out in 1684, headed by William Dunlop, a Presbyterian minister, and Lord

---

[1] *Scottish Colonial Schemes*, 238–9.
[2] There was also a proposal, sometime in Charles II's reign, for a Scottish colony in the Caribbean Islands (General Register House: Scottish Record Office MS., GD103/2/4/42).

Cardross, a Presbyterian sympathizer, and they settled at Stuart's Town, a short distance south of the later town of Beaufort. The settlement was, however, destroyed by the Spaniards two years later. Despite several attempts and projects, therefore, the Scots, unlike so many western European nations, had not succeeded in establishing a settlement of any importance across the Atlantic. Colonization in America did not provide an outlet for the over-abundant vitality of seventeenth-century Scotland or employment for men who were too active and energetic to find occupations in the peaceful and settled conditions now prevailing in their homeland. It is true that Scotland was unable to furnish either the capital or the military and naval support necessary for colonization with success. Besides, in the circumstances of the personal union with England, which meant that Scotland could not pursue an independent foreign policy, she could not have maintained a colony without English diplomatic support, and the fate of the Nova Scotia venture had illustrated this. But it would seem also to be true that there was no great enthusiasm in Scotland itself. There is a very sharp contrast between the ease of raising men by the thousand for service in Europe and the difficulty of raising even a handful to go to Nova Scotia. It can even be said that the interest in colonies was mainly among Scots who were tinged by English thought. Sir William Alexander was an anglicized Scot; the East New Jersey episode was an offshoot of an English project; the Presbyterians who furthered the South Carolina scheme were in close touch with Shaftesbury, the leader of English dissent, who was one of the proprietors of that colony, and at that juncture the factions opposed to the government in both countries shared an interest in colonization—which, indeed, they were accused of using as a cloak to cover subversive designs. There was a strong English flavour at each stage, and native Scots were still looking mainly to the Continent of Europe rather than to America.

The fact is that in the seventeenth century more Scots went to America under compulsion than went of their own free will. The 'transportation' of criminals and political offenders is something we shall hear more about in connection with Australia in the late eighteenth century and the early nineteenth; but there was a good deal of transportation westwards across the Atlantic in the seventeenth century, from Scotland as well as from England.

As early as 1617 and 1618 King James VI and his privy council were considering whether delinquents, including 'the most notorious and lewd persons' on the Borders, should be shipped to Virginia or some other distant territory, and in 1619 the Archbishop of St. Andrews threatened to banish to America ministers who were disaffected to the established Church. But the process of transportation does not seem actually to have begun until, in the course of the civil war between Charles I and his subjects, the Scots found themselves at war with the English parliament and its general, Oliver Cromwell. In August 1648 a Scottish army was cut to pieces by Cromwell in the north-west of England, and in September we hear that Scottish prisoners were to be transported to the plantations. Two years later, the Scots were routed by Cromwell on their own soil, at Dunbar (3rd September 1650), and a few days after the battle it was ordered that 900 Scottish prisoners should be shipped to Virginia and 150 to New England. Exactly a year later again, a Scottish army invading England was defeated at Worcester (3rd September 1651), and once more prisoners were despatched overseas: 1,500 of them were granted to a Guinea merchant for transportation to the mines in Guinea, but some also went to America, and a shipload of about 272 persons arrived at Boston in 1652.[1] In 1653–4 there was a rebellion in Scotland against Cromwell's government, and after its collapse some of the prisoners were shipped to Jamaica, an island newly acquired by England.[2]

When Cromwell was dead, and Charles II recovered his father's throne, the Scottish government itself followed the example which England had set. In 1665, permission was given for the transportation of strong and idle beggars, gipsies and criminals, to Jamaica and Barbados, and in December of that year 'there was sindry sent over to Barbadoes, sum for povertie, utheris for criminal causis'.[3] The policy of transporting criminals and strong and idle beggars to Virginia and Barbados was pursued intermittently until the end of the century.[4] Besides criminals, some of the Covenanters who were in trouble with the government were shipped overseas, from 1666 onwards.[5] It is said that the total number of Covenanters so deported was no less than 1,700, and one of the well-known incidents of the period was the wreck in Orkney of a ship carrying a cargo of 200 Covenanters destined for America, after a covenanting rising had been defeated at Bothwell Brig in 1679. Another instalment of disaffected persons was sent overseas after the failure of a rising led by

[1] Samuel G. Drake, *History of Boston* (1856), 342.
[2] On the whole topic, see Abbot Emerson Smith, *Colonists in Bondage*, 38, 133, 144–6, 152–4, 157, 289.
[3] *Register of the Privy Council of Scotland*, 3rd ser., ii, 101; Nicoll, *Diary*, 443.
[4] *Reg. Privy Council*, 3rd ser., v, 231, vii, 178; *cf. Lauderdale Papers*, ii, 116.
[5] *Lauderdale Papers*, i, 236.

the Earl of Argyll in 1685.[1] It was one of the many compulsory emigrants of this period who was referred to when the Stirling town council recorded the purchase of two fathoms of rope 'to tye Laurence McLairen quhen sent to America'.[2]

Some of the involuntary colonists in the end gained their freedom but, instead of then returning home, remained in America and prospered. We hear of one, several years later, living in New Jersey 'like a Scots laird' and wishing his country well 'though he never intends to see it'.[3] We are also told that 'so many more of the Scots servants which go over to Virginia settle and thrive there, than of the English ... that if it goes on for many years more, Virginia may be rather called a Scots than an English plantation'.[4] There is ample testimony, too, that while they were in compulsory service the Scots gained a good reputation as workers. They were considered so valuable that in 1663, when the English government passed an act which in general prohibited any exports to America from Scotland, a qualification was introduced so that 'servants' could still be sent.[5] However, despite this qualification, the restrictions on trade between Scotland and the colonies did reduce the number of servants sent out, and in 1667 the governor of Barbados complained of the cessation of a traffic whereby 'formerly this and the rest of the islands were supplied with brave servants and faithful subjects'.[6] He also reported to the secretary of state in Scotland that 'some of your nation I find here and those good subjects. I wish there were more of them. . . . 3,000 or 4,000 servants would upon honourable terms be here entertained. . . . This country will be willing to pay for their passage and they shall be freemen after one year's service'.[7] In 1670 the governor of Jamaica urged the encouragement of Scots as 'very good servants';[8] in 1679 the governor of Barbados again made a request for Scottish servants; and in 1680 there was a similar request from St. Kitts.[9] It may have been in an attempt to satisfy such demands that in 1669 two Scottish vessels were authorised to sail to New York with not less than 400 'planters'. One of the ships may have reached her destination safely, but we know that the other,

---

[1] W. H. Carslaw, *Exiles of the Covenant*, 13.
[2] *Stirling Burgh Records*, 1667–1752, 345.
[3] *Scottish Colonial Schemes*, 114.
[4] Defoe, *Tour* (London, 1927), ii, 748–51.
[5] Statute 15 Car. II, c. 7, sect. 5.
[6] G. L. Beer, *The Old Colonial System*, I, ii, 11.
[7] *Lauderdale Papers*, ii, 27.
[8] *Scottish Colonial Schemes*, 123; there are other testimonials *ibid.*, Appendix D.
[9] Beer, *op. cit.*, 21*n*, 46.

after being duly freighted with 'beggars, vagabonds, egyptians [gipsies], whores, thieves and other dissolute and loose persons' from Scottish gaols, was wrecked on the coast of Buchan.[1]

The demand for 'Scottish servants' also stimulated another kind of forced emigration—the seizure of innocent persons and their shipment to America, where they were sold for hard cash. This had begun in the seventeenth century, for in 1688 two ships which had been authorised to convey criminals were searched for kidnapped persons, and the practice became common enough in the eighteenth. Aberdeen, which had a considerable American trade, was quite a centre of this nefarious traffic, and produced the best-known case, that of Peter Williamson, who ultimately published his story as *The Life and Curious Adventurers of Peter Williamson, who was carried off from Aberdeen and sold for a slave*. Born in 1730, Williamson was kidnapped when he was playing at Aberdeen harbour as a boy of ten and was sold for £16 in Philadelphia to work on the plantations. After a time he gained his freedom and acquired a farm of his own at Forks of Delaware, on the Indian frontier. Captured by Indians in a raid, he escaped after some months. Then, in the course of a war between British and French, he was captured by the latter but gained his freedom in an exchange of prisoners and returned to Britain. In York he published an account of his experiences and, proceeding to Aberdeen in 1758, he advertised himself as 'Indian Peter' and made public appearances in Indian garb. As his book had disclosed the interest which some Aberdeen bailies had in the kidnapping trade, Peter was prosecuted for libel, but he raised proceedings against the magistrates and won his case. He then settled in Edinburgh, opened a coffee house, published the first *Edinburgh Directory* (1773) and started a penny post in the city (1776). He died in 1799. This biography shows that there was nothing fanciful about R. L. Stevenson's story of David Balfour, who was kidnapped at the instance of his wicked uncle, Ebenezer, and escaped shipment to America only because the brig *Covenant* of Dysart was wrecked on the Torran Rocks. The *Covenant*, it appears from the disclosures of the half-crazed cabin-boy, made something of a practice of carrying either adults or children who were forcibly removed to America. She was bound for Carolina, and it emerged that Ebenezer had given Captain Hoseason £20, the usual fee, for disposing of David; and 'forbye that', Hoseason 'was to have the selling of the lad in

[1] P. Gouldesbrough, 'An attempted Scottish voyage to New York in 1669', *Scot. Hist. Rev.*, xl, 56–62.

Caroliny, whilk would be as muckle mair, but no from my pocket, ye see', as Ebenezer explained.

In so far as there was any spontaneous interest in America among Scotsmen in the seventeenth century, it arose less from any desire to form permanent settlements than from a concern for the development of Scottish trade. The trading interests of Scotland had been almost exclusively in the Continent of Europe until about the end of the sixteenth century, but at that time we do find a reference to the occasional voyage to Newfoundland, and Edinburgh merchants were soon trading so far afield as the Canaries. It is said that an Aberdeen merchant, in Charles I's reign, was the first Scot to trade with the American colonies, and in the Cromwellian period Glasgow merchants experimented in trading with Barbados. Scottish traders were certainly active in the New Netherlands before that territory was conquered by England. They had been there even in 1648,[1] and in 1657 it was complained that 'they sail . . . to the best trading places, taking the bread as it were out of the mouths of the good burghers and resident inhabitants. . . . They carry away the profits in time of peace, and in time of war abandon the country'.[2]

After 1660, trade between Scotland and the English colonies was in general prohibited, but some Scots did receive licences for trade and there was a not inconsiderable traffic, partly by illicit means, partly indirectly through England. The commodity specially sought was, of course, tobacco, and the tobacco trade, both then and later, required resident agents or factors, so that it led to the settlement of some Scots in America, if not permanently at any rate for long periods. One of the earliest, if not actually the first, letter known to have been written to Scotland from America was sent in 1662 from 'Virginia, in Accomacke', by Patrick Fleming, son of a burgess of Kirkintilloch, to his 'assured friend', James Fleming of Oxgang, in Scotland. The writer was evidently engaged in the tobacco business, and intimated that on his next visit home he would bring a thousand pounds of tobacco with him, but the terms of his letter closely resemble those of countless personal letters written throughout the generations:

> I have received ane letter from you the 25 of Jan. 1662 and I am very glad to hear of your welfare and my sisters and uncle and cousin. Having this opportunity I thought good to write unto you, hopeing that you are in good health as I am at this present writing, thanks be to God. . . . I doe intend, God willing, this nixt ensuing year to come home.[3]

[1] J. R. Brodhead, *History of the State of New York* (1859), 489.
[2] J. A. Doyle, *The Middle Colonies*, 47.
[3] *Court Book of the Burgh of Kirkintilloch* (Scot. Hist. Soc.), 147–8.

It was out of commercial interests and aims that the final attempt to establish an independent Scottish colony arose. This was the well-known Darien venture of the 1690s. The company responsible, often referred to now as 'the Darien Company', was officially 'The Company of Scotland trading to Africa and the Indies', and the Scots of the time often called it 'Our African Company' or 'Our Indian Company'. Initially it owed a great deal to the desires of English merchants to compete with the existing East India Company, which had a monopoly of trade with the Far East, and some Englishmen called the new company 'The Scotch East India Company'. Indeed, at first 50 per cent of the capital was subscribed in England, half of the directors were English, and the headquarters of the company were in London. It was only after the East India Company engineered an attack which made continued English participation impossible that the company was thrown back on Scotland and Scottish capital, and it was only then that Scottish colonial ambitions began to play an important part in the company's schemes. It had already been proposed that, besides sending ships to Africa and the East Indies, the company should establish an emporium for trade on the isthmus of Darien, near Panama, conveniently situated for trade with the Atlantic and the Pacific and with North and South America. This proposed location was now seized on as the site for a colony, and it completely captured the imagination of the Scots, who crowded in to participate. In 1698 and 1699 a total of well over 2,500 persons left Scotland for 'New Caledonia', but none of the expeditions succeeded in maintaining a footing for any length of time. The reasons for the failure were partly climatic, though in the end the Scots were evicted by the Spaniards, who had a long-established right to Central America, but the Scots blamed the king, William of Orange, for failing to support his Scottish subjects, and indeed the whole episode was a lesson in the inability of Scotland to take effective action overseas in a constitutional situation where she lacked the political independence and the power to carry out the decisions of her parliament.

Only a few years after the Darien fiasco, Scotland was joined with England in a complete union, and any possibility of independent Scottish action in the colonial field was at an end. The future of Scottish emigration lay in the movement of Scots to colonies already established by the English—or now, British—government.

The manifold activities of the seventeenth century—compulsory transportation, trading ventures, and a little voluntary emigration—

had, all in all, resulted in the establishment of a fair number of Scots as permanent settlers in several of the American colonies. There were not very many in New England, but it is remarkable that as early as 1657 a Scots Charitable Society, with twenty-seven members, was established at Boston—surely the first of the many such societies which Scots were to found in all parts of the world. It long maintained no more than a tenuous existence, with a small membership,[1] but from time to time Scots did settle in Boston, like David Melville in the 1690s, and Duncan Campbell was a bookseller in Boston in 1686. In Pennsylvania, 5,000 acres of land were granted by the proprietor in 1685 to 'Eneas Mackpherson alias Chatone of Inveressie in Scotland, esquire', whose American estate was to be erected as a manor, called the manor of Inveressie[2]—the first plan for carrying a part of a highland clan to the new world, still under the domination of its chief. But it was probably in and around Virginia that there was the largest number of Scots, since both indentured servants and tobacco factors were plentiful there. Before 1700 there were Scottish settlers in Westmorland and Stafford counties on the Potomac; Scottish interests were dominant in the area where the town of Dumfries grew up; and the town of Alexandria, a little further north, also drew most of its settlers from Scotland. As for New Hampshire, the governor of that colony wrote in 1682, 'There are several Scots that inhabit here'.[3] Writers who have investigated the history of particular Scottish families in America have sometimes been able to begin their chronicles in the seventeenth century; for instance, we find Thomas Crawford in Virginia in 1643 and David Crawford there about 1654, while John Crawford, from Ayrshire, was in Massachusetts in 1672.

Apart from the mainland colonies, there was a good number of Scots in the West Indian islands, and it was said in 1762 that about a third of the European inhabitants of Jamaica were Scots either by birth or descent;[4] many of the Scots in the islands were, of course, indentured servants, but some of them were men of social standing—for instance, one of the Camerons of Lochiel made a fortune in Jamaica, and William MacCulloch, fourth son of William Mac-Culloch of Garthland, was a colonel in the army and settled in St. Kitts.[5] In 1740 Sir James Campbell of Auchinbreck had a

[1] S. G. Drake, *History of Boston*, 455.
[2] Charles P. Keith, *Chronicles of Pennsylvania* (1917), i, 75.
[3] *Scottish Colonial Schemes*, 118.
[4] H. E. Egerton, *British Colonial Policy* (1928), 137–8.
[5] McKerlie, *Lands and their owners in Galloway*, i, 337.

scheme to transport emigrants to Jamaica and Alexander Monteith settled as a master carpenter there in 1749.[1] It was to Jamaica that Robert Burns, the poet, contemplated emigrating in 1786, before the publication of his first volume of verse won him fame at home.

Among the Scots settlers in general there was a considerable social range. It is safe to assume that some of the time-expired indentured servants never rose above the labouring level, but others prospered, and in addition, among the Scots who came freely to America, there were those who were making their mark in the Church, in education and in government. John Gordon, who became Bishop of Galloway in 1688, had been a chaplain in New York in 1682. Francis Makemie (*c.* 1658–1708), an Ulster Scot, studied at Glasgow, was ordained by an Irish presbytery in 1683 and went to America, where he organized churches and presbyteries. The Scots William and Thomas Gordon were founding schools in Middlesex, Virginia, before the seventeenth century was out. They were Aberdeenshire men, and another Aberdeenshire man who had a remarkably varied career was George Keith (1638–1716), a native of Peterhead. As a Quaker, he was associated with the settlement in East New Jersey, and in 1684 was surveyor-general of New Jersey, residing at Perth Amboy. He deserted Quakerism for the Church of Scotland in 1700, and was appointed a missionary among the American Quakers by the Society for the Propagation of the Gospel. That Society had many other Scots on its staff in America, including Robert Keith, Thomas Crawford, Andrew Boyd, George Ross and William Andrews.

The best known Scottish-American churchman of the period was James Blair (1656–1743), who had graduated at Edinburgh in 1673 and had been minister of the Scottish parish of Cranston before going out to Virginia in 1685. At that time the bishop of London was responsible for the oversight of the Church in the colonies, and in 1689 he appointed Blair as his commissary or representative in Virginia. Blair was accused of appointing too many Scots to parishes in the colonies, and in fact at least thirty Scots were so appointed between 1688 and 1710, but the reasons went beyond any personal preferences of Blair, for in a list of ministers who went to America between 1690 and 1811, with the assistance of a bounty from the Bishop of London, there are well over a hundred with distinctly Scottish names.[2] Blair, like so many of his countrymen, was keenly interested in education, and was responsible for the foundation of

---

[1] MSS. in Register House, Edinburgh (Scottish Record Office, GD 14/12, 30/1586).
[2] Gerald Fothergill, *A List of Emigrant Ministers to America* (1904).

William and Mary College in 1693. The master of the grammar school which prepared for the college was also a Scot, Mungo Inglis; and it was yet another Scot, Thomas Blair, who wrote the first book on French teaching ever published in America, in 1720.[1]

Towards the end of his long career, Commissary Blair became governor of Virginia (1740–41). He was not the only Scot to hold the highest colonial office, and some had attained political eminence even before 1700. Andrew Hamilton was governor of New Jersey, and Robert Livingston, whose great estates gave their name to Livingston County, was a native of Ancrum, Roxburghshire, who arrived in America about 1672 and was the ancestor of many legislators, administrators and politicians.[2] When an act of 1696 raised the question of the legality of the tenure by Scots of offices in the colonies, it emerged that among Scottish office-holders were not only Commissary Blair but also Patrick Mein and Alexander Skene in Barbados, Andrew Hamilton in East New Jersey and Robert Livingston in New York. It was Andrew Hamilton, a native of Edinburgh, who organized the first postal service in the colonies, in 1694, and John Campbell (1653–1728), postmaster of Boston, published the first newspaper printed in North America, *The Boston News-letter* (1704).

A vivid picture of most of the Scottish elements in the life of America about the end of the seventeenth century is presented by John Buchan in his novel *Salute to Adventurers*. We meet there a fanatical Covenanter, Muckle John Gib, who after arrest 'was destined for the plantations in a ship of Mr. Barclay of Urie's, which traded to New Jersey'; Andrew Garvald, who learned the American tobacco trade in his uncle's counting-house in Glasgow before going to Virginia as a factor; Ninian Campbell, from Breadalbane in the Perthshire Highlands, a pirate who said, 'they ken me well on the Eastern Shore and the Accomac beaches'. We hear of 'a heap of Scots redemptioners' or time-expired indentured servants; we meet an emigrant who had reached America from Ulster but whose forebears had come from Scotland; and we also meet 'Dr. James Blair, the lately commissary of the diocese of London, who represented all that Virginia had in the way of a bishop' and who 'was full of his scheme for a Virginian college to be established in the Middle Plantation'.

---

[1] On Scottish churchmen in America generally, *cf.* R. Foskett, 'Some Scottish Episcopalians in the North American Colonies, 1675–1750', in *Records of the Scottish Church History Society*, xiv.

[2] H. L. Osgood, *The American Colonies in the Eighteenth Century* (1958), i, 202–3, 238.

4

A NEW ORDER IN THE HIGHLANDS

THE economic and social structure of the Highlands, before it underwent revolutionary changes in the eighteenth century, was still based on the clan. The Highlands were, in fact, a case of arrested development, and the cohesion which had at one time been given to the whole of Scottish society by the dependence of lesser men on greater men lingered on there after it had disappeared elsewhere. The chief was normally, if not invariably, also the owner of the land on which his clan lived, and therefore the landlord of his clansmen, who were his tenants. There were, however, intermediaries between chief and tenants, namely the tacksmen, so called because they held from the chief tacks or leases of large tracts of land. It was usually the tacksman, and not the chief, who let the land out in smaller holdings to the rank and file of the tenants, and he lived on the surplus by which the rents paid to him by the tenants exceeded the rent which he paid to the chief. Usually a farm was let by the tacksman to several families, who occupied it together and co-operated in some of the agricultural operations in the cultivated land, where each family's holding was scattered in strips intermingled with those of others. The tenants had no leases, or any security of tenure, and were legally at the mercy of the tacksmen, though in practice the same holdings would often be held by the same family for generations. The tacksmen were usually related to the chief, and bore his surname, and they often considered themselves to have a hereditary right to their tacks. They acted as lieutenants of the chief in the organization of the clan not only in its agricultural activities but also in its character as a military unit. In the days when a clan had to be ready to defend its territory and its cattle against its neighbours, the most valued function of the tacksman, from the chief's point of view, was to maintain a large body of fighting men on the estate.

As long as the clan was regarded primarily from a military angle the maintenance of large numbers of tenants was a more important consideration than any economic question of the standard of living which could be extracted from the cultivation of the soil and the keeping of flocks and herds, and population was apt to outrun subsistence. Sir Walter Scott says of his highland chief in *Waverley*: 'He stretched his means to the uttermost to maintain the rude and plentiful hospitality, which was the most valued attribute of a chieftain. For the same reason, he crowded his estate with a tenantry, hardy indeed, and fit for the purposes of war, but greatly outnumbering what the soil was calculated to maintain.' The means of sustenance provided by peaceful pursuits had in earlier times been supplemented by raids on other clans and on the more fertile Lowlands, but when law and order came to be generally established throughout the kingdom this source of supply began to dry up. In the eighteenth century, therefore, observers were unanimous that the Highlands already had more people than could be adequately supported, especially as the prevailing agricultural methods were inefficient and the habits of the people were not such as to make the best of a poor soil and an adverse climate. Hitherto, Highlanders had seldom made their way to the Lowlands except in arms, but from this period they began to seek, and to find, peaceful employment there, and their settlement, ultimately in large numbers, in lowland cities, represents perhaps the greatest of all internal migrations within Scotland.

Clans, as ready-made fighting units, had intervened in Scottish civil strife in the seventeenth century, when James Graham, Marquis of Montrose, recruited some of them on behalf of Charles I in 1644 and when John Graham of Claverhouse, Viscount Dundee, enlisted some of them, in 1689, on behalf of James VII and II after that monarch had been deposed in favour of William of Orange. In the eighteenth century some clans again rallied to the cause of the House of Stewart in the Jacobite Risings of 1715 and 1745, on behalf of the Old Pretender, James VII's son, and the Young Pretender, his grandson. It was partly for economic reasons that the Jacobite cause made its appeal to highland clans. There were men on the verge of economic desperation, who had nothing to lose by a rebellion even should it prove unsuccessful, and a rebellion in itself offered the opportunity for a revival of the traditional collection of booty in the Lowlands,

Menstrie Castle, birthplace of Sir William Alexander

'The Emigrants'

on the grandest scale. There were, admittedly, other reasons as well for highland Jacobitism. One of these was sentimental, for the doctrine of the hereditary rights of kings made a special appeal to Highlanders, accustomed as they were to the rule of hereditary chiefs. Another was nationalist, for a certain number of Scots were attracted by the promise of the Stewart Pretenders to dissolve the union with England should they be restored. But much more important in shaping highland Jacobitism was ecclesiastical opinion. While few Presbyterian Scots favoured a Stewart restoration, most Scottish Roman Catholics did, and so did many Scottish Episcopalians—the so-called 'non-jurors', who would not swear allegiance to a Hanoverian king. It was perhaps this factor more than any other which determined the area of Jacobite support. Had the motives been primarily economic, they might have been expected to appeal to all clans equally, but this was far from being the case. In fact it was only some clans which supported the Jacobite risings, and the support came essentially from clans which were Episcopalian or Roman Catholic. By 1700 the Presbyterian church had not made a great deal of headway in the central and west Highlands, except in Argyll, where Clan Campbell, under the Earls and Dukes of Argyll, had long been attached to the Covenanting and Presbyterian cause and had come to be aligned with the Lowlands rather than with the Highlands.

Even in the thirty years between the Fifteen and the Forty-five, the Presbyterian Church was growing stronger, and the area which was Episcopalian and Jacobite in sympathy was shrinking. The Fifteen, indeed, had a good deal of lowland support, in the north-east, Fife, the Lothians and the south-west, and in the Highlands there was general support for that rising in the western isles and in the north as well as in the centre and the west coast. The Forty-five, however, was much less broadly based. This time there was practically no support in the southern Lowlands. The north-east was still important, for Moray, Banff and Aberdeen provided about a fifth of the Jacobite strength, and Perthshire, on the fringe of the central Highlands, contributed many recruits, raised by a few enthusiastic landlords and chiefs. Within the strictly highland area, however, the north was this time mainly on the government side and the Western Isles gave little support to the Jacobites. The main highland strength of Prince Charles's army lay in a relatively small area—Appin, Glencoe, Lochaber, Lochshiel and Moidart, inhabited largely by Stewarts, MacDonalds and Camerons, who were the hereditary foes

4

of their neighbours, the Presbyterian and Hanoverian Clan Campbell.

A great many Scots, highland as well as lowland, not merely held aloof from Jacobitism but were on the government side and fought in the government army, which was not an 'English' army. Thus, among the officers in the force which Prince Charles defeated at Prestonpans in 1745 were men with names like Murray, Farquharson, Campbell, Drummond, Kennedy, Sutherland, Haldane, Mackay, Munro, Stewart, MacNab, Grant and Ross; and famous Scottish regiments fought under the Duke of Cumberland when he defeated Prince Charles at Culloden in 1746. It is therefore a fact to be emphasized that the Jacobite movement was not a Scottish movement in the sense that the nation supported it. Nor was it even a highland movement in the sense that all the Highlands were behind it. The picturesque impressions of Prince Charlie marching at the head of an army of kilted Highlanders, first to victory and then to defeat, and of Prince Charlie hunted among the heather, guarded by incorruptible Highlanders and saved from capture by the gallant Flora MacDonald—these impressions have led to an identification of the Highlanders with Jacobitism which is contrary to the facts. Facile talk about 'the clans' being defeated at Culloden ignores the fact that there were only some 5,000 men in the Jacobite army at that time, when the population of the Highlands was somewhere in the region of 300,000. It was not a military defeat at Culloden which transformed highland society.

That transformation was beginning before the Forty-five, and would undoubtedly have been completed, though possibly more slowly, had there never been a Forty-five. Nor is it true that the military and legislative action taken by the government to pacify the Highlands after both rebellions, and after the Forty-five to ensure that there would be no more rebellions, were the most important factor in changing the face of the Highlands, though what they accomplished was not negligible. The principle of disarming or demilitarizing the Highlands was adopted in 1716, but it was not at that stage put into effect very successfully. From 1725, however, General Wade was in command in the area, and his administration had important effects. His soldiers searched for arms, and seized them when they could find them—though many remained concealed. He was also authorized to recruit for service members of the clans which had been loyal to the government, and in 1739 ten companies of such recruits were formed into the Black Watch Regiment, the first of the many regiments in which Scottish Highlanders have played such a conspicuous part in Britain's wars ever since. But Wade is best known for his road-making. By roads linking Crieff and Dunkeld, which lay on the highland boundary, with Inverness and Fort William, and linking Inverness to Fort William, Wade provided ready access for troops to the nearer parts of the Highlands. After the Forty-five, there were renewed measures for disarming the Highlands, and this time the wearing of the kilt was forbidden as well. There were also acts which aimed at reducing the power of the chiefs over their followers. But the traditional way of life in the Highlands was altered less by any legislation than by social and economic changes.

Such changes had begun before the Forty-five. It was seen that the function of the tacksman as the organizer of armed retainers was now becoming obsolete, and he therefore began to be regarded by the landlord as an unnecessary middleman—a mere encumbrance on the estates, the value of which to the chief would be enhanced if the rents which the tenants had hitherto paid to the tacksmen could be drawn directly by the landlords. The process of completely eliminating the tacksman from the structure of estate management seems to have begun on the Argyll estates in the 1730s, and it went on in various areas for half a century. Alternatively, instead of brusquely ousting the tacksmen, the chief might ignore their hereditary rights and put the leases up to auction, so that an existing tacksman could be displaced by a higher bidder. When this happened, the new leaseholder sometimes found that the enhanced rent would be more easily paid if he took up cattle raising on his own account, and was therefore prompted to turn out the existing tenants from their farms. Whichever of the two alternative courses the landlord took with his tacksmen, the landlord profited, but it was also true that in either event there was dispossession: in the first instance, of the tacksmen themselves, who were left without an occupation, in the second instance of the tenants. The general tendency, obviously, was towards the decay of the clan system and the transformation of the old relation of chief and clansmen into something more like normal commercial landlordism. A landlord who no longer enjoyed influence and power as a chief and who no longer received services from his clansmen expected a more substantial monetary income by way of compensation.

Another change which was beginning in the Highlands even before the Forty-five was the introduction of various industries, in an attempt to train the people in industrious habits and give them peaceful occupations. Lead mines were opened at various places, with considerable energy but little return; there was iron smelting, using the local timber and imported ore; and the linen manufacture was greatly expanded. Some agricultural changes, too, started before the Forty-five, including the introduction of the potato.

After the Forty-five, all those changes were accelerated and intensified. The mere fact that the estates of chiefs who had supported Prince Charlie were annexed to the crown and administered by government commissioners for a period of forty years overthrew the traditional clan structure. When the chiefs finally recovered their estates, neither they, who had learned new ways of life in the interval, nor their clansmen, who had for a generation been tenants of an impersonal commission, could go back to the old ways. But, apart from that major change, the commissioners made many alterations in highland land-holding and agriculture. Tenants were granted leases for fixed terms of years, but at the same time were debarred from the possession of more than one holding, so that sub-letting and the re-emergence of a tacksman class were excluded. The commissioners also made many regulations to ensure good husbandry and the improvement of the arable land. In conjunction with the Board of Manufactures, the commissioners further encouraged the linen industry, and they spent considerable sums on roads and bridges. At the same time, the making of military roads, in extension of Wade's work, went on, and just after 1800 Commissioners of Highland Roads and Bridges were appointed, to extend the road system to even the most remote parts of the mainland.

Other changes took place without direction from any official body, but simply as a result of the operation of economic incentive. Perhaps the most important was the development of sheep-raising in the Highlands, where the tenants had hitherto concentrated on cattle. From the 1760s onwards, first of all in the nearer parts of the Highlands, like southern Argyll and Dunbartonshire, sheep farmers from the Lowlands were brought in to stock the hills with breeds of sheep new to these districts, and within half a century this fashion spread even to Inverness-shire, Ross and Sutherland. The reason was the simple one of profit. In lowland Scotland, and in England, the industrial revolution was leading to a vast concentration of population in new towns, and there was a steadily rising demand for mutton as food, while there was an equally important demand for wool to be manufactured into clothing. Consequently, the change-over from cattle to sheep led to an enormous increase in the value of an estate just in a few years. It also led to vast social changes, for the advance of sheep always involves the retreat of men, as the many tenants and labourers associated with other types of farming are dispossessed in favour of a handful of shepherds.

In arable farming, too, there were changes. Hitherto the system had been one of joint-cultivation, with several families working one farm. Now there was a changeover to the crofting system, which involves a number of small separate holdings, each worked by one family, in combination with grazing rights held in common on large open areas of pastureland. As the population grew, the crofts tended to be subdivided into ever smaller units, and, while it was true that by growing potatoes a very small croft could sustain life in a good year, it could not maintain the cattle by the sale of which the tenants had hitherto acquired their only cash to pay rents and so forth.

For a time, the danger was not apparent, because a new industry had arisen which gave employment along a large part of the west coast and the islands. This was the kelp industry, the manufacture of alkali from the burning of seaweed. It had been growing since before the middle of the century, but it flourished especially for a few years before and after 1800, when there was a heavy duty on imported alkalis and when the long wars with France tended in any event to restrict imports. After the war ended in 1815, however, and the import duty was reduced, the kelp industry soon faced extinction.

The crofting system and the kelp industry both facilitated the increase of population, and in some areas, especially the outer islands, the increase in this period was spectacular. Even Tiree, one of the Inner Hebrides, increased its population from 1,500 in 1747 to 2,700 in 1800 and 4,500 in 1831. Sheep-farming, however, where it prevailed, had a contrary tendency, though even it led largely to redistribution of the population within the highland area, or even within a single county, rather than to a reduction of the population. The population of the highland counties continued to increase for some time: Perth and Argyll reached their maximum in 1831, Inverness in 1841, Sutherland and Ross in 1851.

As soon as the notion was rejected that the land should support the largest possible number of people, irrespective of their standard of living, there was bound to be a drastic change in the Highlands, and this took the form of the 'clearances'. When people speak of the highland clearances, or about evictions for sheep, they usually have in mind particularly what happened in Sutherland in the early years of the nineteenth century. The position was that most of the county was used for low quality farming and cattle raising, by a population who were constantly on the fringe of starvation. The proprietor decided that it would be a sounder economy to turn the inland parts of the county over to large sheep-farms, which would require only a few hands to man them, and re-settle the people in crofts on the coasts, where they could supplement the produce of their crofts by fishing. Economic planning, however, paid insufficient attention to human wishes. The tenants saw themselves driven from holdings which had been their ancestral holdings for generations, in the process of removing them unnecessary brutality was sometimes used, and fishing was an unfamiliar and perilous occupation. There-fore, while the movement was successful in the sense that the county became a great exporter of wool and mutton and the fishing industry was enormously expanded, much bad feeling was engendered. It also happened that, although the bulk of the evicted tenants remained in the county, some of them did leave for the Lowlands or the colonies.

Among the many changes which had transformed the Highlands after the Jacobite period had been certain ecclesiastical developments which could not have been predicted from the past history of the area. Presbyterianism continued to expand, for the Episcopal Church in the Highlands dwindled almost to nothing and the Roman Catholic Church, while it did not lose much ground, made no head-way after the early years of the eighteenth century. But the Presby-terianism which prevailed in the Highlands was not solely, or even mainly, the Presbyterianism of the established Church of Scotland. Instead, there was much dissent, partly because the established Church was accused, not without some reason, of making inadequate provision for the spiritual needs of the Highlands, of sending ministers of poor calibre to the remote areas, and of failing to take into account the wants of Gaelic-speaking congregations. Conse-quently when the Disruption came in 1843, the Free Church obtained a large highland following, which it retained because it provided the Highlands with perhaps more adequate ministrations—when necessary in the Gaelic tongue—than they had ever known before. Thus, when the majority of the Free Church agreed to merge in the United Free Church in 1900, the minority which con-tinued as 'Wee Frees' was especially strong in the Highlands. Not only so, but even the Free Church was not rigid enough for some

Highlanders who had formed the still more conservative Free Presbyterian Church in 1892. All the stern austerity of classical Presbyterianism, long since abandoned throughout most of Scotland, still survives in highland districts where the Free and Free Presbyterian Churches are strong.

It became increasingly apparent, after the collapse of the kelp industry, that drastic measures were going to be necessary if the Highlands were to be placed on a sound economic footing and if their still increasing population was to be secured against the constant danger of starvation. Crofts were being subdivided, there was in general a lack of employment to supplement what the crofts yielded, there were epidemics of disease, there were bad seasons which were fatal to both the food and the fuel of the crofters. A crisis came in 1845, when the potato crop practically failed and when there was famine in consequence.

The existing system of poor relief was quite unfitted to deal with such a situation, and starvation was warded off mainly by charitable subscriptions raised in the Lowlands and by the highland landlords, who spent vast sums in buying food for their tenants. The government was slow to act, but in 1847 set up the Board of Destitution to organize the employment of Highlanders in railroad construction and in the making of the so-called 'Destitution roads', sometimes called 'meal roads' because payment was made not in money (which would have been swallowed up in arrears of rent) but in meal.

While the worst effects of the crisis of the 1840s had thus been overcome, nothing had been done to place the Highlands on a sound economic footing, and another crisis was bound to come sooner or later. When it came it reflected hardly any new cause, though there was one slight change in the situation, in that as the century went on sheep-raising ceased to be profitable, and the letting of shootings did become profitable, so that sheep runs were to some extent replaced by deer-forests.

The process of clearing tenants had by this time spread to the islands, where the collapse of kelp had resulted in a vast unemployed population. Sometimes the removal of tenants did no more than rectify the previous gross inflation of the population, but sometimes it almost stripped an area of inhabitants altogether. Mull's population, for instance, fell from 10,000 in 1821 and 1841 to 6,000 in 1881, and Ulva's from 360 in 1849 to fifty-one in 1881. Tiree, with over 4,500 in 1841, had only 2,700 in 1881, and Coll dropped from 1,400 in 1841 to 600 in 1881. But several areas were still over-populated, and it was plain that substantial reduction of the population was necessary in some districts as the only cure for a fundamentally unsound economy.

The crisis, when it came, once more came as much from natural causes as from any act of man. In 1882 there was a general failure of the potato crop, gales ruined the grain crops, the price of cattle fell and the fishing was unsuccessful. The demand now was for more land, and both in Skye and Lewis there were 'land-raids', when crofters seized certain grazings by force and started to cultivate them. In 1883 a Commission was appointed to inquire into the condition of crofters in the Highlands and Islands, and in 1886 came the Crofters' Holdings Act, which granted security of tenure, appointed fixed rents, allowed compensation to outgoing tenants for improvements and arranged for enlargements of holdings; and the Crofters' Commission was set up to superintend the operation of the new laws and regulations.

For a long time people thought that the 'Crofters' Act' had settled the problems of the Highlands and Islands. It is now apparent that it did no such thing. To give tenants security of tenure while freeing them from any control over the use to which they put the land has resulted in land going out of use and being turned over to sheep instead of being cultivated. There was not even any obligation on a tenant of a croft to live on his holding, and there has been a curious reversal of the earlier situation—instead of absentee landlords turning out tenants and converting land to sheep-runs, we have absentee tenants abandoning cultivation and using the land only to graze sheep. The problem of providing subsidiary occupations was not solved either, and, as fishing on the whole declined, crofters could no longer earn a livelihood. As a result, the depopulation of the Highlands and Islands has continued and has actually accelerated under twentieth-century conditions. The population of Sutherland, for example, reached its maximum in 1851 and did not experience a catastrophic fall until after 1911. The whole problem of providing the Highlands and Islands with a sound economy remains as intractable as ever, and the suggestion has recently been made that certain crofting areas should simply be 'written off' altogether.

5

EMIGRATION FROM THE HIGHLANDS

THE Jacobite risings, just because they are one of the episodes in Scottish history of which everyone has heard, are too readily regarded as the explanation of changes which in truth had other causes, and in particular the reasons for individuals and groups of people leaving the Highlands or leaving Scotland are too often assigned to the aftermath of Jacobitism. This persistent error extends across the Atlantic. It was long a common belief that the numerous settlers in North Carolina owed their origin to the transportation of defeated rebels from Scotland or to the migration of Jacobites who were pardoned on condition that they went into exile. This is far from being the case.

It is true that in the eighteenth century the expulsion of 'undesirables' from Scotland to America which had begun in the seventeenth century continued, and that a certain number of those 'undesirables' were not criminals but perfectly reputable citizens who had simply happened to be on the losing side in the political disputes of the time. Thus, after the 'Fifteen', some six hundred Jacobites were transported as indentured servants to Antigua, South Carolina, Maryland and Virginia, and we find, for example, that in 1716 the governor of South Carolina bought thirty highland rebels at £30 apiece. Most of those expelled Jacobites would no doubt serve for their term of compulsory service, and some of them remained in America after they were at liberty to return home, but so many of them did not remain, and so many seem actually to have escaped before their term expired, that the utility of the policy of transporting them at all was seriously questioned.

After the Forty-five, again, about 800 Jacobite prisoners are recorded as having been transported between March 1747 and November 1748. Their sentence was one of compulsory service for life, but this meant in practice that after serving for seven years they received their liberty, though they were still obliged to remain in banishment for the rest of their days.[1] It was also provided, in the act for disarming the Highlands after the Forty-five, that persons refusing to deliver up their arms might be compelled to serve as soldiers in America, that those convicted of this offence a second time should be liable to transportation to the colonies for seven years and that persons guilty of wearing the highland dress should also be liable to transportation on a second conviction.[2] Legislation against the non-juring Episcopalians, who were among the staunchest supporters of the Jacobite cause, likewise made transportation the penalty for those Episcopalian clergy who held illegal services and for schoolmasters who worshipped in an unauthorized Episcopalian meeting-house.

But such compulsory migration of Jacobites and of other political and ecclesiastical offenders was hardly a significant element in the foundation of the important highland settlements in America. Those settlements owed far more to the social changes in the Highlands which were going on between the two risings and after the Forty-five. Yet, if it is an error to attribute those settlements to Jacobitism, it is no less an error to see the earlier migrants as tenants who had been cleared off their holdings to make way for sheep. It is true that in the eighteenth century we do occasionally hear complaints from emigrants that in Sutherland 'the opulent graziers engrossed the farms' and that men were driven from Appin and Glenorchy 'to make room for shepherds',[3] but these complaints were unusual, and in any event they do not occur earlier than the 1770s.

There were developments which stimulated emigration long before clearance for sheep was so much as thought of. When the tacksman was by one means or another eliminated from his place in the structure of estate management, he often found, or felt, that his only refuge lay in emigration. He had no wish to be depressed to the level of an ordinary tenant and very often he had no real interest in farming, whereas by emigrating he could become a proprietor and raise, rather than lower, his status. This preference of

---

[1] Duane Meyer, *The Highland Scots of North Carolina*, 25.
[2] 19 Geo. II, c. 39.
[3] Ian C. C. Graham, *Colonists from Scotland*, 60.

the tacksman was one cause of the earliest emigrations, from the 1730s until about 1780. Besides, as a more commercial form of land-lordism began to prevail in the Highlands, the general tendency was to raise rents, and at least from 1770 onwards the demand for higher rents was very generally given as the reason for emigration. Accord-ing to official records for 1774–5, this was the reason usually given, and after a number of tenants had left the island of Lewis others said that they too would go unless their rents were restored to the old rates and the excess paid during the past three years was refunded.[1] It is true that as long as the tacksmen retained their posi-tion, any increase would in the first instance affect them, but they in their turn could pass on any increase to their tenants. Besides, there were tacksmen who so strongly resented the demand for higher rents that they were inclined to throw up their tacks rather than pay, and others who chose to find the money for higher rents by becoming stock-breeders and turning out their tenants. Once the tacksman was eliminated, of course, increases in rent would fall directly on the tenants. It may well be, however, that when the tacksmen raised the cry 'higher rents', lesser people would rally round them. A further factor which came along to stimulate emigration was the gradual penetration of new and improved farming methods, which meant that there was less need for labourers on the land.

Highland society being what it was, some tacksmen were naturally willing and able to take their tenants with them to the colonies to work on their new estates. A tacksman might post a notice on the church door, inviting people to join him in emigrating, or a meeting might be summoned to gain support. The tacksman, carrying on his old profession of organizing part of the clan, would then go to a seaport and make arrangements for the voyage. The leadership of tacksmen in emigration declined after about 1775, but it was not difficult for a body of tenants, independent of a tacksman's leader-ship, to imitate the technique which the tacksmen had pioneered. It is also true that as highland society changed, and the clan ties decayed, the chief ceased to be a leader: he was now a landlord, and increasingly an absentee landlord, who no longer required to live on his land in order to enjoy the services rendered and the produce made over to him by his clansmen. But, as we shall see, the High-lander seems still to have felt the need for leadership, and others took the place of chief or tacksman.

The most important area of highland settlement in the first phase

[1] Meyer, *op. cit.*, 62.

of emigration was North Carolina. A few lowland Scots had found their way there before 1700, including William Drummond, the first governor, and Thomas Pollock, an early council member, and there may possibly have been some Highlanders there before the first recorded arrivals in 1732, when three Scots—James Innes from Caithness, Hugh Campbell and William Forbes—received grants of land on the Cape Fear River. The grants were of areas measuring from one to three square miles, and this would suggest that those individuals were leaders of groups. In September 1739, when 350 people from Argyll settled in the Cross Creek area, the same pattern was followed, for large grants of land were made to twenty-two individuals, who clearly had dependents. The party included Duncan Campbell of Kilduskland, Daniel McNeill and Coll McAlister, and other names among the settlers were McLachlan, Stewart, McDougall and McBrayne. In 1740 the governor of the colony gave special encouragement to further settlers by conceding tax exemption to 'foreign protestants'. It is clear from a letter written in 1744 that the number of emigrants was so considerable as to attract much notice, and even to cause a certain amount of alarm, in Scotland: Archibald Campbell of Knockbuy remarked on 'that spirit of deserting this country', and added 'had not the sickness cut off soe many of the adventurers in North Carolina, I believe it [*i.e.*, Argyll] might have been left a disert'.[1]

North Carolina continued to attract large numbers of Highlanders until the early 1770s. Between 1768 and 1772 there is evidence that a number approaching 2,000 emigrated to that colony. By that time the phase of emigration under the leadership of tacksmen was passing, and many of the colonists were now taking small plots for themselves. Besides, some came as unskilled labourers, others as tradesmen, others again became merchants, and the concentration of Scottish settlers also attracted time-expired indentured servants of Scottish extraction who were looking for free employment.

The chief area of settlement was the upper Cape Fear and its tributaries, but there were a few settlers on the South Black River, Big Raft Swamp, Drowning Creek and the lower Cape Fear. The region was variously apportioned among counties at different times, but ultimately most of the Highlanders found themselves in Cumberland County when it was formed in 1754; its name derived from the general who had defeated the Jacobites at Culloden, but this was less inappropriate than it might seem, for so many of the settlers were

[1] Stonefield Papers (H.M. Register House), No. 17.

from Argyll and other non-Jacobite areas. The census of 1790 showed MacLeans, Bryces, Morrisons and MacNeils, among other Scots, in that county. The 'Scotland County' which now exists in North Carolina was not formed until 1899. A town at first named 'Campbelltown' was later re-named 'Fayetteville'.

The first task of the settlers was to fell pine trees, partly to clear the ground and partly to obtain timber to build their houses. There was, however, no need for systematic and complete felling of trees, for the removal of a ring of bark sufficed to kill them and enabled the sun to reach crops which were sown among the trees. The crops were Indian corn, wheat, oats, peas, beans, flax and sweet potatoes, and there was also some cattle-raising. Working as the colonists did, with vast areas of ground at their disposal, there was no need to give the land any attention by manuring it; after one tract of ground had been worked out, cultivation was simply moved to another. Many of the farmers had a small number of negro slaves to help them in their work, and some of them attained such wealth that their slaves numbered up to forty or fifty.

While North Carolina was the most notable area for highland settlement in this period, settlement elsewhere was not insignificant. When General Oglethorpe was founding the new colony of Georgia, he recruited, in 1735, a band of 160 members of Clan Mackintosh to colonize his southern frontier lands and defend them against the Spaniards. A few other Scots also went to Georgia. In 1735 there was a migration of about 200 people, under the leadership of Lieutenant Hugh Mackay, who sailed from Inverness for Savannah, between South Carolina and Georgia. As a result of an invitation by the governor of New York State to 'loyal protestant Highlanders' to settle between the Hudson River and the northern lakes, eighty-three families, largely from the island of Islay, were brought out by Lachlan Campbell of Islay in 1738; and Sir William Johnson, Baronet, planted many Scottish Highlanders on his estates in the Mohawk Valley, New York, before he died in 1774. No doubt partly as a result of movement within America, Scots settled in the late 1760s in the present counties of Fayette, Westmorland, Allegheny and Washington in Pennsylvania; in 1773 there were Scots in Kentucky and by 1779 they had crossed the Ohio River.

These movements belonged in the main to a phase, lasting from about 1730 to 1770, which was not unimportant but which was anterior to the first major exodus from the Highlands. That exodus is fairly well documented in contemporary sources, and it was also the subject of some comment from Dr. Samuel Johnson, who toured the Western Highlands and Islands with James Boswell in 1773. Even before Johnson and Boswell reached the Highlands, their attention had been drawn to the amount of emigration which was taking place, and they discussed the matter at Monboddo, in Angus, where Johnson remarked, 'To a man of mere animal life, you can urge no argument against going to America but that it will be some time before he will get the earth to produce. But a man of any intellectual enjoyment will not easily go and immerse himself and his posterity for ages in barbarism.' The visitors discussed emigration again in Glenmoriston, in the central Highlands, a district from which seventy men had gone to America in the previous year. When they were in Skye they heard of people sailing from Lochboisdale for America, they saw a ship, the *Margaret*, pass by with a number of emigrants on board, and they learned that the annual departure of an emigrant ship from Portree was accepted as normal. In Raasay they heard a song which was 'a farewell composed by one of the islanders that was going, in this epidemical fury of emigration, to seek his fortune in America'. The reasons usually given were increased rents, and a farmer in Glenmoriston told Johnson that he intended to emigrate because his rent, which had been only £5 twenty years ago, was now £20 and he thought he could afford no more than £10. But Johnson saw clearly enough that there was an element of mob-psychology not entirely capable of rational explanation; 'there seems now, whatever be the cause', he said, 'to be throughout a great part of the Highlands a general discontent' which led to emigration. He also discerned how the movement grew: 'the accounts sent by the earliest adventurers ... inclined many to follow them; and whole neighbourhoods formed parties for removal.'

The movement which Johnson witnessed had started about five years earlier, so far as the evidence shows, for in 1768 the *Scots Magazine* reported emigration from the Western Isles to Carolina and Georgia, and again in 1769 and 1770 there were many sailings from the West Highlands: in the latter year no less than six vessels, with 1,200 persons, left for America. In 1771 500 persons sailed from Islay and 370 from Skye, for North Carolina; in 1772, 200 sailed from Sutherland for North Carolina; and in 1773 there were three main groups—250 from Fort George (Inverness), 308 from Fort William and 775 (gathered from Moray, Ross, Sutherland and Caithness) from Stromness in Orkney. The total number of emigrants in those few years must have been many thousands. Skye, where the tacksmen had just been asked for higher rents, was particularly affected, and between 1769 and 1773 many tacksmen went off to North Carolina with their tenants, to the number, so it was said, of 4,000; the number is no doubt exaggerated, but that it should be put so high accounts for the impression made on Johnson and Boswell. Notable among the Skye tacksmen who emigrated at this time was Allan MacDonald of Kingsburgh, along with his better-known wife, Flora MacDonald, who landed in North Carolina in 1774 and settled at Cross Creek, now Fayetteville, where he bought a 475-acre plantation. It appears that bad harvests in 1773-4 had reinforced the pressure caused by rising rents, and Allan Mac-Donald of Kingsburgh had lost 327 cattle in the three winters before he left Skye.

In 1774-5 the emigration was mainly from Argyll (including 200 people from Appin) and Inverness-shire, but there were isolated groups from Caithness, Moray, Perthshire, Ross and even Shetland. The ports from which emigrants sailed were Greenock (6 ships), Fort William (6), Skye (5), Stromness (4), Gigha (2), Stornoway (2), Islay (2) and Dunstaffnage, Jura, Loch Erriboll, Thurso, Dornoch, Kirkcaldy and Port Glasgow (one each).[1] It is hard to understand why some were able to sail from ports near their homes, while others travelled to ports in the south before they embarked, but possibly it sometimes suited the convenience of Clyde-based American traders to carry emigrants on the outward voyage. Advantageous terms can be the only explanation of the exploit of 200 people from Aviemore who marched all the way to Greenock to embark, in 1775. Some of the sailings may, however, have been of Lowlanders.

The conspicuous emigrants at this stage were still tacksmen and men of substance, no doubt mostly with their followers. In 1771 John MacDonald, laird of Glenaladale in Moidart, bought land in 'St. John's Island' (Prince Edward Island) for a hundred natives of South Uist, and in 1773 he sold his estate and himself joined those emigrants as leader of a party from Moidart. These Highlanders were Roman Catholic, and a priest, James MacDonald, accompanied them; later on, the laird's brother, who was also a priest, joined the settlement. MacDonald of Glenaladale raised a loyal regiment, the 84th or Royal Highland Emigrant Regiment, when the American War of Independence broke out, and he died in Nova Scotia in 1811. In 1773 about 300 Roman Catholics from Glengarry, Glenmoriston,

[1] Meyer, *op. cit.*, p. 60.

Glenurquhart and Strathglass emigrated, apparently under the leadership of a tacksman who thought in terms of reproducing in America the social conditions familiar in Scotland. Even in Caithness, which was not highland, the same pattern was followed, for in 1774 James Hogg, a tacksman from Caithness, arrived in North Carolina with 280 people. The departure of such men of substance as lairds and tacksmen was lamented because it was taking money out of the country, but it can hardly be doubted that the rank and file of the emigrants were by no means wealthy, and that poverty pressed on them. One of the emigrants from Caithness in 1774 was a shopkeeper who said he was leaving because the people were too poor to pay their debts to him. The tacksman could obviously realize a large sum on his departure by the sale of stock, but the others could probably do no more than raise the cost of their passage. It was estimated about 1800 that an ordinary tenant could raise about £10 by the sale of his stock, and when the passage money for an adult was about £3 10s., this sum just about sufficed for a family.

When the fashion, or craze, for emigration reached the height it did in the early 1770s, the causes were not to be sought only in the factors which made people feel badly-off at home. There was also a positive 'pull' from overseas. For one thing, as Dr. Johnson had indicated, emigrants, even in those days, communicated with their kinsfolk and encouraged them to follow. The minister of North Uist, referring to the emigrations from that island in the 1770s, said, 'Copies of letters from persons who had emigrated several years before to America . . ., containing the most flattering accounts of North Carolina, were circulated' and went on to explain that those who emigrated in the 1770s 'in their turn gave friends at home the same flattering accounts that induced themselves to go'.[1] But it was also true that Scottish regiments had been engaged in campaigns in America in the Seven Years' War (1756–63): the Black Watch fought at Ticonderoga in 1758, the Royal Scots Fusiliers were at the capture of Belle Isle in 1761 and the Royal Scots took part in the capture of Louisbourg and the subsequent conquest of Canada. Then, after the war, the Cameronians were stationed for a time in Canada. When warriors from those regiments returned to Scotland they did something to make the prospects overseas known to their friends at home. Three men from Barra, for example, who had seen Cape Breton in the campaign of 1758, persuaded some of their

[1] *Old Statistical Account of Scotland,* xiii, 317.

Between decks on an emigration ship. This illustration depicts the interior of a steamer running Irish emigrants in 1851, and represents conditions vastly superior to those which obtained in the earlier sailing vessels.

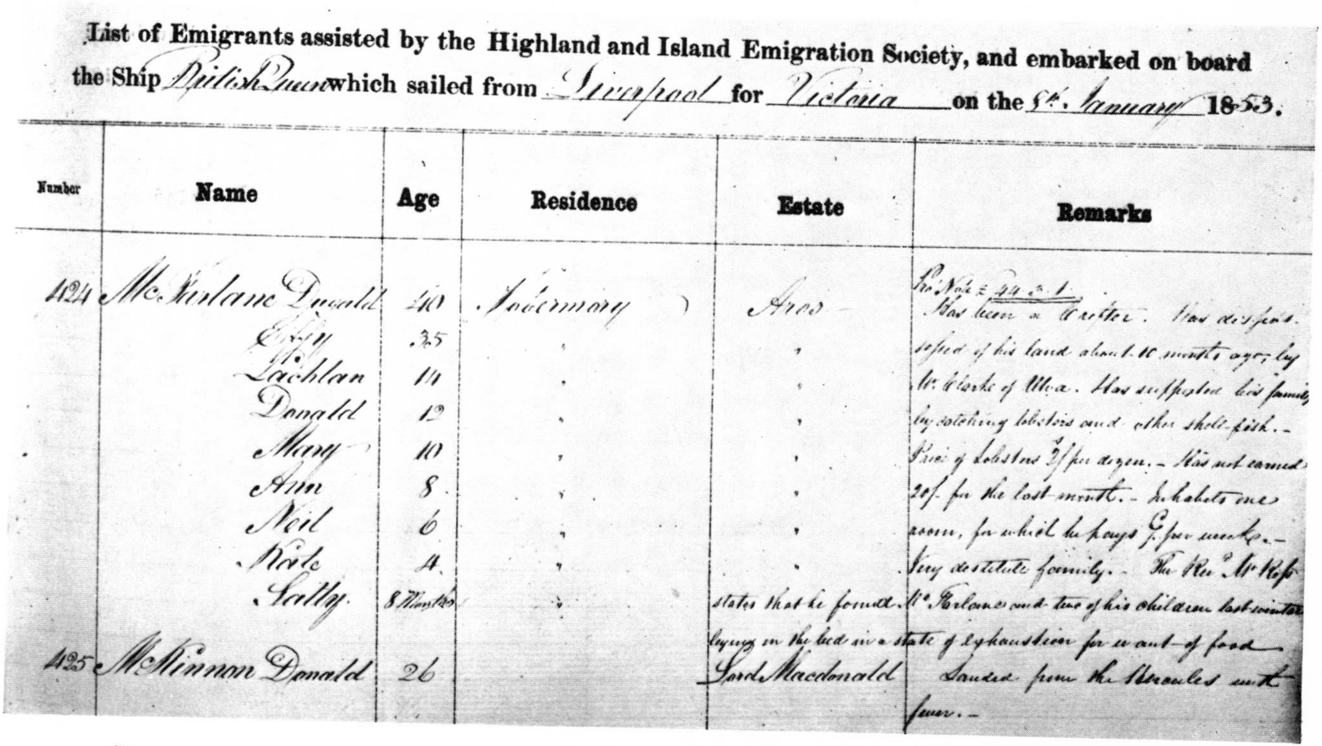

List of Emigrants assisted by the Highland and Island Emigration Society, and embarked on board the Ship British Queen which sailed from Liverpool for Victoria on the 8th January 1853.

Number	Name	Age	Residence	Estate	Remarks
424	McFarlane Dugald	40	Tobermory	Aros	Pro Note = 44 3.1. Has been a Crofter. Was dispossessed of his land about 10 months ago, by Mr Clarke of Ulva. Has supported his family by catching lobsters and other shell-fish.— Price of lobsters 2/- per dozen.— Has not earned 20/- for the last month.— Inhabits one room, for which he pays 6/- per week.— Very destitute family.— The Revd Mr Ross states that he found Mr Farlane and two of his children last winter laying on the bed in a state of exhaustion for want of food
	Effy	35	"	"	
	Lachlan	14	"	"	
	Donald	12	"	"	
	Mary	10	"	"	
	Ann	8	"	"	
	Neil	6	"	"	
	Kate	4	"	"	
	Sally	8 Months	"		
425	McKinnon Donald	26		Lord Macdonald	Landed from the Hercules with fever.—

From a page of the List of Emigrants sent out by the Highlands and Islands Emigration Society fellow-islesmen to go and settle there. Not only so, but some high-land soldiers who had been discharged at the end of the war and had been granted land in America, mainly in New York and Prince Edward Island, formed nuclei which attracted other settlers. Apart, however, from such spontaneous encouragement to emigration, shipping agents had discovered that it was a profitable business, and looked for passengers, while some lowland Scots had apparently become agents of some kind for territories overseas, and in 1772 we find advertisements in Scottish newspapers inviting colonists to Nova Scotia. There was certainly a good deal of propaganda, which must have encouraged emigrants. There was, for instance, a tract by *Scotus Americanus*, called 'Information concerning the province of North Carolina', which commended the fertility of the soil, and some prospective emigrants had been informed that in Carolina the land yielded three crops a year. Again, in the *Edinburgh Advertiser* for 4th January 1774 we read, 'A day labourer can gain thrice the wages he can earn in this country. . . . There are no beggars in North America. . . . There are no titles, proud lords to tyrannize over the lower sort of people, men being there more upon a level.'[1]

While one group of Scots after another made their way to America, the crisis was approaching which, in 1776, led the colonies to declare their independence of the mother country. In the war which followed, the great majority of the highland settlers were loyal to the British cause. To those who have identified the Highlanders with the Jacobites who had twice in the century raised a rebellion in their own country against the British crown, this has been something of a surprise, but there is, in truth, no mystery about it. For one thing a good many of the emigrants had come from areas like Argyll which had not been Jacobite and whose people had been accustomed at home to align themselves with the Lowlanders. It may be, too, that there was something in the highland outlook which felt a dis-taste for republicanism, and in any event by 1776 a generation had grown to maturity which had never known any effort in Scotland to unseat King George. But it was also true that Highlanders who had been Jacobite rebels before they emigrated had seen the consequence of unsuccessful rebellion at home and had no wish to inflict such sufferings on themselves and their families in America. The fortunes of the Scottish loyalists in America will be traced in Chapter 9.

The immediate effect of the outbreak of the American War in 1776, by cutting off what had hitherto been the principal outlet for

[1] Meyer, *op. cit.*, 43, 53.

5

highland emigrants, was to check the emigration altogether for a time, but, shortly before the war ended, there was a disastrous harvest (1782–3), leading to famine conditions in the Highlands, and emigration was soon in full swing once more. Again, the war with France, beginning in 1793 and continuing until 1815, on the whole curbed emigration from Scotland, but there was from time to time a substantial exodus from the Highlands. Figures of emigration are hard to come by, for many sailings were from ports where no records were kept, but the estimate was 779 persons in 1801 and 3,401 in 1802. In 1801–3 it is said that twenty-five vessels sailed with emigrants from Skye alone. Between 1783 and 1803 there must have been 20,000 emigrants from Scotland as a whole, the majority of them from the Highlands. From 1790 onwards a number of people, variously estimated at up to 700, left Moidart, Arisaig, Ardnamurchan and Sunart, and about 1812 most of the Kinlochmoidart tenants are said to have emigrated to America. It had not yet occurred to many minds that emigration might be advantageous, and contemporaries were much concerned: one section of a report on the Highlands in 1802 was headed 'The causes of emigration and the means of preventing it', and there it was alleged that the emigrants of 1802 took £100,000 with them, raised by the sale of their cattle.[1] Road-making in the Highlands and the construction of the Caledonian Canal were initiated at this time partly with a view to providing employment and checking emigration. Besides, as will appear in the next chapter, the Passenger Act of 1803, designed to improve conditions on emigrant ships, had some effect in checking emigration because it raised the cost of passages, but it did not stop the movement: 'Some individuals who cannot afford to pay the increased freight have already enlisted in the Canadian Fencibles, on condition of having their wives and children carried free to America; and many single families will probably engage passages on board of ships that, by taking out only a few, will not come within the operation of the act'. In 1805 the spirit of emigration 'about Lochaber and the island of Skye has manifested itself more openly', for four or five vessels had sailed from there, and other passengers had made their way overseas by way of the Clyde.[2]

The objective in this period was those northern parts of the North American continent which were later to become the Dominion of Canada, for one consequence of the successful American revolution

[1] Parliamentary Reports, 1802–3, vol. ii.
[2] Cregeen, *Argyll Estate Instructions* (Scottish History Society), 201n.

was to turn the thoughts of highland emigrants for a time away from those territories which had now become the United States of America and to direct them to areas further north which remained loyal to the British crown. Emigration to Prince Edward Island and Nova Scotia had, indeed, just started before the America War. In 1767, when the lands of Prince Edward Island (which had been finally ceded to Britain in 1763) were allotted to proprietors who decided to encourage Scottish settlers, a party from the Highlands and Dumfriesshire arrived as colonists, and in 1770 another two parties landed. The tradition of settlement once established, more emigrants followed, like John McNeill, from Argyll, who settled at Cavendish in 1775. There were plans for settlement in Nova Scotia in 1768, but it seems that the first band of emigrants, numbering a hundred, did not go until 1770. In 1772 two hundred emigrants arrived in Nova Scotia from South Uist, and it was in Prince Edward Island that the laird of Glenaladale, as mentioned before, settled his people. One migration shows the relation between Highlanders and lowland *entrepreneurs*, for a Greenock merchant who had shares in a company which had been allotted 200,000 acres in Pictou County, Nova Scotia, offered a free passage, land and a year's provisions, to Scottish Highlanders. In 1773 families from Inverness-shire, Wester Ross and Sutherland settled at Pictou, where in 1777 they were joined by some Scots from Dumfriesshire who had settled in Prince Edward Island three years earlier. These early settlements in Nova Scotia and Prince Edward Island helped to encourage other Scots after the American War was over, and in any event those maritime provinces were attractive because it cost less to reach them than to penetrate to the inland areas of the Continent. There were, however, two developments which helped to foster settlement in Canada proper. The 78th or Fraser's Highlanders, who had taken an active part in the capture of Quebec from the French in the Seven Years' War, were disbanded when the war ended, and, with a section of the 42nd Highlanders or Black Watch, formed a Scottish nucleus in Montreal, Quebec and elsewhere. They attracted others.

Secondly, Scottish highland settlers who had not supported the revolutionary party in the American War of Independence found that there was no place for them in the United States after 1783 and, in common with other United Empire Loyalists, removed to the northern areas. For example, the Highlanders from Glengarry who had emigrated to the Mohawk Valley in 1773 moved during the war to 'Glengarry County', Ontario, on the St. Lawrence River and

Lake St. Francis, adjoining the counties of Stormont and Dundas. In 1785, 520 Highlanders from Knoydart, with their priest, Alexander Macdonnell, joined their clansmen in that new Glengarry. A little later families came from Glenelg to this district, and then some from Lochiel, which also gave its name to a county in the area.

Emigration from the Highlands tended, at least for many years, to be peculiarly communal or corporate, reflecting the close-knit character of highland society. Moreover, it was usually a movement under leadership, as one would expect of people accustomed to clan life. In the earlier phases, we have seen how tacksmen acted as leaders, and this continued down to about 1775. There was one later example of leadership by a chief, the peculiar one of Archibald Macnab, of Kinnell (near Killin in the Perthshire Highlands), who, as a fugitive from his creditors in Scotland, arrived in Upper Canada in 1822 and arranged the acquisition of 5,000 acres of land in the county of Renfrew, on the Ottawa River adjacent to Fitzroy. In 1824 about a hundred emigrants went out, undertaking to repay the cost of their transportation and entering into a bond on their lands in Canada. Macnab lorded it over them very much as a tyrannical chief in Scotland might have done. Sometimes the emigrants found their leader in a clergyman. Thus, Alexander Macdonell, who had accompanied so many of his parishioners to Canada in 1785, apparently conducted a second party to Canada in 1791. Angus MacEachern, another priest, led his people from North Uist to Prince Edward Island in 1790, and many more Roman Catholics followed to build up a community. Angus became bishop of Prince Edward Island in 1821. In 1802 Roman Catholics from Barra settled at Antigonish, and no less than 800 of them, with their priests, Augustine and Alexander MacDonald, chiefly at Arisaig. In 1801 the Glengarry Fencibles, which had been raised during the French war and had served against the Irish rebellion in 1798, were disbanded at Ayr, and in 1803, with their families, 1,000 strong in all, were led by Alexander MacDonnell, their chaplain, to Upper Canada, where 200 acres of land were granted to each family for their settlement in Glengarry County near Montreal. MacDonnell became bishop of Upper Canada in 1826 and a member of the legislative council in 1831. In the middle of the nineteenth century the Moidart priest, Ronald Rankin, advocated emigration and promised to go with his people wherever they might settle; in 1855 he rejoined those of his flock who had gone to Australia.

Another type of leadership was represented by Thomas Douglas, eighth Earl of Selkirk (1771–1820). He was the seventh son of his parents, but through a series of deaths he unexpectedly succeeded to the title in 1799. His father was a man of liberal and humanitarian outlook, and Earl Thomas, although a Lowlander both by descent and by his landed interests, developed a concern for the well-being of the Highlands and their people. Accepting emigration from the Highlands as inevitable, he combined a solicitude for destitute Highlanders with a desire to develop British North America rather than see emigrants go to the United States.[1]

Selkirk already owned a tract of land on Lake Ontario, but it was now within the boundaries of the independent republic, and in 1803 he obtained the government's sanction for settlements in Prince Edward Island and Upper Canada. In that year he led across the Atlantic three shiploads of emigrants, about 800 in number, from Skye, the Uists and the mainland of Ross, Argyll and Inverness. They landed at Orwell Bay in Prince Edward Island, and are commemorated in the parish church of Belfast on the south side of the island. Selkirk's personality gave the people the leadership they needed, and he said himself that the venture had 'a little resemblance to the old feudal times'.[2] The work of the settlement followed the usual pioneering pattern, and the first task was to fell timber and clear the ground for growing crops. The colony prospered, and it was the only one of Selkirk's schemes to be wholly successful.

Leaving his colonists in Prince Edward Island, Selkirk went on to prospect in Upper Canada, and in 1804 he established a settlement, in Dover and Chatham townships on Lake St. Clair, which he named Baldoon after his paternal estate in Scotland. Some of the small number of settlers were loyalists from the United States, including certain of the Glengarry MacDonnells, and some were Scots previously settled in Montreal, but others came out from Tobermory to join them. The settlers encountered a disastrous harvest and disease which caused many deaths, so that the whole venture ended in failure.

But Selkirk had been interested even earlier in a colony much further west, 'at the western extremity of Canada, upon the waters which fell into Lake Winnipeg'.[3] Reverting to this idea in 1808, he bought up shares in the Hudson's Bay Company and hoped that his proposed settlement would aid that company in its competition with the North-West Company. In 1811 he acquired from the Hudson's

---

[1] In 1805 Selkirk published his *Observations on the present state of the Highlands of Scotland.*
[2] John M. Gray, *Lord Selkirk of Red River*, 22.
[3] *Ibid.*, 53.

Bay Company, for a nominal payment, no less than 116,000 square miles of land—an area as large as the British Isles—and proposed a settlement on the Red River. As part of the bargain, he gave an undertaking to provide 200 servants a year for the Company and to develop an agricultural colony. The area was one into which French explorers and fur traders had penetrated before 1763, and since 1763 both French and British traders had been operating; there was, in consequence, a certain population of half-breeds as well as a very few settled Europeans.

Selkirk already had recruiting agents in the west of Scotland and in Ireland. In 1811 an assortment of Orcadians, Glaswegians and Highlanders was mustered (not without some desertions) at Stornoway, where they embarked, and after many difficulties they at last reached Red River in August 1812. Another party, of Scots and Irish, sailed from Sligo and arrived in October 1812; in 1813 a party of about ninety evicted tenants from Kildonan, in Sutherland, sailed under Selkirk's auspices from Stromness, but were stranded at Churchill, on Hudson Bay, for a year; and in 1815 a fourth party sailed from Helmsdale, in Sutherland.

The North-West Company was strongly opposed to the settlement, for, as they saw it, an enormous tract of land, which had previously been regarded as a common hunting ground, had now been conveyed to Selkirk as private property. Already in 1815 the settlers were driven out by agents of the North-West Company, but they re-established themselves before the end of the year. Meantime Selkirk had sailed from home for New York, whence he went on to Upper Canada and, in preparation for an expedition to Red River in the following spring, collected a force of disbanded soldiers to assist him to maintain his colony. He was too late to avert a further disaster, for in 1816 a party of half-breeds, instigated by the North-West Company, again destroyed the settlement, with many fatal casualties. But Selkirk came west with his force, and, in his capacity as a magistrate, arrested the leaders of the North-West faction and sent them to Montreal for trial. More high-handedly, he took possession of the North-West's post at Fort William, on Lake Superior, and wintered there. The North-West Company replied with a warrant for the arrest of Selkirk, on charges of theft of the Company's property and forcible seizure of Fort William. Selkirk resisted arrest and in the spring of 1817 he proceeded to Red River. Some settlers had already returned there, and more joined them. Selkirk left Red River before the winter and returned to Lower Canada.

Trials at Quebec disclosed that the North-West Company was influential enough to interfere with the course of justice, for one accused person was acquitted in face of the evidence and others were quietly released or allowed to escape. In the trials for murder, Selkirk's activities were misrepresented as nothing more than an effort on behalf of the Hudson's Bay Company in its competition with the North-West Company. The counter-trial of Selkirk himself was inconclusive. After it, he returned to London to seek justice there, but his health gave way and, seeking recovery in the south of France, he died at Pau in 1820.

In spite of disasters, the western colony had not been a complete failure, and it had successfully overcome many of the difficulties which had been pointed out when it was first proposed. Thus, so far from there being danger to the settlers from the Indians, the latter had shown themselves favourably disposed. Again, so far from the land being incapable of growing crops, it had been proved to be very fertile. And, finally, while the climate was certainly severe, the colonists had been able to survive through the winters. The continued security of the colony was at last assured when the merger of the two trading companies in 1821 brought their rivalry to an end.

Yet another kind of leadership of Highlanders is typified in the story—one of the most remarkable in the long history of Scottish emigration—of Norman MacLeod (1780–1866) and the people whom he led from his native Assynt first to North America, then to Australia and finally to New Zealand.[1] We have already seen how a priest like Angus MacEachern could act as a leader and even commander, but Angus was a very mild version of the tyrannical Presbyterian Norman MacLeod. After six years of University study, first at Aberdeen and then at Edinburgh, Norman MacLeod decided that he could not in conscience become a minister of the Church of Scotland as he had originally intended. Much of his future career was to be determined by the strength of his dissent, which he carried to inordinate lengths in later years. 'I flatly deny,' he declared, 'having ever claimed the status of a minister of the Church of Scotland, and in all humility and sincerity desire to bless heaven for having enlightened my mind to dread and abhor that state';[2] and his view was said, probably with truth, to be that there was not a minister of Christ in the Church of Scotland. He was never formally attached to any sect, and can only be described as a 'Normanist'; he did himself

---

[1] The story is told by Flora McPherson in *Watchman against the World* (Hale, 1962).
[2] *Ibid.*, 114.

use the term 'Normanism' to describe his tenets. For many years, after going to America, he acted as an entirely unauthorized preacher until, in 1827, he obtained ordination from a presbytery in the state of New York—a place suitably distant from his own sphere of operations in Cape Breton. He was perfectly frank about his rejection of any kind of discipline: 'Being placed at a distance, I have never experienced the least restraint or control. . . . Otherwise, I would not have thought of joining the clergy for all my life in the world.'[1] Needless to say, such an attitude was the very negation of orthodox Presbyterian thought, which lays great stress on the subordination of the minister to the courts of the church. It was hardly surprising that later, in 1840, Norman refused to join the local Church of Scotland presbytery in Cape Breton.

After he completed his university studies, Norman had become a schoolmaster at Ullapool, under the auspices of the Scottish Society for the Promotion of Christian Knowledge. He was soon in trouble with the local parish minister, to whom he was supposed to be responsible but with whom he was almost at once in competition, for Norman began to preach as well as to teach. Seeing that schoolmastering, as well as the ministry of the established Church, was closed to him in Scotland, he decided to emigrate, and worked at the fishing station at Wick for a time in order to accumulate the necessary funds.

In 1817 Norman sailed from Loch Broom for Pictou, in Nova Scotia. He urged his compatriots to follow his example, and in 1818 another 150 sailed from Assynt. At Pictou there was already a prosperous community of Scots, engaged in lumbering and shipbuilding. Over 800 Presbyterians had settled there in 1802, so there were already Presbyterian churches and, inevitably, a school, or rather 'Pictou Academy'. Norman, of course, formed his own spiritual community, which he dominated by his sermons, and he began to conceive of it as a fellowship which he could control and which he could seclude from the influence of the outside world. In 1820, therefore, he transferred a party of settlers to St. Ann's, Cape Breton, from which the original French settlers had long since withdrawn and where few others had taken their places. Others followed from Pictou to St. Ann's in 1821, others came from Scotland to join the community.

At St. Ann's a settlement could be almost entirely self-supporting on an agrarian basis, though at a rather low level of comfort. Land

[1] *Ibid.*, 73.

was granted free to the settlers, up to an area of 200 acres; beyond that there was a nominal charge. Log cabins were built, potatoes were planted among the stumps of the felled trees and could be grown much more easily than grain, which could hardly be cultivated until the ground was completely cleared. Potatoes and fish therefore formed the staple diet in the early days. When corn did become available, it was at first ground in hand-querns as it had been at home in Scotland. There was ample grazing for the cow which each family soon acquired, and also for sheep, which provided wool for clothing just as the cows provided hide for shoes. So far the settlers could depend on their own produce. Luxuries were to be had from a store, but at this Norman looked askance, and when he quarrelled with the store-keeper about the latter's dealings in smuggled brandy he forbade his people to have any dealings with the store, even although in a bad season they could have avoided much misery by drawing on imported goods.

Norman's domination was complete. He became officially magistrate of his community in 1823. He was from the outset its preacher and spiritual leader, and with his ordination in 1827 he became its official minister. Likewise, he had been conducting a school from 1822, and in 1827 was officially licensed as schoolmaster. The school had hitherto been supported entirely by the parents' subscriptions, and it continued to be mainly so supported, though it now received an official grant. As both minister and schoolmaster, Norman received payment not in money but by labour services on his farm and in his other undertakings. There was indeed 'a little resemblance to the old feudal times', as there had been in Selkirk's ventures; and one can only conclude that the Highlanders were so habituated to leadership and domination that they meekly acquiesced in Norman's tyranny.

In Norman's community, Sabbatarianism was carried to inordinate lengths, even by Scottish and Presbyterian standards. Potatoes for use on Sunday had to be peeled on Saturday, the dishes used on Sunday were not washed up until Monday. It was not even permitted to bring fresh water into the house on Sunday; water brought from the well on Saturday had to serve. Norman's denunciations from the pulpit seldom, if ever, had to touch on the more serious sins, for his people were too terrified to commit any, but he found trivialities to denounce, and his own wife came under censure for wearing a hat which he thought unduly gay. This minister never celebrated Holy Communion, for he presumed to judge his congregation unworthy to receive it. It is not surprising that an observer of Cape Breton remarked that Norman's flock were 'the most sober and orderly settlement on the island'.[1]

In 1849, at a time when Cape Breton had suffered from a very bad season, a report arrived from a son of Norman who had gone to Australia, giving a very favourable account of conditions in that continent. Plans were made to remove, and in order to do so the people had in the first place to build two ships, one of 300 and another of 180 tons. One ship left in October 1851 with 140 people on a seven months' voyage to Adelaide, which they found disappointing. They then moved to Melbourne, and landed there in the midst of a goldrush, which was not to Norman's taste either. The second ship, leaving Cape Breton in May 1852, reached Australia in five months, but the people on board were disappointed to find that the first party had not yet formed a permanent settlement.

New Zealand seemed more promising than Australia, and in 1853 over a hundred persons set out for there. Norman followed in a second voyage. The community settled on the Waipu River, and now invited their brethren who were still at St. Ann's to follow them. Between 1855 and 1860 a further four shiploads of them did. In New Zealand the people found agriculture much easier than it had been in Cape Breton, for burning the bush produced right away a soil of incredible fertility. Many of them, however, turned to occupations other than agriculture, and, mingling with the other Scottish settlers in New Zealand, made a name as shipbuilders and mariners.

Norman MacLeod's activities make a picturesque story, but the migration of his people was not in itself unusual in that period after 1815. Between 1815 and 1820 many others went overseas from Sutherland and other parts of the West Highlands. A visitor to Stornoway in August 1816 noticed that 'there are two vessels lying here with emigrants for America, each with eighty people on board, of all ages from a few days to upwards of sixty'.[2] Many made for Nova Scotia and Quebec, but the colonization of Upper Canada went on too. A settlement at St. Anicet, Godmanchester township, was made in 1820 and was developed in the next two or three years by a heterogeneous band of Scots. Duncan McNicol came from Glengarry County in Canada, three brothers MacMillan came from Lochaber in Scotland, Donald Rankin from Argyll and John Harvey and William Brodie from the Scottish Lowlands. In 1823 another

[1] *Ibid.*, 122.
[2] R. L. Stevenson, *A Family of Engineers*, 185.

Highlander from Lochaber, John Macpherson, left Fort William by
sea and his ship lay for a time at Tobermory awaiting other emigrants. In the same year about 600 Highlanders in all from that area
of the West Highlands are said to have made their way to Upper
Canada. New ground was broken in 1825, when some Highlanders
set out for Venezuela under the auspices of the Columbian Agricultural Association, but they found conditions unfavourable and transferred themselves first to the United States, then to Upper Canada.
In the 1830s, Australia became a serious objective of highland emigrants, and about a hundred people are said to have gone there from
Arisaig and Moidart in 1837–8.

It was, indeed, not uncommon for emigrants to reach their ultimate destination only after two or three moves, as Norman Mac-
Leod's people had done. The simplest case was, of course, when the
first move was from the Highlands to the Lowlands. For example,
Hugh MacDonald, born in the parish of Rogart in Sutherland in
1782, moved to Glasgow, where he married and where his third son
was born in 1815; in 1820 the family emigrated to Kingston, Ontario, and the boy who had been born five years before, John Alexander MacDonald, became first prime minister of the Canadian
Confederation in 1867. Similarly, Alexander MacDougall, born in
Islay in 1845, was taken by his parents to Glasgow when he was
seven years of age and to Canada when he was nine. What may well
be a typical instance of movement within the American continent is
that of two families from Islay who sailed from Greenock to North
Carolina in 1818 and settled, one in Cumberland County, the other
in Richmond County, where cousins of theirs were settled already.
But, encouraged by another man from Islay who had settled in
Canada and came to visit them, they sold off and made their way
overland to Eldon, Ontario, about 1830.

Not for the first or the last time, emigration from the Highlands
was, between 1815 and 1820, denounced by those who regretted the
loss of man-power to Britain, and David Stewart of Garth's *Sketches
of the Highlanders of Scotland* (1811) was a military history which was
also designed as propaganda against emigration. This was a variant
of the old theme that the highland population should be fostered to
provide fighting men, though now as cannon-fodder for British
armies. However, by the 1820s, the clearance or eviction of tenants
for the sake of sheep farming was well under way, and emigration
began to be looked on with a fresh eye. Many now thought it desirable, as providing an outlet for over-numerous tenants who were a

burden on the estates. Already in 1825 we find the proprietor of the island of Rum, whose rents were £300 in arrears, solving his problem by cancelling the debt and paying the passages of those of his tenants who were prepared to go to Canada. From 1826 onwards there were many requests from landlords for government assistance towards the removal of their tenants to the colonies, but the government was reluctant to act, and such assistance was but rarely given at this stage. Even after 1837, when a Committee on Unemployment and Poverty in the Highlands recommended emigration, nothing was done by the government. Some landlords, however, continued to organize emigration—one is said to have aided nearly 2,000 persons to emigrate between 1837 and 1841—but down to 1840 there were still landlords who thought humanity demanded that they should encourage their people to remain—a policy which many thought mistaken. The critics of the 'humanitarian' landlords were justified when economic disaster came to the Highlands in the 1840s. Some of the societies which were then formed to offer relief to starving Highlanders also helped in this way: the Scottish Patriotic Society, besides striving for improved conditions at home, also assisted emigration, and the Highlands and Islands Emigration Society began its operations in 1852. The Highland Destitution Committee also was involved. In 1851 the government conceded, by the Emigration Advances Act, that landlords should be entitled to borrow from public funds to defray the cost of removing tenants who wished to emigrate.

The history of the Highlands and Islands Emigration Society requires special notice.[1] It appears that early in 1852 committees had been formed in both London and Edinburgh to promote emigration from the Highlands and Islands and were appealing for subscriptions. The movement found a director in Sir Charles Trevelyan. As an Assistant Secretary to the Treasury he had administered Irish relief in 1845–7 and his experience of the Irish situation had given him emphatic views on the desirability of 'a *final* measure of relief for the Western Highlands and Islands by transferring the surplus of the population to Australia'; his contention was that 'the only immediate remedy for the present state of things in Skye is emigration, and the people will never emigrate while they are supported at home at other people's expense. This mistaken humanity has converted the people of Skye, from the clergy downwards, into a

[1] The Letter Books of the Society, and its Lists of Emigrants, are in the General Register House, Edinburgh. Succeeding notes refer to the Letter Books. *Cf.* D. S. MacMillan, 'Sir Charles Trevelyan and the Highland and Island Emigration Society, 1849–59', in *Royal Australian Hist. Soc. Journal*, xlix, 161–88.

mendicant community.[1] The Society was formally founded at the end of April, with Prince Albert as patron, and the queen gave a donation of £300 from the privy purse. Sir Charles himself was active in soliciting subscriptions, and a circular setting forth the aims of the Society was printed in May 1852. It was stated that 'The surplus population of the Western Highlands and Islands is from 30,000 to 40,000. . . . The expense of sending men, women and children will on an average be at least £5—that is to say it will be upwards of £3 for the outfit and deposit of each person—and £15 for the proportion (which, however, I hope will not be a large one) which will not be eligible for free passages. On the other hand, we may calculate on half the expense being defrayed by the emigrants and the landowners, and as our Fund is a reproductive one we may begin to get back our repayments from the colony before the whole of the original sum is expended.'[2] The target for subscriptions was £100,000. The Society worked under the rules of the Colonial Land Emigration Commissioners, who provided passages on receipt of a deposit, usually of £1 or £2. The Society was to make good any deficiencies in the sums required; proprietors were to pay one third of the sum disbursed by the Society; and the emigrant, by a promissory note, undertook to repay the advances.

The first sailing organized by the Society took place on 26th January 1852, and the passengers included a characteristic family—John McDonald, aged forty, his wife, aged thirty-nine, and eight children of ages from nineteen to two. The Society worked systematically, by estates, so that in general people from the same estate went together on the same ship and preserved the integrity of their community. The chief areas from which it drew emigrants were Skye and Mull, but it drew some also from Coll, Morvern, Ardnamurchan, Iona, Moidart, St. Kilda, Kintail, Uist, Harris, Sutherland, Kintyre, Lochiel, Tiree, Lewis and Ullapool. In all nearly 5,000 emigrants went out under the Society's auspices. The ships sailed mostly from Liverpool, but one at least from Campbeltown, and they carried numbers of passengers ranging up to more than 700.

Some of the comments in the Society's records on the people assisted are worth quoting: 'Very poor family. A proper object for the aid of the Highland Society'; 'eligible couple'; 'very poor family; chief support shellfish'; 'man small of stature and has suffered greatly from want of food. Eldest daughter healthy eligible looking

[1] 3rd April 1852 and 20th January 1852.
[2] 22nd May 1852.

girl'; 'a very industrious woman; good family for Australia'; 'strong woman; fine grown children'. A vivid picture of the misery which the Society sought to relieve is given in the description of Donald McFarlane of Tobermory: he had been a crofter, but had been dispossessed of his land about ten months before by Mr. Clark of Ulva. He had supported his family by catching lobsters and other shellfish, but, as the price of lobsters was only 2s. per dozen, in the last month he had not earned 20s. He and his family inhabited one room, for which he paid 7d. a week. 'A very destitute family: the Rev. Mr. Ross states that he found McFarlane and two of his children last winter lying in the bed in a state of exhaustion from want of food.'

On the emigrant ships, as well as in the prior arrangements, there was co-operation between the Emigration Society and the Emigration Commissioners; in July 1852 the Society appealed to the Religious Tract Society for books, 'especially books suited to the capacity of the young', to supplement the small libraries which the Commissioners provided on the ships. After several years of work, the balance of funds in the hands of the Society (amounting to £865) was in 1858 handed over to the Board of Supervision, which was the central body in Scotland for the administration of poor relief, and the Society's affairs were finally wound up in 1859.

The principal areas from which emigrants went out between 1840 and 1860 were Strathconon, Glencalvie and Newmore in Ross, Glenelg and Knoydart in Inverness-shire, Glenquaich in Perthshire, Glenorchy in Argyll and the islands of Skye, Lewis, North and South Uist and Barra. Some of the totals were very high—700 or more from Skye, over 2,000 from Lewis, 1,000 from Harris, North Uist and Benbecula, 1,500 from Barra and South Uist. In 1851 alone, 3,500 Scots were assisted by their landlords to emigrate to Canada, including 986 from Lewis by Sir James Matheson and 1,681 from South Uist and Barra by Colonel Gordon of Cluny. The majority of all the emigrants went to various parts of Canada, where the maritime provinces still had their attraction for Highlanders, but quite a number, including those sent by the Highlands and Islands Emigration Society, went to Australia.

It has become firmly implanted in folk memory that much of the emigration from the Highlands was 'compulsory' and that'clearance' or 'eviction' commonly meant dispossessing tenants and shipping them off to America. It has already been made clear in this volume that this is by no means the whole story, or even an important part of it. Much of the clearance involved nothing more than re-settling tenants on new holdings within the same county, sometimes even within the same parish, and the notion that scheming landlords, for their own financial profit, shipped to America tenants who were living in plenty, or even in comfort, at home, is preposterous. The truth is that people who had experienced the miseries of life in the Highlands in the 1840s clamoured for assistance to enable them to leave the country: for example, in 1847, 136 heads of families in the grossly-overpopulated island of Tiree addressed the head of the Board of Supervision, lamenting their 'great destitution' in an island 'where there is no fuel and not an inch of waste land which the inhabitants could not drain and trench in a few months' and begging for assistance so that they could participate in 'the enjoyments and comforts, they are from day to day informed, their friends in Canada enjoy';[1] and the people of Barra, in a similar petition, remarked that from America 'their relatives are daily sending intelligence calculated to encourage them to follow'. Desire to emigrate was also stimulated by a Gaelic periodical, published monthly, drawing attention to the advantage of emigration.

When the next highland crisis came, in the 1880s, emigration was once more regarded as an obvious remedy. Again there was private enterprise: Lady Gordon Cathcart assisted over sixty distressed crofting families from her estates in the Hebrides to settle on land south of Wapella and Moosomin in Saskatchewan. But it was also true that the Napier Commission, which investigated crofting conditions and made recommendations so favourable to the tenants, reported in favour of emigration, aided and directed by the state, as the only remedy for the over-population of certain areas. In Britain, therefore, an Emigration Board was appointed with power to expend £10,000; New Zealand in 1884 made provision for the setting apart of 10,000 acres for crofter settlers, each of them to have ten acres free and more on payment; and Canada made provision for such settlers in Manitoba and the North-West. James Macandrew, in advocating the New Zealand scheme, spoke rhetorically of '40,000 families of these crofters, physically one of the finest races on the face of the earth—and withal sober, industrious, frugal. . . . It would be an exodus such as the world has not seen since the days of Moses'.[2] But little came of the proposal. Not many Highlanders went to Canada either under this scheme, and those who went (in

---

[1] *Scotland as it was and as it is,* by the Duke of Argyll, Appendix.
[2] McLintock, *Otago,* 645.

1888) were successful in Killarney (Manitoba) but unsuccessful in Saltcoats, about 200 miles north-west of Killarney.[1]

As was explained in the previous chapter, the new régime inaugurated by the Crofters' Commission did nothing to check migration from the Highlands, and since the 1880s far more people have left the Highlands of their own volition than were ever forcibly removed by wicked landlords. From 1861 to 1931, it has been calculated, the Highlands lost some 230,000 people in net outward movement, and possibly 150,000 of them migrated to places outside Scotland. This, however, was only part of a wider movement of people away from the rural areas in every part of Scotland, and the depopulation of the Highlands was no greater than that of some parts of the Borders, for example. To that extent, emigration from the Highlands after the nineteenth century merges in the general picture of emigration from Scotland as a whole, and even before the end of the nineteenth century it had ceased to have the distinctive features which justifies giving it separate treatment in its earlier phases.

[1] For the Canadian settlements, see *Canada and its Provinces*, vii.

6

SCOTLAND'S CHANGING
INDUSTRIAL ECONOMY

THE union of Scotland with England, in 1707, meant the removal of the restrictions which had previously hampered Scottish trade with the English colonies in America and, in the words of a Glasgow merchant in Scott's *Rob Roy*, 'opened us a road west awa' yonder'. Within a few years the results were spectacular. By the middle of the eighteenth century millions of pounds of tobacco were coming to the Clyde each year, and Glasgow became the premier tobacco port of Great Britain. Most of the tobacco was for re-export to the continent of Europe, for the colonies were forbidden to export tobacco directly except to Britain and other British possessions. In exchange for their exports to Scotland, which included sugar and rum as well as tobacco, the colonists wanted manufactured goods, for they themselves had few manufactures and were indeed restrained from the manufacture even of some of their own raw materials. Consequently manufactures sprang up in Scotland to meet the demand. Among them were wrought iron work, leather goods, pottery and crystal, rope-making, hat-making and furniture.

The most important manufacture exported, however, was linen, and it would scarcely be an exaggeration to call the eighteenth century, or at least part of it, the linen era in Scottish industry. The many processes involved—the preparation of the raw flax by separating the fibre from the stalk, spinning, weaving, bleaching and dyeing—were, one or more of them, carried on in nearly every parish in the kingdom. The industry was mainly a domestic one, and was often the part-time occupation of men and women who spent most of their time in agricultural work, but, while spinning long remained a part-time occupation, weaving, even though still done in the home, came to be full-time and to be largely concentrated in particular areas like Glasgow, Paisley, Dundee, Dunfermline and Perth, and the finishing processes were even more localized. The production of linen rose about twelve-fold between 1728 and 1800.

This phase of the Scottish economy came to a sudden end when the American War of Independence (1776–83) brought about the collapse of the lucrative tobacco trade. After the colonies became independent, tobacco was, of course, once more imported, but only for Scottish consumption, as the Americans were now free to send their tobacco directly to markets anywhere. In the new situation, most of the Scots who had been engaged in the tobacco trade had to find other outlets for their energy and resources. The industry which came along, just at this time, to absorb attention, and to make use of the skill in textile manufacture already acquired by Scottish linen-workers, was the cotton industry, which was to dominate the Scottish economy for over half a century. Within a few years of the end of the American war there were by Scottish riversides, especially in Renfrewshire and Lanarkshire, many cotton spinning mills, worked by water-power. The weaving looms were still worked by hand, and as the production of cotton thread increased the weavers enjoyed a time of great prosperity.

The serious beginnings of the Scottish iron industry are usually dated from the opening of the Carron Works near Falkirk in 1760. But for a long time thereafter development was very slow, and it was not until the invention of the hot blast in 1828 made it easier to make economic use of Scottish iron ore that there was a great increase in production. Until that time, iron was a negligible item in comparison with linen and cotton.

The eighteenth century saw, besides these commercial and industrial changes, a revolution in Scottish agriculture as well. One of the greatest weaknesses in Scottish farming had been the lack of winter feeding for cattle, but now root crops like turnips began to be cultivated on a large scale and new grasses were introduced to yield abundant crops of hay. As cattle and sheep could now be better fed in winter, it was possible to improve the stock by breeding heavier animals. There was a tendency to make farms larger, and to enclose the fields by dykes. Tenant-farmers were now granted long leases of their holdings, so that they were no longer in any danger of being deprived of their farms before they could reap the benefit of any improvements they had made. The land was more carefully fertilized, and one of the elements in the new husbandry was a thought-ful rotation of crops to make the best use of all the constituents in the soil. Finally, better implements, like a lighter and more efficient plough, and threshing-machines, made their appearance. Thus equipped for more efficient operation, Scottish farmers made a great deal of money at the end of the eighteenth century and the beginning of the nineteenth. At that time, not only had the growing populations of the towns to be fed, but the long French wars meant that armies had to be clothed and the navy had to be supplied with salted meat, and also that imports were restricted.

The dominance of cotton in the Scottish economy continued until the middle of the nineteenth century and even a little later. About 75 per cent of the output came from mills in Lanarkshire and Ren-frewshire, and there was an especially heavy concentration of cotton factories in Glasgow and its immediate neighbourhood. After 1800 power was increasingly applied to weaving as well as spinning, and the handloom weavers in general suffered severely from the change, though some of them were able to make a good living by producing some specialized products, like the famous Paisley Shawls, which were beyond the capacity of the power looms. The point of maxi-mum expansion of the industry as a whole seems to have been reached by the 1850s, and after that there was a standstill, or even a slight decline, before the prosperity of this great Scottish industry was shattered, as the tobacco trade had been shattered in the eighteenth century, by events on the other side of the Atlantic. This time it was the American Civil War (1861–5), which cut off the supplies of raw cotton on which the Scottish factories had relied. After the war, recovery was only partial, for Lancashire became the centre of the cotton industry in Britain, and only certain specialized branches of cotton production continued to flourish in Scotland.

The linen industry, unaffected by the disaster which had over-taken cotton, remained important until the twentieth century. It became mechanized, so that here, too, the handloom weavers were driven out of business, and, after it had been displaced in the west by cotton, it came to be concentrated mainly in Angus and Fife. Even within that area, there were degrees of specialization, and a new textile, jute, became the main industry of Dundee, while Kirkcaldy concentrated on linoleum.

However, while some textiles thus retained their importance, the emphasis of the Scottish economy, especially in the west of the country, moved away from textiles to the heavy industries—coal,

iron, steel, engineering and shipbuilding—which came to dominate
the Scottish scene in the later nineteenth century. The demand for
coal was increased by the introduction of steam engines, in ever
increasing numbers, to textile factories, by the appearance of steam
locomotives and steamships, by the expansion of iron smelting and
by the use for lighting and heating of coal gas and, later, electricity.
The total output of coal in Scotland rose from $7\frac{1}{2}$ million tons in
1854 to 39 million tons in 1908. Scottish iron, as was mentioned
earlier, began its career of expansion with the invention of the hot
blast in 1828. In ten years the number of furnaces more than doubled,
and production increased more than 500 per cent. By 1860 a million
tons of pig iron were being produced annually, and production
remained at a little above that figure until 1914. Cast iron was used
for a wide range of articles, and by the middle of the century malle-
able iron came widely into use. Then, very shortly afterwards, the
production of steel on a large scale became possible and the new
metal soon superseded iron for many purposes.

Engineering of every kind developed in this period, as skills were
acquired by experience and training, and precision tools were
invented for working on metals. The extension of the use of the
steam engine was at first hampered by inefficiency in working in
metals, but once the difficulties had been overcome the craftsmanship of Scottish engineers was applied to steam engines for ships and
for locomotives on the railroads. The Glasgow area, and Clydeside
generally, took a foremost place in the production of steamships and
locomotives, many of them for export to all parts of the world, and
Clydeside engineers were associated with almost every improvement
in the marine engine in the later nineteenth century.

While what are known as the heavy industries thus predominated
in the west, and indeed in the industrial economy of Scotland as a
whole, there were many other industries in which use was made of
Scottish natural resources and of Scottish skill, and which contributed to the wealth of the country in the nineteenth century.
Quarrying, especially of granite in Aberdeenshire, was one, and
another industry involving the extraction of minerals was shale-
mining and the production of oil from the shale, an industry which
had a brief but extraordinarily successful career, especially in West
Lothian, at the end of the nineteenth century and the beginning of
the twentieth. Among lighter industries, the manufacture of paper
was important, and Scotland was also famous for printing and book-
production. Brewing and distilling had been going on for centuries,

but they were put on a commercial footing at the end of the eighteenth century and the beginning of the nineteenth and provided substantial exports to England and overseas.

The general pattern of Scottish industry in the nineteenth century therefore, is one of progress and prosperity and of great opportunities for Scotsmen of capacity. Yet within the general trend there were booms and slumps, and during the phases of depression, either generally or in particular industries, some men's minds naturally turned towards emigration. Thus, there was a financial crisis in 1824–5 and there were hard times in the 1840s, which were 'the hungry forties' partly because of bad harvests and partly because the weavers found conditions more difficult than ever before. On the other hand, in the 1850s, wars in the Crimea and in India absorbed men and stimulated certain branches of industry, and a general increase in prosperity in Great Britain coincided with a commercial crisis in the United States, with the result that emigration fell off for a time. At the end of the 1860s there was considerable distress following the changed fortunes of the cotton industry in consequence of the American Civil War, and there was a period of general depression once more between about 1875 and 1879.

While Scotland was no longer predominantly a rural country, the changes in agriculture in the nineteenth century were important, too. Steam-power made its appearance in the farmyard for the operation of threshing-mills; the skills of the engineers made possible the production of efficient reaping machines and a whole range of other mechanized implements. The war-time boom had fallen off after 1815, as foreign foodstuffs were again imported, but the prosperity of the farmers was on the whole maintained until nearly the middle of the century, partly because the Corn Laws gave their products protection against serious competition from abroad. Then, in 1846, the Corn Laws were repealed, in order to provide cheaper food for the populace, and this step became detrimental to British agriculture when wheat could be imported from the virgin plains of North America more cheaply than it could be produced at home. Later in the century, the price of cattle suffered in a somewhat similar way, when refrigeration and canning facilitated the import of beef and mutton from South America and New Zealand.

Many of the agricultural changes led to a surplus of manpower in the countryside and, consequently, to migration. It had been true even in the eighteenth century that the creation of larger farms, in place of smaller, less economic, units, and the introduction of labour-saving machinery were tending to displace men from the land. The nineteenth century developments had more far-reaching effects. Even apart from the slump in agriculture after the middle of the century, which itself led some tenant farmers to give up and to seek their fortunes elsewhere rather than work as landless labourers, there were other changes which led to some redistribution of man-power. Scottish estates passed into English hands, by marriage or by sale, Scottish landowners tended to be absorbed into a British upper class centred on an English social round; consequently, there was increased absenteeism among landowners, and the old tradition of a landlord taking pride in keeping men as retainers finally passed away. In any event, the increased industrialization of Scotland and the decline in agriculture meant a steady fall in the proportion of the population employed on the land.

It was some compensation for the decline in the prosperity of farming that the nineteenth century and the early twentieth saw an unprecedented development of the Scottish fisheries. Herring were latterly being caught in prodigious quantities and salted for export to the continent, while the steam trawlers were able to reap a harvest from distant grounds previously inaccessible.

The population of Scotland as a whole increased during the nine-teenth century from about one and a half millions to nearly four and a half. But the increase was not evenly distributed; indeed, many counties were showing a decrease long before 1900, whereas the big cities and even medium-sized towns showed spectacular increases, so that Glasgow, a small town with 12,000 people in 1707, had a million inhabitants in the present century. This vastly increased urban population meant that problems arose of housing and public health which were only slowly dealt with. Old houses, once the mansions of the wealthy, were abandoned in favour of poorer occu-pants and divided and subdivided; new houses equally provided only the minimum of accommodation. Many working class families had only one room, and the great majority of them had no more than two. Houses in the older areas of a town were often without water or sanitation of any kind, and even the newly built blocks were quite inadequately served, with facilities shared among many households. These conditions bred disease, and for a large part of the nineteenth century several types of fever were persistent and there were occa-sional epidemics of cholera in the 1830s, 40s and 50s.

It was indeed usually possible for a working man, with steady employment, to better his position, to rent a more comfortable house or even (with assistance from a building society) to buy one. But the Scots as a nation have been reluctant to devote an adequate proportion of their earnings to housing, and the unwillingness of many people to pay reasonable rents has continued right down to the present day, to make impossible the provision of satisfactory houses for all. Besides, in the nineteenth century there were many workmen with very low wages and no security of employment. For example, apart from the effect of the power-loom on the earnings of the weavers, that industry had attracted starving Irishmen who were willing to accept a lower wage than a Scot could live on; and women also took up weaving and helped to force down wages. Thus the weavers' wages fell below subsistence level. There was until the twentieth century no assistance from the state for the unemployed, and the traditional Scottish system of poor relief, based on the parish and financed largely by the collections taken at the church door, was not unfitted for a rural society but broke down in the growing towns. In 1845 new legislation made it almost compulsory for a parish to levy an assessment for the relief of the poor, and more adequate sums then began to be paid out.

One of the essentials to combat disease in the towns and reduce the heavy death-rate was the provision of a piped water supply and of suitable drainage. It was noted, for instance, that as soon as Glasgow began to obtain pure water from Loch Katrine, in 1859, the deaths from epidemics greatly decreased. Under various acts of parliament local authorities were empowered to take action in the interests of public health, such as insisting on the notification of infectious diseases and on the removal of 'nuisances' which might be a danger to health. Improvements in housing were made steadily from about 1860 onwards. The worst slums were demolished, broader streets were constructed, the number of one-roomed houses in the country was halved between 1861 and 1911. Even so, however, Scottish houses, solidly built of stone, tended to last too long and to degenerate with age, so that a heritage of unsatisfactory property always remained, and the last of it has not been cleared away even today.

Political radicalism in Scotland had originated in the later eighteenth century, as a reaction against the hopelessly unrepresentative character of the parliamentary and local franchises, and it was stimulated to militancy by the successes of the French revolutionaries, with whom some of the Scottish political reformers were in direct correspondence. A measure of political reform came in the

1830s, but it benefited only the middle classes, and agitation for a further extension of the franchise went on until the further reform acts of 1868 and 1885. Radical tendencies with such political origins were strengthened and stimulated by the appalling housing in some of the urban areas, by the long hours of work in squalid conditions and by the periodical slumps in one industry or another. It was noted, for example, that the Corn Laws, while they benefited one privileged section of the community, meant dear bread for the people at large. When half-educated working men fell on evil times they were very apt to align themselves with left-wing political movements like the Chartism of the middle of the nineteenth century and the Labour Movement which arose at its close. This has to be kept in mind as explaining some of the appeal of conditions in lands overseas, where—so at least it was believed—there was less political and social inequality as well as better economic conditions.

After the First World War the economic picture in Scotland was one of a widespread and prolonged industrial depression such as the country had never experienced before. Depression was not, of course, peculiar to Scotland, and at its peak in 1931 the slump was part of a world-wide economic crisis. But Scotland, or at any rate parts of Scotland, suffered with exceptional severity, because the heavy industries and textiles on which they relied were especially affected. At no time between 1919 and 1939 was the percentage of unemployed in Scotland less than 10, and in 1931 it was over 27.

The cause came at least in part from changes in other countries rather than from any internal change in Scotland itself. In the period before 1914, Britain had been ahead of most other countries in her industrialization, and the result had been that practically the whole world had been a market for British and Scottish products. But, as other countries overtook Britain, they began to supply themselves and also began to compete with Britain in supplying the remaining markets. With a world-wide development of heavy engineering and of steel-making, Scotland could no longer be a provider of the world's needs in ships and locomotives as she had been before 1914. The linen industry suffered because of changes of fashion and through competition from Belfast. The coal industry languished because of the competition of imported coal and of oil, which has become the fuel for ships and locomotives. For a long time, no compensation for the decline of old industries was found in the establishment of new industries, because the manufacture of motor cars and aeroplanes, for example, did not take root in Scotland.

Scottish agriculture was not in a healthy state between the World Wars, and, although it has been more prosperous since the Second War, increased mechanization has meant that fewer hands have been needed on the land. There has also been a kind of revulsion against rural ways of life, encouraged in every way by the government and its legislation, which is designed to suit city dwellers. One of the most disastrous developments, for example, is the regulation requiring that all children, on reaching the age of twelve, shall have a secondary education of a standard which, in the main, can be provided only in towns. Thus, country-raised children, when they reach the age of twelve, are taken away from their parents and their homes and educated for an urban way of life; they never return to the country. Not infrequently, the parents, rather than see their family broken up, migrate to the town when the eldest child reaches the age of twelve. Thus rural depopulation goes on apace, and problems of housing and employment in the towns are aggravated.

The fisheries have been as unfortunate as the heavy industry. The continental markets for cured herring were very largely lost as a result of the dislocation caused by the First World War, and in any event the herring have deserted the grounds where they used to be caught in such enormous quantities. White fishing has proved more stable, but did not expand in Scotland in proportion to the expansion which took place in England.

Ultimately a measure of recovery was made. Already before World War II, and more conspicuously since it, a variety of new industries, especially in the field of lighter engineering, has been introduced to Scotland, and many of the older industries have revived, with the result that in recent years the average percentage of unemployment has been only about three or less. Even so, however, the Scottish economy is in a less healthy state than that of Southern England, which continues to absorb manpower and capital from the whole of Britain.

7

EMIGRATION AS A BUSINESS

To recount only the conditions in Scotland, economic and other, which prompted people to emigrate would be to produce a one-sided and distorted picture of the history of emigration. In addition to the 'push' arising from conditions at home, there was a 'pull' from outside, in the shape of the attractions held out by those who, for one reason or another, wanted to entice Scots into crossing the sea and settling in new lands.

One aspect of the 'pull' has been alluded to more than once already, and it is a feature never to be overlooked—namely the letters written by successful emigrants to their friends and kinsfolk at home. For example, letters from Canada in the early 1830s contained sentences like these: 'We have plenty of good food and grog . . . we dine with our masters. . . . We have no poor rates nor taxes of any consequence. . . . We shall never want timber nor water. . . . Bricklayer is a good trade here. . . . A poor man can do a great deal better here than he can at home.'[1] Sometimes the successful emigrants went further, and remitted money to pay for the passages of their correspondents. Naturally, it was especially common for male emigrants, after they had made good, to send money to enable their wives or their fiancées to join them, or—especially in the United States—to send home a prepaid passage ticket. Within a family, there was a kind of snow-balling effect, and it was a common occurrence for a pioneering member of a family to be followed by his brothers and sisters, their wives and fiancées, and not infrequently in the end by parents as well. Apart altogether from blood relation-

[1] Craig, *Upper Canada*, 228.

ship, however, the ancient ties of the clan and the name were still potent, and behind them all was a sense of community among all Scots. This found expression in the many societies and associations established by Scots overseas,[1] and some at least of them made it their business to welcome immigrants, to help them to feel at home and even to assist them in hard times: for instance, in the winter of 1841–2, the St. Andrew Society of Montreal cared for 229 destitute immigrants from Lewis. The fellow-feeling among Scots was undoubtedly a contributory factor in easing the path of the emigrant or would-be emigrant.

But there were many other aspects of the 'pull'. Individuals not infrequently became enthusiasts for the attractions of one area or another, and produced books or pamphlets to publicize its advantages. As early as 1773, for example, there were pamphlets circulating in Ayrshire which explained how in Prince Edward Island leases were being offered at rents which were to rise during seven years from 2*d*. to 2*s*. an acre 'and never after to be raised'.[2] At a more official level, there was the perfectly honourable and reputable desire of colonial governments to assist the development of their territories by encouraging emigration through propaganda and even by assisting it financially. One of the earlier examples was the action of Canada in the years after 1815, when that colony felt it necessary to counter the attractions both of the United States and also of a new competitor, Australia. There were many instances later on, and it need only be mentioned as an example that in 1910 the offices of the Dominion of Canada in Britain advised close on 30,000 personal callers, received and despatched 100,000 letters and sent out many tons of booklets, besides distributing maps and lantern slides and arranging exhibitions. Equally, the British government from time to time took action to assist emigration, either with a view to fostering the development of a particular colony or in order to alleviate distress at home.

Before the second quarter of the nineteenth century, government action in favour of emigration had hardly ever gone beyond the transportation of undesirables. On the whole the view had been that an increase in the population of Britain was welcome, and in particular it was so strongly felt that skilled workmen should not be allowed to change their allegiance that an act of 1782 (passed on the eve of the victory of the American colonies in their fight for inde-

[1] See pp. 44, 104, 126–8, 151, 163, 180.
[2] R. M. Campbell, *Scotland since 1707*, 8.

pendence) forbade such persons to emigrate to foreign countries and made it an offence to solicit any such person to emigrate to a country not under the British crown. The act was much evaded, and it did not prevent people reaching the United States by way of Canada, but it was not repealed until 1825. Further, Britain took a generation to recover from the shock of the loss of the American colonies, and it was felt for a long time that, as any other colonies would in the end be lost as they had been, it was not worth while doing anything to foster colonization. There was therefore little official interest in colonies or in emigration.

One factor which did begin to stimulate some interest was the influence of Malthus (1766–1834), for his writings induced a new thought—a fear of over-population, a fear that population might outrun the means of subsistence. There was also, during the period of economic difficulty which followed the end of the war with France in 1815, interest in emigration as a possible means of curing unemployment and alleviating distress. In 1815, therefore, the government, in order to encourage emigration to Canada, offered assistance with transport, free grants of land, and salaries for ministers and teachers, and several hundreds of persons from several parts of Scotland were conveyed to Quebec and other parts of Canada; in 1817 a hundred families, mainly from Breadalbane, were assisted under a similar scheme. In 1819 there was a vote of £50,000 to assist emigration to the Cape, and in 1821 a vote of some £70,000 for emigration from Ireland to Canada and the Cape, followed by smaller sums in some succeeding years. These faint beginnings were followed by further measures, partly because of the stimulus given by the writings of Robert John Wilmot Horton, Under-secretary for War and the Colonies, who from 1823 to 1830 advocated the removal of paupers to Canada on the ground that this would in the long run cost less than maintaining them at home. The next measures by the government, therefore, although they included the repeal of the act restricting the emigration of artisans, were mainly concerned with the removal of paupers. In 1823, 1825 and 1827 there were grants for the settlement of paupers in Canada (where allotments of 70 acres each were made) and in the Cape (to which labourers were sent). In 1826 a Select Committee on Emigration reported that in Scotland, as also in England, and more notably, Ireland, there were districts where the population was 'redundant' and from which able-bodied labourers could be removed to the colonies; it was therefore recommended that aid should be given to remove paupers to British North America, Australia and the Cape. This policy, which was unkindly described as 'the shovelling out of paupers' to places 'where they might die without shocking their betters with the sight or sound of their last agony',[1] did not long continue.

The distress which occasioned some of the governmental interest in emigration in this period led also to the formation of societies to aid emigration by co-operative means. In Scotland, it was weavers who were mainly affected by economic change, and most of the societies were in the Clydeside area—thirteen of them in Renfrewshire and twenty-two in Lanarkshire, representing among them some 13,000 persons; and weavers from Langholm in Dumfriesshire were among the emigrants of 1820. In 1826 more than thirty Scottish societies petitioned the Emigration Committee for aid, and there were many more petitions in succeeding years; the request was usually for free land in Canada. Other agencies were at work to help, for as early as 1821 the Committee of Management on Emigration in Glasgow assisted nearly 2,000 people to reach America.

The many 'companies' interested in emigration which appeared for the first time in these years originated with men of substance, and often of wealth, who were philanthropists as well as philosophers and economists. Although most of the companies were British rather than specifically Scottish, they had a dual Scottish connection. Not only did some of them make a special appeal to Scotland for emigrants, but several of the leading figures in the movement either were Scots by birth or had been educated in Scotland: for example, Edward Gibbon Wakefield had received part of his education at the Royal High School of Edinburgh; Charles Buller and William Molesworth had been students at Edinburgh University and Molesworth had a Scottish mother; Robert Stephen Rintoul, a close friend of Wakefield, was a Scottish journalist; and James Mill was also Scots by birth.

Apart from such Scots who played their part in the encouragement of emigration on the British stage, there were others who were actively interested within Scotland itself. John Crawford, a Paisley solicitor, wrote his *Philosophy of Wealth* in 1837 and advocated emigration, especially to New Zealand. Patrick Matthew, one of the Chartists, who brought forward a programme of somewhat radical constitutional changes, was also interested in emigration schemes, and Alexander Campbell, another radical, was for a time organizer of a New Brunswick emigration agency.

[1] Quoted McLintock, *History of Otago*, 152.

It was John Galt, the Scottish novelist, who formed the Canada Company in 1824, and it was chartered in 1826. This company had agents in Edinburgh and Glasgow as well as in towns in England and Ireland, and its business was in effect to advertise Canada to prospective emigrants. The British American Land Company, chartered in 1834, pursued a similar policy and made special appeals to Scottish Highlanders. The New Brunswick and Nova Scotia Land Company, founded in 1831, also appealed to Scots.

Meantime the views of Edward Gibbon Wakefield were becoming influential. In his writings, which began to appear in 1829, he propounded the view that cheap and abundant land in a colony meant that too few people, of a uniform type, tended to settle, and he argued that the issue of land to emigrants should be restricted, to ensure that there should be an adequate force of landless labourers. Therefore, he concluded, land should not be given away free, but should be sold at a price determined by the condition of the labour market in a colony at any given time. Thus emigrants would have to work for a time as labourers before they could acquire land. The money raised by the sale of land, besides, should be used to assist emigration of poor labourers. Emigrants should be judiciously selected, with some emphasis on a balance between the sexes and among various social strata, so that a varied society should exist from the start. Views similar to those of Wakefield were held by Robert Gourlay, who has been described as 'a crack-brained Scotch Canadian'. As Gourlay attributed the lack of prosperity of Canada to the superabundance of land, he wanted land to be sold, in limited quantities, rather than given away free, and he proposed that there should be a land tax, which, along with the money realized from the sale of land, should be used to bring out emigrants.

The government was impressed by Wakefield's theories to the extent that his ideas were put into effect, in greater or less degree, in New South Wales, South Australia and New Zealand, and an unsuccessful attempt was made to put them into effect in Upper Canada. Regulations made for New South Wales in 1831 followed Wakefield's principles so far as the sale of land was concerned, and the treasury advanced £10,000, against future land sales, to assist emigration. In the same year the government appointed an Emigration Commission, which arranged to assist emigrants to Australia by loans, and in the end it became the practice to pay the whole passage-money as a free grant (1835). The emigrants so assisted were supposed to be selected as Wakefield had proposed, with a proportion of mechanics as well as labourers, but selection was not very effective. A report of 1838 which condemned transportation of convicts to Australia also recommended that land should be sold at £1 per acre to prevent labourers from becoming landowners too soon. In South Australia land was in fact sold as Wakefield had proposed.

In 1840 the British government appointed Colonial Land and Emigration Commissioners, primarily to operate these schemes which followed Wakefield's proposals, but also to issue information about conditions for settlers in the British colonies generally and to supervise the conditions under which emigrants travelled. The Commission was not renewed after 1878, when the government ceased for a time to make any financial provision for the assistance of emigrants. The function of supplying information to intending emigrants was, however, assumed in 1886 by the Emigrants' Information Office.

By about 1840, when economic and political discontent was focussed in the Chartist movement, emigration as a cure for all ills was being generally advocated. In 1839, Thomas Carlyle wrote, in his *Essay on Chartism*: 'On a certain rim of our small Europe, . . . the "tide of population" swells too high. . . . And yet, . . . does not everywhere else a whole vacant Earth, as it were, call to us, Come and till me, come and reap me.' Four years later, in *Past and Present*, he demanded 'an Emigration Service', an 'effective system of Emigration: so that . . . every honest willing workman who found England too strait . . . might find likewise a bridge built to carry him into new Western lands. . . . A free bridge for Emigrants . . . every willing worker that proved superfluous finding a bridge ready for him.'

At a time when there was so much interest in, and vigorous thinking about, colonization, it was natural that societies should be formed to further various schemes for emigration. A National Colonization Society was founded in 1830. A fresh impetus was given to interest in 1839, when Dr. Thomas Rolph, an English Canadian, came to Britain with Dr. MacDonnell, the Roman Catholic bishop of Lower Canada, to try to revive migration to Canada, which had been interrupted by the effects of a rebellion in Upper Canada in 1837. Rolph published a letter to the President of the Highland and Agricultural Society of Scotland suggesting colonization in Canada as a remedy for highland destitution. He interested several notables in Scotland, among them the Duke of Argyll. In 1840 various organizations interested in emigration combined to form the North American Colonial

Committee, of which Argyll and various members of parliament were members. Then, in 1841, the British American Association for Emigration and Colonization was formed, with a predominantly Scottish membership, including Argyll as president, four marquises (including Huntly, Bute and Lorne), four earls, seven barons, thirty-nine baronets and the lord provosts of Edinburgh and Glasgow. A characteristic product of this phase was a pamphlet, *Short Account of Prince Edward Island designed chiefly for the information of agriculturists and other emigrants of small capital* (London, 1839).

The highland crisis in the 1840s produced a fresh crop of societies to aid emigration, as has already been mentioned. But the 'hungry forties' saw the creation of many emigration societies in the lowlands as well. Some of them were based on narrowly localized interests: thus there were societies in places like Ceres, Kennoway and Cults, in Fife, and in the far north a 'Shetland Female Emigration Fund' was projected.[1] In the decade of the Disruption of the Church of Scotland, sectarian feeling ran high, and some of the societies were on a denominational basis, like the Protestant Emigration Society of Glasgow (1840), the Glasgow Protestant Canadian Emigration Society (1841) and the Glasgow Wesleyan Emigration Society (1841). Besides, some of the societies which had been formed among the weavers in the 1820s continued, or were revived, and in 1843 nineteen organizations, comprising the United Emigration Societies of Paisley and Renfrewshire, petitioned for aid. Weavers' societies continued to assist emigration until the 1860s. Some Trade Unions from time to time encouraged emigration in the belief that it would relieve unemployment in Great Britain and even, by reducing the labour force available at home, lead to higher wages. For example, in 1858 the Scottish Typographical Union organized emigration on behalf of the printing unions of Edinburgh, Glasgow and other towns.

The activities of such organizations, and of the individuals who inspired them, were disinterested to the extent that financial profit arising from the exploitation of emigrants was not their aim. It was very different with some other individuals and organizations. To shipping agents, shipping companies, and all concerned in actually transporting emigrants across the oceans, emigration was a business

---

[1] Edwin Guillet, *The Great Migration*, 28, and William H. G. Kingston, *How to Emigrate* (1850), 285; cf. W. S. Shepperson, *British Emigration to North America*, 123, 125.

and emigrants a source of revenue. This was discovered quite early. In the phase of renewed emigration at the close of the American War of Independence, in 1784, we come across references to 'the avarice of the Glasgow merchants', to shipmasters who grant passages on credit and then exact from the emigrants 'a sum more than double what they would have paid for their passage', and also to the 'merchants of Aberdeen', whose 'terms are high' and who, by charging fourteen guineas cabin and seven guineas steerage, seem, from what we know of fares in later times, to have been exacting more than a fair profit.[1] That emigration was business, and big business, was plain from the claim of one agent that he had been responsible, between 1821 and 1831, for the transport of 12,000 Highlanders to Nova Scotia, Prince Edward Island and Upper Canada.

No doubt from an earlier stage, and certainly about 1790, agents of shipping companies or of shipowners were working hard to entice Highlanders and Lowlanders alike to emigrate to Nova Scotia and Prince Edward Island. Sometimes no more was involved than honest business, for instance when in 1820 local newspapers in the southwest of Scotland carried advertisements notifying 'passengers going to America' that ships were about to sail from the Solway for Philadelphia, St. John's (New Brunswick) and Pictou (Nova Scotia). But some of the agents were quite unscrupulous in their propaganda, and deserved the description of them as 'artful and unprincipled men'.[2] In 1801, we learn, a party of emigrants from the Chisholm territory were deceived into believing that in Nova Scotia they would find a tree to yield sugar and soap as well as fuel and that America was only a short voyage beyond the western isles. Indeed, some, on sighting the Outer Hebrides, optimistically inquired, 'Is this America?' One hopes that the 'Guide for the Emigrant to North America', published in Gaelic in 1841, was more accurate in its information, but there is no doubt that, as in the earliest days, the most glowing accounts of conditions overseas continued to be circulated. In the middle of the nineteenth century it was being said that in America wages were 50 per cent higher and food prices one third lower than in Britain and that one day's work in America would keep a family for three days.

One does feel that, had there not been advertising and propaganda, designed to encourage people to make light of the voyage and the difficulties they might encounter on arrival, far fewer Scots

---

[1] *William and Mary Quarterly*, xi, 283, 286.
[2] Cowan, 148.

7

would have undertaken an enterprise which in truth often brought them much misery. It does seem that far too few emigrants understood sufficiently the conditions they had to face and the preparations they ought to make, but they would probably have taken more trouble to obtain accurate information if they had not been subjected to a good deal of salesmanship. Neither the 'push' at home nor the 'pull' from overseas would in themselves have produced so many emigrants.

The perils of the sea voyage were occasionally brought home to people when an emigrant ship was wrecked. In October 1773, for instance, the *Batchelor* left Leith for North Carolina and called at Thurso to take some 200 emigrants on board. After sheltering for a time at Stromness, in Orkney, she put to sea but was driven towards Shetland and sought shelter again in Vaila Sound, but her anchors failed to hold and she ran aground. Apart from some children who were suffering from smallpox and were suffocated in the hold, there was no loss of life, but the emigrants had to stay in Shetland until the following spring when they were sent back to Leith.

The length of the voyage, even if it was in the end successful, made migration across the Atlantic a formidable undertaking. A case often cited, and no doubt exceptional, was that of a party bound from Dornoch to New York on the brig *Nancy* in 1773; they spent three months on the voyage, and eighty-one out of a total of 280 persons died on the way. But a three-month voyage was not unknown even a good deal later, for in 1843—that is, just before steamships began to ply regularly across the Atlantic—the time taken between British ports and Quebec ranged from twenty-seven to eighty-eight days, with an average of forty-four. As soon as steam came into use there was a rapid improvement, and by the 1870s a ten-day crossing was quite normal.

Conditions on these long voyages were bad in every way. Food was obviously one problem, and, in spite of British experience in victualling naval vessels which, with large numbers of men on board, were accustomed to keep at sea for long periods, this problem was not satisfactorily tackled on emigrant ships. If the food was provided by the shipowners, their interest was to provide the cheapest and scantiest rations, and in 1774, we are told, a party of Orcadians on a voyage to America found the food supplied to them to be quite inedible and had to fall back on raw potatoes. In general, however, passengers provided their own food, at least in sufficient quantity for a normal voyage, but shipmasters were accused of prolonging voyages deliberately so that they could sell provisions at a profit after the emigrants' own food was exhausted.

The next great evil was overcrowding, with consequences not only in discomfort but in disease. We read in the early days of a ship of 270 tons carrying 400 passengers from Skye to Canada. Admittedly, in estimating what those and similar figures mean, we have to remember that comparison with a steamship is not appropriate, for in a sailing ship there was no space taken up by engines and boilers, so that the carrying capacity was much greater; but, even so, on that ship of 270 tons there can have been little more than standing room. The first act of parliament which proposed to improve conditions was the Passenger Vessel Act of 1803, which was in fact passed in an attempt to check emigration, of which there was much criticism at the time. By this act it became illegal for the number of emigrants to exceed half the number of tons of the ship's burden—in other words, one passenger for each two tons; by this standard the vessel referred to above would have had three times the permitted number of passengers. In 1816 and 1817 there were acts which were designed to encourage emigration to British colonies rather than to the United States, for by their terms, whereas vessels carrying emigrants to the United States were limited to one passenger for every five tons, British vessels going to British colonies could carry one person for every $1\frac{1}{2}$ tons and therefore provide a much cheaper passage. Further acts, in 1823 and 1825, had the effect of so raising the cost of conveyance that they temporarily checked emigration, and they were repealed in 1827. A milder act of 1828 laid down that there were to be only three passengers to every four tons; there was to be a clearance of $5\frac{1}{2}$ feet between decks; 50 gallons of water and 50 pounds of bread, biscuit and oatmeal were to be carried for each person. By an act of 1835 the quota of passengers was reduced to three to every five tons and the quantity of provisions increased to 70 pounds; it was also laid down that spirits were not to be sold. Further improvements were made by acts of 1842 and 1848. Finally, by an act of 1855, 18 square feet of deck space were to be allowed for each adult passenger, there were to be seven feet between decks, and many other improvements were prescribed. The earlier acts at least had proved difficult to operate, partly because some ships sailed from remote points where there were no officers to inspect them, but even elsewhere ships were sometimes allowed to sail which did not fulfil the conditions laid down, as the alternative would have caused even more suffering to the intended emigrants. The enforcement of the

1855 act ultimately fell to the Board of Trade, and later regulations, concerned with safety as well as comfort, included the introduction of the load line or 'Plimsoll line' by the Merchant Shipping Act of 1876.

It is only right to say that some ships offered considerably higher standards than the minimum laid down by law, at least to judge from their advertisements. In December 1839 an Edinburgh newspaper carried an announcement that the *Isabella Watson*, of 520 tons, was loading at Leith for Melbourne, Port Phillip and Sydney, New South Wales. It was explained that 'Her poop accommodation will be found equal to any vessel in the kingdom, being fitted with baths and every convenience. Has also a great height between decks for the comfort of steerage passengers. . . . A few respectable married and single mechanics, and male and female agricultural and domestic servants, on producing satisfactory certificates of character and qualifications, may have a steerage passage to Sydney by this ship on payment of Three Pounds each.'

It has to be remembered that in the early days genuinely passenger ships were unknown for the emigrant traffic and, as that traffic was a one-way traffic, it could most economically and cheaply be conveyed by vessels which carried cargo in the opposite direction. To the shipowner, emigrants represented a clear profit, for the alternative to carrying them was to make the voyage in one direction in ballast. For a long time the usual pattern was the carriage of timber eastwards across the Atlantic and the carriage of emigrants westwards, but later, after the repeal of the Corn Laws, grain was a usual eastward cargo. In the emigrant ships, therefore, there was a rule neither light nor ventilation except when the hatches were open. The beds, so-called, were shallow wooden boxes, usually in tiers of two or more, made from rough wood rudely knocked together. It is true that James Boswell remarked, 'The accommodation for the emigrants was very good . . . a row of beds on each side, every one of which was . . . fit to contain four people',[1] but everything depends on one's definition of a bed. In Galt's novel *Lawrie Todd*, the hero was shipped to New York in 1794 in a ship which 'betwixt decks was only four and a half feet in height, with two tiers of sleeping berths, and three persons slept in every berth'. It was sometimes pointed out that certain emigrant ships provided more cramped accommodation than the ships in the slave trade.

In such conditions, disease raged and the death-rate was some-

[1] Boswell, *Tour*, ed. Pottle, 156.

times high. This was especially true in the late 1840s, when some of the emigrants were already in poor physical condition, after semi-starvation at home, before they started on their voyage. Various infectious diseases, including typhus, developed on board. It did not improve matters in relation to either feeding or health that there were sometimes long delays before the emigrants, after assembling at a port, were able to board their vessel, or delays before the vessel sailed, and sometimes the emigrants were detained when they reached their port of destination. It was not until 1835 that responsibility was put on the shipping companies for maintaining emigrants who were delayed in such ways through no fault of their own. Even on arrival in a colony, their troubles were by no means over, for there might be no preparation made to receive them and they would simply be put ashore on uncleared lots of land. Worse than that, major immigration centres like New York, Quebec and Montreal were infested with adventurers and rogues of all kinds waiting to prey on the new arrivals.

Competition among shipping companies forced down prices. The cost of a transatlantic passage about 1824 was not usually more than £5, and some Scots reached Nova Scotia for as little as £2 10s. In 1831 and the following years the cost of a steerage crossing without food might be as low as 30s. Costs rose somewhat after 1840 and from the middle of the century were 65s. to 75s. Some emigrants obtained their passages on credit, and later on, when payment was demanded, they might have to part with cattle or even with land.

Apart from the improvements brought about by legislation, there was a tendency towards better conditions arising simply out of the development of shipping itself. Regular sailings, for example between Glasgow and New York in 1823, were established, and shipping lines were founded even before the advent of the steamship. Thus Alexander Allan (1780–1854), originally a ship's carpenter, became captain and part-owner of a brig which ultimately traded between Greenock and Montreal, and so founded the Allan Line in 1820. In 1830 the *Canada*, of 329 tons, was built for the Atlantic traffic, and another ship was added in 1837. The first of the line's steamers did not come until 1854. The Anchor Line, trading from Glasgow to New York, appeared in 1856. The Cunard Line had started in 1840. All of those lines helped with better-quality emigrant traffic. By 1863 most transatlantic emigrants, and nearly half of all emigrants, were travelling in steamships; by 1866 the percentage for all emigrants was 81. Steamers were, of course, more expensive than sailing vessels.

There is one literary account of the experience of an emigrant, who travelled from Scotland to America by steamer in 1879, by Robert Louis Stevenson in his *The Amateur Emigrant*. He paid eight guineas for the ten days' voyage as a second cabin passenger, and compared his position favourably with that of the steerage passengers who paid two guineas less and had to supply their own bedding and dishes and either bring or buy food to supplement their rations. He was not impressed by the quality of the emigrants. Their average age was quite high, and they were largely men who had lost employment as a result of industrial depression, especially in Glasgow. But there were other reasons: one was fleeing from a drunken wife, another from a drunken father, another hoped to escape from his own drinking habits. Stevenson remarked, 'So far as I saw, drink, idleness and incompetency were the three great causes of emigration', and he speaks of 'a shipload of failures'. Yet, despite their own background and the horrible conditions on the ship—in the steerage 'the stench was atrocious; each respiration tasted in the throat like some horrible kind of cheese'—their spirits rose when the weather was fine, so that there would be music, song and dancing, and America was the land of hope, the land of plenty—'In America you get pies and puddings' one of them remarked. From New York Stevenson set out westwards across the continent. Special arrangements were made for the many emigrants then making the long overland journey, and from the Missouri they travelled in a special emigrant train. He describes graphically the conditions, none too comfortable, for sleeping on the long journey, on which the railroad would 'bear an emigrant for some twelve pounds from the Atlantic to the Golden Gates'. But most of the emigrants were *from* the eastern states and from Canada, and Stevenson remarks on the pathos of emigrants from Europe arriving in parts of America which were being abandoned by those who had settled in them earlier on the score of 'hard times'. And, worse than that, there were emigrant trains bearing people *back from* the west.

At this stage, migration had become such a regular feature in the life of western man that it was almost something kept going for its own sake. An age of mobility had arrived, and the answer to every problem, every difficulty, seemed to be to move on.

8

EMIGRATION TO THE UNITED STATES

APART from the Highlanders who came in such numbers, expecially to North Carolina, there were also lowland Scots who arrived during the eighteenth century, as they had already arrived in the seventeenth, to swell the Scottish element in the British colonies which were to become the United States. Even in North Carolina not all the Scottish settlers were Highlanders, and for decades there was a casual trickle to America of indentured servants and the arrival of hundreds of tobacco factors and agents (many of them only temporary residents). It is significant that in Aberdeen, a city which had many trading links with America, there are records called 'Propinquity Books' which contain many references to Aberdonians settled in the colonies about the middle of the eighteenth century.[1] In the years just before the War of Independence broke out, there was something of a movement of Lowlanders to America which is one of the earliest examples of economic distress leading to emigration. The failure of the 'Ayr Bank' of Douglas, Heron and Company, in 1772, ruined many Scots and had an adverse effect on industry, leading to unemployment which caused the emigration of weavers and others from the Clyde area in 1774. It may be, too, that the raising of rents which had so much effect on the Highlands had some effect on the Lowlands as well. It certainly affected Orkney and Shetland, and led to the first emigration from those islands, and it may have been for the same reason that John Ross, a native of Tain in Easter Ross, went to America. We do know that in 1773-4 a good many lowland farmers left for America. Following an example set in

---

[1] Victoria Clark, *The Port of Aberdeen*, 70.

Wigtown in 1773, associations were formed to provide assistance to emigrants, and among the weavers of Renfrewshire and the farmers of Stirlingshire 'companies' or 'societies' were formed for the co-operative purchase of land in America. Caledonia County, in Vermont, originated with those emigrants. The total Scottish emigration for the years 1763–75 has been put as high as 25,000.

There was a trickle of Scots into almost all the colonies, including New England and even Maine (where one Adam MacCulloch arrived about 1766), but the most important areas of Scottish settlement during the eighteenth century were the Cape Fear Valley in North Carolina, the Mohawk and Upper Hudson valleys in New York and the Attamaha valley in Georgia. On the whole the Scots were admired for their better qualities: 'The Scotch . . . are all industrious and saving; they want nothing more than a field to exert themselves in, and are commonly sure of succeeding.'[1] But their very success in business was apt to arouse jealousy among those who had, perhaps, been less enterprising and energetic. And, of course, once controversy arose between the colonies and the mother country, the many Scots who were loyalist incurred bitter reproaches. In 1774 there were 'ill-bred invectives' against the Scots in Virginia, and even a petition for expelling them all from the country.[2]

The successful Scot was usually ready to assist his less fortunate countrymen, and it was partly for charitable objects that in the eighteenth century a number of St. Andrew's Societies were formed, like the Charitable Society which Scots had established in Boston in 1657: they appeared in Charleston (1729), Philadelphia (1749), New York (1756) and Savannah (after 1750). The published *Historical Catalogue of the St. Andrew's Society of Philadelphia, 1749–1913*,[3] gives biographies of many members who attained distinction in various walks of life, but also preserves the memory of otherwise forgotten emigrants, like John Inglis, who was born in Scotland in 1708 and died in Philadelphia in 1775. Apart from the charitable purposes for which those societies had been founded, they served social and convivial ends, not least with their annual St. Andrew's Day dinners, and in 1774 fifty people in Charleston sat down to consume £50 worth of food and £200 worth of liquor.[4]

The Scottish settlers continued to make their various contribu-

---

[1] *William and Mary Quarterly*, xi, 170.
[2] *Ibid.*, 291.
[3] Printed for the Society in two volumes, 1907–13.
[4] Graham, *Colonists from Scotland*, 132.

tions to American life as they had started to do in the seventeenth century. One of the oddest contributions was made by Lachlan MacGillivray, an Argyll man who became a trader in Georgia and had a son, Alexander, by a French-Indian half-breed woman. When the colonies became independent Lachlan returned to Scotland, but Alexander (*c.* 1759–93) joined his Indian kinsfolk in Alabama and, as a Creek chieftain, tried to play off Spain against the United States. The closest parallel to MacGillivray's career is that of Sir Alexander Cuming, a Scottish lawyer who sailed for America in 1729 and become 'lawgiver' and spokesman of the Cherokees. Between 1707 and 1783 thirty or more governors and lieutenant-governors of American colonies were Scots, though some of them were not colonists or even residents. William Keith, son of the third baronet of Ludquhairn in Aberdeenshire, was surveyor-general of customs and then lieutenant-governor of Pennsylvania, and it was a Patrick Gordon who succeeded him in 1726. Robert Aitken (1734–1802), born in Dalkeith, was a printer and publisher in Philadelphia in 1769, one of the first of many Scots who made their mark in printing and publishing in America. David Hall (*c.* 1714–1772), a native of Edinburgh, had been trained as a printer at home before he emigrated to America, where he entered the employment of Benjamin Franklin, who wanted an especially skilled man. John Smibert, born in Edinburgh about 1684, went to America in 1728 and attained fame as a portrait painter; and Cosmo Alexander, who flourished about 1766, was another portrait painter of Scottish extraction. It is only right to add that some men of ingenuity took refuge in America after meeting with failure at home. James Tytler (*c.* 1747–1805) wrote many books and printed some of them himself when he was in the debtors' refuge at Holyrood; he made large contributions to the second and third editions of the *Encyclopaedia Britannica*; and he was a pioneer aeronaut (in a balloon). But his whole career was a failure, and in the end he had to flee to America to escape arrest.

Scottish association with education in America was no less now than it had been earlier. James Innes, a native of Canisbay, Caithness, left his estate to found a school in North Carolina. William Smith, born in Aberdeen in 1727 and educated at King's College there, went to New York as a tutor in 1751 and then to Philadelphia; he returned to Britain to take Anglican orders (1753) and in 1755 became provost of the 'college, academy and charity school' of Philadelphia, which was the predecessor of the University of

Pennsylvania, erected in 1791. A contemporary of Smith was the well-known John Witherspoon, born at Gifford, East Lothian, in 1723. Witherspoon graduated at Edinburgh in 1739 and was a minister in the west of Scotland for a time before going to America, where he became principal of the College of New Jersey—Princeton University—in 1768, an office he held until 1794. There were also, among others, John Beveridge, who was a teacher in Edinburgh about 1766 and later became a professor in the College of Philadelphia under Provost Smith; James McClurg (*c.* 1747–1825), professor of medicine at Williamsburg; and William Small, an Aberdeen graduate, professor of natural philosophy there from 1758 to 1764.

There were, besides, many Scots engaged in education in much humbler and less distinguished ways, for it was said in 1773 that the Virginians had 'all their tutors and schoolmasters from Scotland'. One of them was John Harrower, whose fascinating *Journal* has recently been published.[1] A native of Shetland, he found in 1773 that his business as a merchant in Lerwick had failed and he set out for the south, hoping to find work in England or possibly Holland. His only capital was a small supply of Shetland knitted stockings, which he gradually sold off, sometimes at less than they had cost him. Every halfpenny of his meagre income and expenditure is carefully noted in the *Journal*, and he faced worsening prospects and increasing poverty with serene courage and no word of complaint. When it became apparent that he would not find work in Britain he took the desperate step of indenturing himself for service in America, as many others were doing at the time. In his own words, he 'engaged to go to Virginia for four years for bed, board, washing and five pounds during the whole time'. Joining a ship at London, he spent no less than sixteen weeks on board, though the passage after she finally cleared the land took less than two months. On arriving in Virginia, he was engaged as a tutor by Colonel William Daingerfield, and served him at his home, Belvidera. Harrower was considered a very successful teacher, not only of Daingerfield's sons but of some other children as well, including a deaf and dumb boy, and he also gave instruction to some of the negroes. He was entitled to fees for some of his work, and his hope was to save enough to bring out his wife and family to Virginia. However, he died in 1777, but by that time he had accumulated some £70, which Daingerfield undertook to remit to Mrs. Harrower in Lerwick.

[1] *The Journal of John Harrower*, ed. Edward M. Riley (Colonial Williamsburg, 1965).

Scottish clergy, too, of both the Presbyterian and the Episcopalian persuasions, went to America. For example, George Gillespie
(1683–1760), born in Glasgow, became a minister in New Jersey and
Delaware. William Hooper, minister of the West Church organized
in Boston in 1737, was a native of Ednam, Berwickshire, and had a
number of Scots in his congregation, including the painter John
Smibert and a James Scholie whose name suggests the Orcadian or
Shetland Scollay. On the other hand, Alexander Garden (1685–
1756), born in Edinburgh, became rector of the Episcopal church of
St. Philip in Charleston, South Carolina, and Dr. Auchmuty was
rector of Trinity Church, New York. Undoubtedly the majority of
the Scots, even the Highlanders, who emigrated in this period, were
Presbyterians, and this gave them a bond with the Dutch in New
York and with some of the New Englanders, but they do not seem
to have found it easy to obtain ministers from home. The North
Carolina Highlanders tried to persuade a minister to come out from
Argyll in 1741, but they had no permanent pastor until 1758, when
they began to be served by James Campbell, who had previously
been in Pennsylvania. One gathers that on the whole the ministers
who had really high qualifications—especially if they were also
ambitious—preferred to remain in Scotland. One minister, James
Munro, was recommended on the somewhat tepid ground that 'he
would answer any congregation in America that loved orthodox
preaching and was not too polite';[1] he did, in 1785, become a
minister in Maryland, but later removed to Nova Scotia. Even in
the early nineteenth century, it is still exceptional to find a man like
Alexander Denoon, a native of Campbeltown, who was minister of
the Presbyterian church at Caledonia, New York, in 1827. A French
traveller remarked in 1765 that Norfolk and Portsmouth (Virginia)
were 'chiefly inhabited by Scotch, all Presbyterians', although they
had no church of their own.[2] On the other hand, it was said of the
Scots in Georgia that 'they all kept whores and condemned religion'.[3]

Presbyterian zeal among so-called 'Scotch' reminds us that the
eighteenth century saw an enormous influx into America of those
who were in some sense secondary Scottish emigrants—the so-
called 'Scotch-Irish', descended from the lowland Scots who, as we
saw, settled in northern Ireland in the seventeenth century. They

[1] *William and Mary Quarterly*, xi, 285.
[2] *American Historical Review*, xxvi, 739–40.
[3] Graham, *Colonists from Scotland*, 139.

were themselves emphatic that they were not Irish, and can more suitably be called 'Ulster Scots'. The reasons for their further migration were that they found themselves in one way or another frustrated in Ireland. There were repressive trade laws, imposed in the interests of England, in some ways not unlike those which subsequently caused friction between the American colonists and the mother country. The linen industry of Ulster, on which the province largely depended for exports, declined for a time in the eighteenth century. The tenant farmers often suffered from rack-renting, and the whole agrarian community found themselves in difficulties in times of bad harvests, like 1727, 1740 and 1770. Finally, a very large number of the Ulster Scots were Presbyterians and resented the privileged position of the Episcopal Church of Ireland; at the beginning of the century the Presbyterians were actually disqualified from public office, in terms of an act of 1704. Even with all these motives for emigration, it may be doubted if so many Ulstermen would have left for America had they not, once the movement was well under way, been encouraged by shipowners and by agents operating on behalf of the colonies. As happened with emigration generally, there was something of an epidemic about it, something of a snowball effect. Some, especially linen workers from Londonderry, settled in Massachusetts, but the primary objective of most of the Ulstermen was Pennsylvania, a colony noted for religious toleration, and, after settling mainly as farmers in the east, many of them moved into the frontier areas in the hinterland of the coastal colonies and others dispersed to more southerly colonies, especially Maryland and Virginia.[1] It is estimated that a total of some 200,000 people left Ulster between 1720 and 1776, and they must account for a large proportion of the 189,000 people of 'Scottish origin' who were estimated to be in the United States in 1790, for we know that nothing like that number had yet come from Scotland, and the same estimate puts those of Irish descent at only 44,000. Ulstermen provided many ministers for Presbyterian congregations in America.

The numerical strength of those 'Scotch-Irish' has to be kept in mind in any assessment of Scottish emigration to the United States, because they were often confused with Scots direct from Scotland although their outlook and their contribution to American life were in many ways quite distinct. This became very clear when the colonies entered on their struggle for independence, because the

[1] Wayland F. Dunaway, *The Scotch-Irish of Colonial Pennsylvania* (University of North Carolina Press, 1944).

Scotch-Irish were revolutionary almost to a man, and it was their part in the revolt which caused the government forces to brand Presbyterians generally as rebels. The record of the Scots was different. In the main they were loyal, and the Highlanders conspicuously so; it was almost in vain that the provincial congress of North Carolina decided in 1776 to publish a manifesto in Gaelic to appeal to them on behalf of the revolution. So conscious was the revolutionary party that it did not have Scottish support that an early draft of the Declaration of Independence actually accused King George III of sending against his American subjects 'not only soldiers of our common blood but Scotch and other foreign mercenaries'.[1]

At the same time, some Scots, both of highland and lowland descent, did support the revolution. Peter Mackintosh, a blacksmith in Boston, was a ringleader in riots against the British government in 1765, and Daniel Malcolm, a Boston trader, was prominent in a mob in 1768. There were even a few Scots who played leading parts in the revolution, notably John Witherspoon, principal of Princeton, who was one of the framers of the Declaration of Independence, though he had to admit that so many Scots were on the other side that 'the word Scotch was becoming a term of reproach in America'.[2] To assess the total part played by men of Scottish descent is impossible owing to the difficulty of disentangling the true Scots from the Scotch-Irish, but the facts for the two groups combined are as follows: out of Washington's twenty-two brigadier generals, nine were of Scottish descent; out of fifty-six members of the congress which adopted the Declaration of Independence, eleven were of Scottish extraction; of the first thirteen governors of states, two-thirds were of similar origin. Hugh Orr (1717–98), born in Lochwinnoch, cast guns and shot for the army, and John Paul Jones (1747–92), the founder of the American navy, was the son of a Kirkcudbrightshire gardener.

The attitude of the Scots to the revolution had its effect on the course of Scottish emigration after the war was over. At a time when so many Scots settlers in America were having to leave the United States because of their loyalty to the crown[3] there was little encouragement to other loyal Scots to come out, and on the whole the ties between Scotland and the United States were temporarily weakened.

[1] Julian P. Boyd, *The Declaration of Independence*, 34–5.
[2] Meyer, *op. cit.*, 150.
[3] See Chapter 9.

However, there were those in Scotland itself who had sided with the revolting colonists, and they were very anxious to revive emigration. One of them was Charles Nisbet, the minister of Montrose, who had gained some notoriety by denouncing the British government from the pulpit. He was a close friend of Benjamin Rush, whom he had met when Rush was a medical student in Edinburgh, and he was also in touch with John Witherspoon, who visited Britain in 1784 to solicit funds for the college at Princeton. Nisbet was very ready to encourage emigrants to head for the States and to give them letters of introduction addressed to Rush. As early as August 1783 Nisbet gave such a letter to David Napier, a linen manufacturer, who was leaving for Philadelphia, and in succeeding months similar letters were given to a cooper, two milliners, a clerk, a teacher and a farmer. Among the emigrants who went from Scotland at this time were Hugh Ross, a merchant of Montrose, who settled in 1784 at Pittsburgh, where he went into business as a distiller and ship-owner, and Ralph Bowie, a lawyer, who went to the United States about 1783 and practised first at Philadelphia and then at York, Pennsylvania. According to Nisbet in 1784, 'many hundreds, I might say thousands, on this coast would willingly emigrate to America, could they find any opportunity of getting a passage'; and again, 'I had a letter yesterday from Banff, informing me that great numbers of poor people in that neighbourhood declare themselves willing and ready to indent for America'.[1] Nisbet found, however, that by 'America' the would-be emigrants did not necessarily mean the United States to which he personally was so attached; and it is not easy to determine how far his propaganda was successful in turning emigrants from Nova Scotia, which his countrymen did prefer at that time, although he declared that colony 'unpopular among intended emigrants, who . . . are not ambitious of enjoying any more of the blessings of his majesty's government'.[2] Nisbet practised what he preached, for in 1785 he accepted the presidency of Dickinson College and went to Philadelphia. In company with him were Alexander Addison, a Presbyterian minister who settled at Washington, Pennsylvania, then studied law and afterwards became a judge, and James Thompson, another minister, who, however, did not remain long in the States.

Nisbet and those who thought like him did not have great success in inducing Scots to migrate to the United States. Yet there was a

[1] *William and Mary Quarterly*, xi, 283, 286.
[2] *Ibid.*, 286.

certain movement in the 1780s and 1790s. William Maxwell, for example, left Paisley for New York about 1790. In the case of John MacLean (1771–1814), a physician and surgeon in Glasgow who emigrated to the United States in 1795, there was the significant feature that he was associated with political agitation in Scotland and chose the United States as his new home because of his preference for a republican government. There was also the case of Grant Thorburn, who was born in Dalkeith in 1773 and is said to have left Scotland in 1794 for political reasons. Thorburn supplied information to John Galt for his novel, *Lawrie Todd* (1832), one of the few attempts to portray a Scottish emigrant in fiction. The hero, born in Midlothian, was in trouble with the authorities for his radical opinions, and in 1794, at the age of twenty, was shipped off to New York by his father. As a novel, *Lawrie Todd* is not very successful, for the author's interest was in character rather than in conditions or circumstances, and some of the most telling pieces of characterisation in the book appear in parts of it which deal with the hero's experiences in Scotland when he revisited his native land.

However, by making his hero spend some years in New York (which he found 'full of Scotchmen'), and then move inland to settle in the backwoods of the Genesee country, 'a hundred miles west of Utica', Galt reminds us of a significant development of the years just before and after 1800. The United States was expanding rapidly beyond the confines of the original thirteen colonies: between 1800 and 1830 the population of Ohio increased from less than 50,000 to almost 1,000,000 and that of Indiana from a mere 5,000 to 340,000. A considerable contribution to this development was made by Scots, many of them, like Todd, making a secondary emigration from the coastal states. The life was one of pioneering in the strictest sense, for the settlers had literally to create their farms out of forest-land, and their first task was to fell trees or strip off girdles of bark to make them die. The fictitious Todd was, of course, successful, and, moving on from farming to store-keeping, he became a leading citizen of a growing town. In Indiana a site for a colony was acquired in 1824 by Robert Owen, the famous owner of the New Lanark Cotton Mills in Scotland, a man who combined success in business with an acute social conscience. In association with William Maclure, Owen formed the New Harmony Society to organize the social life of the colony, but the venture was a failure.

This phase of emigration of course carries us on for a generation or more after the point at which the United States had gained their independence and Charles Nisbet had been trying to encourage Scots to settle there rather than in British possessions. Despite the efforts of Nisbet and those who thought like him, it was in fact several years after 1783 before the United States became an important reception area for Scottish emigrants. For various reasons the loyal provinces of British North America, especially Nova Scotia, Prince Edward Island and Upper Canada, long remained far more popular. Besides, the period of the long wars with France (1793–1815) was not one of heavy emigration at all; and Britain was actually at war with the United States from 1812 to 1814. In the peace which followed, emigration again became substantial, but for almost a generation after that—until about 1845—Canada was roughly of equal importance with the United States: in some years one, in some years the other, received the greater number of British emigrants. After 1845, however, emigration to the United States gained momentum, and that country retained its lead over all competitors, usually by a very large margin, for the rest of the nineteenth century.

For generations, therefore, the United States were unquestionably the most important of the receiving areas for emigrants from Britain. From 1815 to 1910, 10,000,000 people went to the United States, as compared with 3,000,000 to British North America. But the proportions were not constant throughout that long period. In 1853–60, 61 per cent of British emigrants went to the United States, 10 per cent to British North America, 28 per cent to Australia and New Zealand. From 1861 to 1870, 72 per cent went to the United States, 8 per cent to British North America, 17 per cent to Australia and New Zealand. In the early years of the twentieth century, the British Empire, and Canada in particular, again became a serious challenger: in 1891–1900 only 28 per cent of emigrants from the British Isles went to the Empire, between 1901 and 1912 the number increased to 63 per cent and in 1913 it was 78 per cent. At this point there was an increasing consciousness of, and loyalty to, the British Empire.

The Scottish pattern differed little from the British pattern, except that it was later before the United States gained their ascendancy among Scots. So late as 1854, for example, 6,706 Scots went to British North America and only 4,888 to the United States, whereas only 6,064 English went to British North America and 37,644 to the United States. However, in time the ascendancy was established, and between 1870 and 1920 53 per cent of Scottish emigrants went to the United States, which were thus receiving more Scots than all the other receiving areas together. Even so, the early twentieth century saw an increased interest in the Empire among Scots as well as English, and by 1907 more Scots were again going to Canada than to the States.

The census of 1920 showed that 254,570 of the inhabitants of the United States had been born in Scotland, as compared with 813,853 born in England. The total number of Scots who entered the United States between 1820 and 1950 was at least 800,000, compared with 3,000,000 English and nearly 5,000,000 Irish, and the figure of Scots for the period 1861–1901 is about 500,000. These are not, however, figures for permanent settlers. For one thing, some who entered the States subsequently returned home, perhaps to the extent of a quarter or a third of those who entered America. In periods when the American economy was affected by industrial recession, as from 1858 to 1860 and from 1874 to 1878, and during the years of the American Civil War (1861–5), the outward movement to the United States was itself checked, but another effect of such phases was to cause some settlers to return home. Moreover, there was often a movement between the United States and Canada, even in early times, and such movement was facilitated as communications improved. Thus, if conditions were bad in one country, emigrants moved to the other, and many tried their fortune first in one before trying again in the other. Some 'Scotch Canadians' transferred from Lord Selkirk's colony across to Minnesota. The highest estimate of immigrants who re-emigrated from Canada to the United States is 60 per cent, but this is an over-all figure, and it is suggested that the Irish labourers were more apt to move than the Scots, who settled more readily and had more persistence to struggle against adverse conditions.

Among the reasons which led so many Scots to choose the United States, rather than a British colony, as their new home, there is no doubt that the republican government and the—at least formally— egalitarian society of the United States did have their attractions. A desire to escape from 'the blessings of his majesty's government' had been imputed to Scottish emigrants by Charles Nisbet in 1784, probably with little reason, but, as has already been pointed out, there are some grounds for believing that in the radicalism of the 1790s there would be Scots who did prefer a republican constitution. Again, in the 1840s, when there was another radical wave, associated with Chartism, Scots could chant:

8

> To the West, to the West, to the land of the free,
> Where the mighty Missouri rolls down to the sea;
> Where a man is a man even though he must toil,
> And the poorest may gather the fruits of the soil.[1]

Just as one or two of the agitators of the 1790s had chosen to find new homes across the Atlantic, so Allan Pinkerton (1819–84), a young Glasgow cooper involved in the Chartist troubles, fled with his wife to the United States and set up a coopering business in Dundee, near Chicago.[2] Nor can we overlook the fact that the best-known of all Scottish emigrants to the States, Andrew Carnegie, came of a family with a strong distaste for hereditary power and titles and with a marked admiration for republicanism.

Yet it would be nonsense to see political or social preference as a serious factor in stimulating emigration to America. The main stimulus was economic, and it is important to determine what place all the thousands of Scottish immigrants took in the American economy in the nineteenth century. Few of them were countrymen at home, and, although they were entering a predominantly agrarian country, few of them became farm workers in America. Between 1873 and 1918 not 2 per cent of all the immigrating English, Scots and Welsh stated that they had been farm labourers at home, though it may be that some farm workers are concealed among the 25 per cent who declared themselves as unspecified 'labourers'. However, the 1890 census listed only 3 per cent of those immigrants as agricultural labourers. It was not the vision of easy possession of limitless acres of fertile land which drew most of the Scots who went to America in this period. All the evidence rather suggests that a very large proportion of the Scottish emigrants to the United States had been skilled workers at home and found employment in similar crafts and trades on the other side of the Atlantic. The tradition was established, or at least anticipated, even in the eighteenth century. Thus John McAllister, born in Glasgow in 1753, was trained at home as a woodworker and turned his skill to account first of all in New York, where he was from 1775 to 1781, and then in Philadelphia, where he died in 1830. Archibald McNeil, who had a rope-walk in Boston in 1770, was carrying on a trade with a long history in Scotland. Galts's Lawrie Todd, too, had been trained as a nail-maker in Scotland and started his career in New York in that trade.

[1] Saunders, *Scottish Democracy*, 127.
[2] Sigmund A. Lavine, *Allan Pinkerton, America's First Private Eye* (1965).

It is not hard to see why there was a special demand, and why there were special opportunities, for the skilled Scottish artificer. In the first half of the nineteenth century, when the United States was energetically developing the cotton manufacture, she urgently wanted skilled workers. The machinery for spinning cotton which had been invented in Britain in the late eighteenth century was jealously protected against export, and the emigration of skilled workers was forbidden as well, so that America had to import a great deal of cotton thread and cloth from Britain. The repeal in 1825 of an act against the emigration of trained men from Britain[1] removed a legal obstacle, and Scotland began to export skilled workers in large numbers. They were encouraged, for example, by James Montgomery, who arrived in New England in 1836 and became the owner of a cotton mill and who wrote a pamphlet to stimulate the emigration of textile workers. This movement went on more or less throughout the nineteenth century, and increased sharply during and after the American Civil War, when the cotton industry of Scotland slumped as a consequence of the cessation of imports of raw cotton and when, simultaneously, the United States imposed tariffs which protected its own products and led to a rapid expansion of the manufacture of cotton. Many of the workers found that they had to labour much harder, but they found that the wages were much higher too. One special branch of the cotton industry was the manufacture of cotton thread for sewing machines, and in this there were special links between Scotland and America. Scottish firms set up branches in America and staffed them with experienced workers from their factories at home; thus George A. Clark, from Paisley, founded works at Newark, New Jersey, and the more famous Paisley firm of Coats founded works at Pawtucket, in the 1860s. Wages were nearly double those paid in Scotland.

Other textiles were affected in much the same way. Scottish clothworkers went to American factories. Carpet weavers trained in Kilmarnock played a large part in factories in New England and the middle Atlantic states. In Lowell were weavers from Paisley and the Connecticut village of Thompsonville was largely peopled by carpet workers from Kilmarnock. Much the same happened with silk workers and with the makers of the so-called 'lace' (actually cotton) curtains.

If it was true that Scotland could teach America a good deal in the textile industries, it was even more true that she could teach her

[1] See pp. 91-2.

something in the field of heavy industry. It was in general true that Scotland, like Britain as a whole, obtained a lead over nearly every other country owing to her early and rapid industrialization, so that there was a period when the world was a market for their products and the world was eager to learn their methods. British engineers therefore brought their skill to the American iron and steel industries. Angus Neilson Macpherson, for example, born in Cluny, Inverness-shire, in 1812, served his apprenticeship in Scotland as a shipbuilder and followed that trade in Philadelphia. Other Scots were working machinery in businesses like paper-making. Type-founding in New York was said to be almost exclusively in the hands of Scottish workmen. George Mackenzie, a Scottish immigrant to the United States, directed the sewing machine company which Isaac Singer had founded.

Even in a less skilled occupation like coal mining the Scots had a part to play. Whereas the coal mines of the eastern states recruited mainly Welsh and Irish miners, the Scots played a large part else-where, west of the Alleghenies. In Illinois, Braidwood was largely Scottish, as was What Cheer in Iowa. During Scottish depressions, many colliers emigrated, and they were to be found by the thousand in states from Maryland and Pennsylvania to Illinois and Ohio. Many Scottish miners, however, went out only for the summer season, because the wages in America were so high that they were still in pocket even after they had paid their passages.

New England granite was worked by Scots, especially after an American tariff in the 1860s reduced the import of granite from Aberdeen, and the masons established communities in Quincy and Ware in Massachusetts, Vinalhaven and Rockland in Maine and Concord in New Hampshire. With their expert knowledge they were employed not only on building-stone but on the shaping of tombstones and memorials. Scottish stone masons worked also in sandstone quarries in Northern Ohio and were employed in the erection of many public buildings throughout the country. As with coal mining, wages were so high that they attracted a good deal of seasonal migration.

In many Scottish households, the name of one American town above all others meant prosperity or fortune, and that was Pitts-burgh. In the eighteenth century there had been on the site the French Fort Duquesne, which the British took and renamed Fort Pitt. In the neighbourhood there was to be found boundless wealth of iron and coal. From its early days Pittsburgh had among its inhabitants men from Scotland and more particularly from Fife, for one of its first inhabitants had been John Forbes, who was born at Pittencrieff in Fife in 1710. By the middle of the nineteenth century, at which time the value of the local mineral deposits had not yet been discovered, there were several Scots, engaged in various trades and professions—one 'Mr. Blackstock, an old Scotsman', John Hay, a manufacturer of bobbins, David Bruce, a solicitor, and James D. Reid, superintendent of the Pennsylvania Railway.

But the best known name associated with Pittsburgh is, of course, that of Andrew Carnegie, perhaps the most famous of all Scottish emigrants. As he was ultimately one of the wealthiest men the world has known, and as his biography is one of the outstanding success stories of all time, he can hardly be described as typical, yet there are many features in his career which were typical of nineteenth-century Scottish emigration.[1] Born in Dunfermline in 1835, the son of a damask weaver, he came of a family which knew the vicissitudes consequent on industrial changes: his grandfather, a leather merchant, was ruined, like many others, when peace and demobilization came in 1815; his father had prospered to the extent that he had four or five looms in the lower storey of the house, with the living quarters upstairs, until 'The change from hand-loom to steam-loom weaving was disastrous to our family'. His father found himself without employment, his mother had to open a small shop, but two sisters of hers were already in Pittsburgh, and the Carnegies made the decision to sell off their looms and other movables and emigrate too. Even after they had realized all they could, they still had to borrow £20 to make up the sum they required. When they left in 1848, they travelled from Glasgow on a sailing ship, rather than a steamship, in order to economize, and had a seven weeks' voyage. These were the beginnings of the man who during his later life gave away over 350,000,000 dollars.

Carnegie's family had a strong tradition of radicalism and unorthodoxy. Some of his kinsmen had been involved in agitation against the Corn Laws, and Dunfermline was something of a radical centre, where it was not uncommon to express a preference for republican America. Even when Carnegie prospered and himself lived in a castle, he never surrendered his dislike of monarchy, as was discovered by those who once asked him to subscribe to a memorial to Scotland's patriot king, Robert Bruce. He replied as follows:

[1] This account is based on Carnegie's *Autobiography* (New York, 1920).

Dungeness, Ga., Mch. 12.87

My Dear Sir,

I cannot feel much interest in Kings or in any who occupied or do occupy positions, not by merit, but by Birth. Let the successors of such build monuments to their predecessors, or those who can live contentedly under institutions which deny them equality.

I am too staunch a Republican, Hate with a bitter hatred and resent as an insult to my manhood, the Monarchical idea.

A king is an insult to every other man in the land.

You see, my dear sir, why, entertaining such sentiments, I cannot give you 30£ to commemorate even one who was better than his class. Perish Kings and Queens and privilege in all its forms.

If you have a Man of the People who is thought worthy of a monument—or of assistance and you obtain subscriptions for this man, I'll send my 30£ to that fund, but not a penny for all the Kings and Queens in Christendom.

Sincerely yours,

Andrew Carnegie.[1]

Carnegie's patriotism was undoubted, and Dunfermline, the burial place of King Robert, was a place where the name of Bruce was held in honour; indeed, Scottish patriotism was a constant inspiration to Carnegie and gave him something of a link with anti-English Americans, but his preference as between the two great Scottish national leaders was for William Wallace, who had been a mere laird and not a king. The Carnegie background was radical in religion as well as in politics, for Andrew's family were not orthodox Presbyterians and some of them ultimately became Swedenborgians. All in all, the element of protest, in economics, politics and religion, clearly played a large part in the Carnegies' decision to emigrate to the United States.

In New York, where they landed, the Carnegies met other weavers from Dunfermline, but went on to Pittsburgh, where Andrew obtained his first job, as a bobbin boy, at 1 dollar 20 cents a week. He next became a telegraph messenger and then transferred to a rapidly expanding branch of industry, by entering the service of the Pennsylvania Railroad Company. By 1859 he was superintendent of the Pittsburgh Division of the Railway. He never lost his interest in railways, and was a pioneer in the provision of sleeping cars, but

[1] In the papers of the Burgh of Kirkcaldy. Printed in the *Scotsman* 27 May 1964.

during the Civil War there was an enormous demand for new rails and for locomotives and Carnegie entered the iron and steel business. He went on to the building of iron bridges, the pioneering of the use of steel and the exploitation of oil in Pennsylvania and Ohio. Ultimately an enormous steel combine was in his hands. He had many Scots among his collaborators—Robert Pitcairn, who had been a fellow-messenger in early days, James Scott, George Lauder and Charles Lockhart, who were all associated with the steel industry, one Macpherson who was in charge of the project of a bridge across the Mississippi at St. Louis and a 'Mr. Chisholm', from Dunfermline, at Cleveland.

In his boyhood in Dunfermline, Carnegie had often admired the beautiful grounds of Pittencrieff Glen, which were in private hands, and he fulfilled a long-standing ambition when his wealth ultimately allowed him to purchase these grounds and present them to his native town. In his early days in America, when he was educating himself, he owed much to the generosity of a gentleman who opened his library to working boys, and this determined the line in philanthropy with which Carnegie's name is perhaps most often linked— the provision of Free Libraries. It was noble, too, in a man who himself had no professional training, that he established the Carnegie Trust for the Universities of Scotland, which for many years assisted the majority of Scottish students to pay their fees, in the days before grants from other sources were available, and which more recently has concentrated on aiding research. Carnegie's other benefactions were many and various, but his native town was always closest to his heart: it was in Dunfermline that he established his first free public library, as early as 1881, and the Carnegie Dunfermline Trust continues to benefit the town in a variety of ways. He remarked that 'what Benares is to the Hindoo, Mecca to the Mohammedan, Jerusalem to the Christian, all that Dunfermline is to me'.[1]

Apart from the larger fields of industry, there were many Scots who carried specialized skill to America. One of the first of them was Thomas MacBean, who was trained as an architect under the Aberdonian James Gibbs (architect of St. Martin-in-the-Fields in London) and who designed St. Paul's Chapel in Broadway, New York, between 1764 and 1766. Thomas Carstairs, born at Largo, in Fife, in 1759, was an architect and builder who followed his profession after he arrived in Pennsylvania in 1784. A later example was Charles Burt, a pupil of the famous engraving firm, W. H. Lizars of

[1] *Autobiography*, 319n.

Edinburgh, who became an engraver in the Treasury Department in Washington.

As industry developed within the United States, the value of Scottish expertise gradually dwindled, for equivalent skills were acquired by Americans and American production of a whole range of commodities was able not only to supply the home demand and make the country independent of imports, but even in time to supply exports to markets which had previously relied on Britain. Thus, in iron and steel America no longer needed Scottish guidance by about 1870; in the mining of coal and iron the turning point was about ten years later; and the importance of the Scottish contribution to textile processes came to an end about 1900. This was one reason for the falling off in emigration to the United States after 1903. There was always, however, ample scope for Scots with initiative and experience, for example as shopkeepers and merchants who had acquired experience at home and set up their own businesses in the States. It is not so clear that many Scottish professional men transferred their skill to America, for although many physicians, teachers, journalists and lawyers in the United States had been born in Scotland most of them were trained in America.

As has already been indicated, Scots were not backward in moving to the west as the Republic gradually extended its frontier. In the early years of the nineteenth century, the Scot John Bradbury was one of the first to visit the Missouri valley, and his *Travels in the interior of America in 1809, 1810 and 1811* was written partly to inform prospective emigrants. Some of the descendants of the North Carolina settlers subsequently pioneered in Tennessee and Mississippi. Further north, the development of Ohio and Indiana was followed by that of Illinois (which increased its population between 1810 and 1840 from 12,000 to 476,000) and Michigan (which increased in the same period from 5,000 to 212,000). Morris Birkbeck's *Notes on a Journey from the coast of Virginia to the territory of Illinois* (1817) and his *Letters from Illinois* (1818) were among the first 'advertisements' for those areas to appear in Britain. Scots reached Illinois at an early stage in its development and among the founders of Chicago were John Kinzie (1763–1828), son of a Mackenzie, and Alexander White (1814–72), a native of Elgin. By 1850 there were nearly 5,000 Scots in Illinois. In 1837 we hear of an Illinois Investment Company, in which Aberdeen and Edinburgh firms were interested. John Regan, an Ayrshire school teacher, visited America in 1842 and, returning later, settled in Illinois, where in 1857 he was editor and proprietor of the *Messenger*; in 1852 he produced *The emigrant's guide to the western states of America*, published at Edinburgh. A 'Scotland County' was formed in Missouri in 1841. Scots began to arrive in Texas in 1848–9, only three years after that state had been received into the Union. In Iowa there were 700 Scots in 1850, 3,000 in 1860, pursuing the usual pioneering life and dwelling in log-cabins or 'sod-houses' which were built of turf in a manner not dissimilar from some of the primitive habitations of the western Highlands and isles. One of the earliest immigrants to Iowa was Samuel Muir, 'a graduate of the university of Edinburgh and a Scotchman to the core, who proved himself a tenacious frontiersman'.[1]

Even earlier than such settlements in the Middle West, Scottish interest had been aroused in the Far West. In 1839, Alexander Forbes, a Scottish merchant of Tepic in Mexico, published a history of California in which he strongly recommended the colonization of that province, and in the same year there was created the Puget's Sound Agricultural Company; the stock was held by the Hudson's Bay Company, a Scot, Dr. William Tolmie, became manager, and a few settlers began to farm. The development of California did not begin, however, until the discovery of gold there in 1848; in 1849 80,000 people—the 'forty-niners'—came into the area, 30,000 of them by land from other parts of the United States and 50,000 by sea. As California developed, it acquired a strong Scottish element, and John McLaren (1846–1943), a native of Bannockburn, was largely responsible for the creation of the Golden Gate Park in San Francisco.

One element in the spreading of Scots throughout the vast areas of the continent arose from the making of canals and railways, for the contractors frequently sent to Britain for labour. Besides, there was sometimes a Scottish element in the management: the Scots-Canadians, Norman Kittson, Donald Smith and George Stephen were associated in raising the capital for the Great Northern Railroad Company in the United States. It was also important that some of the railroads had land to dispose of, and therefore wanted settlers. Such railways as the Chicago and North-Western advertised to encourage settlement on farm land in Central Dakota—'2,000,000 farms of fertile prairie lands to be had free of cost', a gift from the United States government. The Illinois Central was another conspicuous example, and did a lot of propaganda in the later 1850s.

[1] Thomas D. Clark, *Frontier America* (1959), 593.

Later, after the Civil War, the two companies responsible for extending the railway system from the Missouri to the Pacific were liberally endowed with land and opened up for human use vast areas of fertile soil. It is to be remembered, too, that, during the Civil War, the Homestead Act of 1862 offered citizens of the United States holdings of 160 acres each, in return for only a small payment at the end of five years.

There was, after all, a minority of Scottish emigrants to whom the prospects of acquiring land did appeal, and clearly the United States offered similar agrarian attractions to those of Australia, New Zealand and the western states of Canada. Certainly the pattern was less predominantly industrial in the Middle West and the Far West than it was in the eastern states, but there were Scottish farmers scattered here and there throughout the entire area of the Union. We find, for example, that Scots came to farm in Caledonia, Le Roy and Scottsville in western New York about 1820 and a group of families from Kintyre were among the early farmers in Argyle, Illinois, in the late 1830s. Other Scottish farmers were at Dundee and other places in Illinois, in Wisconsin, in Iowa and in Florida. In 1871 Scots established a settlement in western Minnesota interested in the raising of pure-bred cattle. And even in the older states there continued to be occasional agrarian settlers: between 1866 and 1874 Scottish as well as English gentlemen brought groups of their countrymen to south-central Virginia. In 1920, of the natives of Scotland then numbered among the inhabitants of the United States, 195,614 were in urban areas and 58,956 in rural areas, but a large proportion of the latter were probably in mercantile or professional occupations and not in farming.

Two Scots of high rank made their mark on the land in the United States. John Sutherland Sinclair emigrated in 1875 at the age of seventeen and he was a farmer on a large scale in North Dakota by 1891, when he inherited the earldom of Caithness. He continued to reside in America, though he visited Scotland occasionally and voted as a Scottish representative peer. The eighth earl of Airlie went out to America for the first time in 1864 and later planned to introduce Aberdeen-Angus cattle to a ranch in the States; he returned to America in 1881 and invested extensively in land, becoming Chairman of the Prairie Land and Cattle Company. He set up his son on land he had bought in Colorado and himself died at Denver, Colorado, in 1881. A remarkable feature of this period was the amount of Scottish investment in the American west. The Scottish

American Investment Company financed, among other companies, the Wyoming Cattle Ranch Company and Western Ranches, Limited. There was also a Scottish American Mortgage Company directing similar investments, and in December 1882, at Dundee, the Matador Land and Cattle Company was founded. Cattle companies in Texas, Montana, Wyoming, Nebraska, Colorado, Kansas and New Mexico were backed by Scottish bankers. It was estimated in the late 1870s and the 1880s that three-quarters of the foreign investment in ranching in America came from Scotland.[1]

The general pattern of the distribution of Scottish emigrants in the United States is shown by the statistics given by the census of 1920 for persons both of Scottish birth and Scottish descent. The heaviest concentration was in the Atlantic, and especially the Middle Atlantic, states, with the highest numbers of all in New York, Massachusetts and Pennsylvania. Next in importance was the east-north-central group of states—Ohio, Illinois and Michigan particularly—and after that came the Pacific coastal area, especially California, a state which came fifth (after New York, Pennsylvania, Massachusetts and Illinois) in the number of inhabitants of Scottish origin. Among the great cities, the largest numbers of Scots were in New York, Chicago, Philadelphia and Detroit.

Many indications have already been given of the contributions made by Scottish settlers to American life, and G. F. Black's book, *Scotland's Mark on America*, lists some 1,500 Scots who made their mark in America in government, the armed forces, the professions, industry, finance and the arts. Over a hundred men of Scottish descent are enumerated as governors of states since the Revolution, and of fifty judges of the Supreme Court from 1789 to 1882 at least fifteen were of Scottish extraction. Among the legislators may be mentioned John McDougal, a native of Dumbarton, who was a member of the Ohio legislature from 1813 to 1815; David Bremner Henderson (1840–1906), born at Old Deer, Aberdeenshire, became speaker of the House of Representatives; William Grant Laidlaw, born near Jedburgh in 1840, was a member of Congress from 1887 to 1891. The tradition of military service by Scots (including Ulster Scots) which had been established in the Revolutionary War was maintained, and the first and second generals who led northern armies into battle in the Civil War bore the names of McDowell and McClellan. In every part of the world where Scots have settled,

---

[1] There is an article by W. G. Kerr on 'Scotland and the Texas Mortgage Business' in *Economic History Review*, 2nd ser., xvi, 91–103.

they have been associated with printing and journalism, and in the United States the outstanding names are those of George Bruce, who introduced the stereotype, Adam Ramage, who invented a printing press, and James Gordon Bennett, founder of the *New York Herald*. Among American literary figures, the outstanding one of Scottish descent was Washington Irving (1783–1859), who was the son of an Orcadian farmer. In recent years the most distinguished American of Scottish descent was Adlai Stevenson, a Presidential candidate in 1952 and 1956, who was descended from an eighteenth-century emigrant from Stirlingshire.

If Scots have left their mark on the history of the United States, they have also left their mark on the geography of the country, as a glance at any atlas or gazetteer will show. Leaving aside the better-known examples of duplication of Scottish place-names in America, the following may be noted. Paterson town, in Putman County, New York, takes its name from Matthew Paterson, a Scottish stone mason who settled there in the middle of the eighteenth century. George McDuffie, governor of South Carolina from 1838 to 1840, gave his name to McDuffie County in Georgia. There are in the United States eleven counties and eighteen towns and villages bearing the name Crawford. Leith, the port of Edinburgh and before its amalgamation with that city in 1920 a substantial town of 80,000 people, has given its name to four tiny villages in the United States, scattered in Alabama, Arkansas, Nevada and North Dakota.

Among the many immigrants to the United States, those who came from Great Britain on the whole assimilated themselves readily to the American nation, mainly because it has always been hard to think of people speaking the same language as being different nationalities, and they were apt to identify themselves with other Americans of British descent as against those of other national origins. The Scots, in particular, had always had a great gift for assimilation, and most of them readily adopted the American idiom and ways of life, though there were always the representatives of the more angular type of Scot who delights in making himself conspicuous. In general, however, while the Scot became an American he became an American Scot, insistent that he was distinct from English, Welsh and Irish, and where there were Scottish communities they carefully fostered—and sometimes exaggerated—what they could preserve of Scottish life and Scottish ways.

Not least significant was the retention of many of the characteristics of Scottish church life. The rigid discipline of the Presbyterian system was maintained in the United States at least as long as it lasted at home. Antiquated customs in worship survived, like the practice of 'lining out' the metrical psalms, a practice which meant that the precentor (who led the singing when instrumental music of any kind was abhorred) read each line, after which the congregation sang it. In America as in Scotland, church services were provided in Gaelic for highland congregations. One hears of them at Elmira in Illinois, at Boston and elsewhere, but the last Gaelic sermon in North Carolina is said to have been preached in 1860 and the language is now extinct in that area.

The Scottish genius for schism went overseas with the emigrants, and several of the Presbyterian secessions were perpetuated there. Thus, the 'Log College' at Neshaminy in Pennsylvania was rent by disputes in the 1740s parallel to those which at that time divided the Scottish seceders among themselves. John Banks (*c*. 1763–1826), a native of Stirling, ministered to 'Associate Congregations' (that is, the 'Burgher' branch of the 'Original Secession') in various parts of the States. John Mason was sent by the Associate Synod in Scotland to a congregation in New York City, where he settled and was succeeded by his son. It was in reflection of an actual situation that in Galt's novel one of Lawrie Todd's fellow passengers on his way to America was 'an anti-Burgher minister' (that is, an adherent of a rival branch of the seceders). One of the smaller sects founded in eighteenth-century Scotland had been the Glassites, and their thought was developed by Robert Sandeman (1718–71), a native of Perth; his writings became so well known in America that in 1764 he was invited across to preach in Boston, where his followers, the 'Sandemanians', built a meeting-house. The strict adherents of the Covenant, the Cameronians, were represented in America, and there as in Britain they declined to acknowledge the authority of an uncovenanted government or to exercise the franchise.

Not only were Scottish schisms reproduced in America, but Scottish emigrants even established sects unknown at home. One which had arisen in Prince Edward Island was popularly known as the MacDonaldites, but its members claimed to be the true Church of Scotland, and a group of Prince Edward Islanders brought this sect with them to Cambridge, Massachusetts, in 1895. The 'Campbellites', who styled themselves the 'Disciples of Christ', were founded by Alexander Campbell (1786–1866), an Ulster Scot, and Walter Scott, a native of Moffat, Dumfriesshire; one of their later leaders was Archibald MacLean (1849–1920), of Skye descent. John

Alexander Dowie (1847–1907), who founded the 'Christian Catholic Apostolic Church in Zion' in 1896, was born in Edinburgh. He arrived in San Francisco from Australia in 1888 and then settled in Chicago, near which he built 'Zion City' for his followers, who were required to forgo liquor and tobacco and submit to a régime of almost unparalleled puritanism. It hardly surprises one to learn that Mary Baker Eddy (1821–1910), the founder of Christian Science, claimed Scots descent.

The Protestant Episcopal Church in the United States had peculiarly close associations with the Scottish Episcopal Church. In 1784 its first bishop, Samuel Seabury, was consecrated by Scottish bishops in Aberdeen, and an undertaking was given that the American Communion service would follow the pattern of the Scottish Liturgy. Scottish Episcopalians who went to America therefore felt themselves at home, and Scottish immigrants provided some clergy for the American Church: James Bonner, for instance, born in Edinburgh in 1810, was a teacher in Scotland before he emigrated in 1835 to America, where he took orders and ministered in a succession of churches in Pennsylvania, New York, Ohio and Maryland.

In the secular sphere, Scots kept up their festivities at Hogmanay [New Year's Eve] and New Year's Day, and also the traditional 'guising' and other customs connected with Hallowe'en. St. Andrew's Day was observed in the United States in generations when it was almost forgotten in Scotland—a curious example of the triumph of national sentiment over ecclesiastical standards which had at the Reformation renounced the observance of saints' days. Another anniversary which came to be of even greater importance was the birthday of Robert Burns (25th January), which was celebrated in the United States at least as early as 1820, with a banquet in New York. The first Burns Club in America was established in New York in 1847, and now one finds Burns Clubs in places like Akron (Ohio), Atlanta (Georgia), Buffalo (New York), Charlotte (North Carolina), Flint (Michigan) and St. Louis (Missouri). No other Scottish author captured the imagination to quite the same degree, but Sir Walter Scott was not forgotten on the centenary of his birth in 1871.

The reputation of Scottish Highlanders for athletic prowess, which they were wont to display in periodical contests, led to 'Highland Games' in America. In 1836 the Highland Society of New York held its first 'Sportive Meeting' and within a few years

Scots in Boston, Philadelphia and elsewhere were holding 'Highland Games'. The traditional contests took place, and sometimes Scottish champions came across the Atlantic to demonstrate their skill and strength. One of the biggest events of this kind is the Scottish Gathering and Games held each year at the end of August by the Caledonian Club of San Francisco, when many thousands of people assemble to watch the athletic contests and the piping competitions. In 1867 international contests were held for the first time between the Caledonian Club of the United States and its opposite number in Canada and three years later the two federated as the North American Caledonian Association. Scotland has never had a national game in the sense of one which interests the whole nation; shinty is peculiar to the Highlands, rugby football found favour particularly in the Borders, golf has always attracted great interest, though its special home is on the natural 'links' of the east coast. But, for some unknown reason, the national imagination has been captivated by curling, a game which has in truth a kind of scarcity value, since it requires sheets of frozen water which in many parts of Scotland may be quite unknown in a normal winter. In America, however, curling could be played with a regularity unknown in Scotland, and in 1867 the Grand National Curling Club was formed, with about thirty constituent local clubs; there is also the United States Men's Curling Association. It should be said that the Scots also took golf to America. Its introduction is assigned to 1888, when a New York linen merchant of Scottish birth, Lockhart by name, returned from a holiday in Scotland with clubs and balls and, with John Reid, a native of Dunfermline, formed the St. Andrews Golf Club of New York.

No doubt many highland emigrants quite naturally and unaffectedly took their genuine native culture and traditions with them, and nothing artificial or false lay behind occasional ebullient demonstrations like an incident in 1873 when mine workers on strike at Blossburg marched behind a pipe band playing 'The MacGregors' Gathering'. But the recent cult in Scotland of 'clans' and tartans has been assiduously copied in the United States. In 1878 the Order of Scottish Clans was founded at St. Louis, but it soon had its most important centre in New England and the middle Atlantic states. The 'clans' which composed it were in reality lodges which adopted the names and tartans of highland families. There were other 'Orders' in schism from the 1878 foundation. The Scottish-American women organized their 'Daughters of Scotia' in 1898. An annual

'Kirkin' o' the Tartan' fills the National Cathedral at Washington. It is, however, curious that so early as 1765 George Bartram, a native of Scotland who had become a cloth merchant in Philadelphia, was advertising 'Best Scotch plaids for gentlemen's gowns and boys' Highland dress';[1] this might suggest that the cult of the tartan actually flourished on the far side of the Atlantic earlier than it did in Great Britain.

The St. Andrew's Societies founded in the eighteenth century were the forerunners of the clubs and societies without number which in later years have been founded for one purpose or another by American Scots. A great many of them bear the name of some clan, and sometimes several local societies of the same clan are federated. Thus the Clan Donald Society of America (Inc.) has branches in Illinois, Louisiana, Missouri, New York, North Carolina, South Carolina, Pennsylvania, Texas and Washington. Some Scottish societies, again, are grouped on a regional basis: the United Scottish Societies of Southern California embrace some thirty-five constituent societies. Some societies are based on a common interest in some feature of Scottish life, rather than on a family name: the Boston Gaelic Club, the Scottish Country Dance Club in New Hampshire, and Pipe Bands in states from Pennsylvania to California. The time-honoured name of St. Andrew's Society is borne by associations in Baltimore, Chicago, Idaho, Kansas, Los Angeles, Milwaukee, New Mexico, New York, Oakland (California), Oklahoma, Philadelphia, Oregon, San Francisco, Washington and elsewhere. Whatever their professed purpose, all those organizations keep American Scots in touch with each other and usually foster an interest in the ancestral homeland as well. A remark made in Pittsburgh in 1904 can be applied, in substance, to wide areas of America: 'Scotland is still the land of dreams to many, although the steel corner of Pennsylvania is the land of dollars.'[2]

---

[1] *Historical Catalogue of the St. Andrew's Society of Philadelphia.*
[2] John Hogben, *First Impressions of America* (Leith, 1904), 82.

Abandoned croft-house in Scotland

Cape Breton scenery

John Strachan

William Lyon Mackenzie

9

EMIGRATION TO CANADA

THE possibility of settling in any territory other than the colonies which were to form the United States seldom occurred to any Scottish emigrant before 1783, and indeed such a possibility hardly existed. There were as yet no British possessions of any consequence outside America, and within America most of the vast areas which were later to become the Dominion of Canada were still unoccupied and even unexplored and the parts of them which were best known had only recently passed under the British flag. Most of Nova Scotia had indeed been ceded by France to Britain in 1713, but it was not until 1749 that any serious British settlement there was attempted and it was only in the 1760s, after many of the French settlers had been dispossessed, that Scots first began to find their way to Nova Scotia in any numbers.[1] What was then known as 'St. John's Island', and was to be re-named Prince Edward Island in 1798, had not been included in the cession of 1713 and remained a French possession until 1763. Cape Breton Island, with its great fortress of Louisbourg, had likewise not been ceded in 1713 and did not finally pass into British hands until 1763, when the French province of Canada, properly so called—that is, what came to be Lower Canada, with its capital at Quebec—was also surrendered by France.

The impetus to the settlement of Britons in the northern parts of the continent arose out of the attainment of independence by the thirteen colonies which became the United States. What had been the main, almost the only, outlet for emigration had suddenly

[1] See Chapter 5.

become an independent, a foreign, country, and emigrants who wanted to live in British territory had to go elsewhere. But what .really transformed the situation in Canada was the problem of finding homes for the 'United Empire Loyalists', those who had been on the losing side in the late War of Independence and who declined to continue to live in a country not acknowledging the British crown. Some of the loyalists had left the United States, mostly under compulsion, before the war was even over, and by the spring of 1783 they were pouring over the frontier in their thousands; before the end of 1784 the total number who had moved was at least 35,000, and it is believed that before the migration was completed no less than 50,000 left their old homes. Some of them went to the West Indies, some of them returned to Great Britain, but the great majority had to be accommodated on the mainland of North America. Lower Canada, or Quebec, under British sovereignty since 1763, provided a home for some of the loyalists: they made settlements especially in the hitherto unoccupied 'Eastern Townships', bordering on Vermont. But the province of Lower Canada was, and remained, predominantly French, and in the main accommodation for loyalists was found elsewhere.

The British government decided that loyalists should have free allotments of land in Nova Scotia and Ontario, and surveyors were appointed to make allocations, varying in size according to the rank which the colonists had held in the loyalist forces, and ranging generally from 1,000 acres for officers down to 100 acres for privates. For many of the migrants, the Nova Scotia area was the more accessible, and for New Englanders the stretch of less than four hundred miles of sea across the Bay of Fundy provided a ready means of transport. It is hardly surprising, for example, that most of the resident members of the Scots Charitable Society of Boston went off to Halifax, carrying the records of the Society with them. Such numbers moved into the Nova Scotia region that in 1784 New Brunswick, which had previously been almost uninhabited but had suddenly acquired 5,000 people, was formed into a separate province. But Upper Canada, too, the future Ontario, was designated as a British colony at this time. As yet it was almost wholly unpeopled by Europeans. There were a few soldiers at Niagara, and some inconsiderable French settlements near Detroit, but settlements which had existed earlier at Kingston and Toronto had for some years been abandoned, and the whole expanse of land which lies along the upper waters of the St. Lawrence and the northern shores of Lake Ontario was available for colonization. Part of this territory was ready for settlement by loyalists in the summer of 1784, and the 4,000 persons who arrived there in that year were later joined by many more. The existing seigneurial system of Quebec was extended into Upper Canada at this point, but Upper Canada was formed into a separate province in 1791. In the 1790s an attempt was made to attract additional settlers from the United States, with a certain amount of success, producing those who are called the 'later loyalists', though in truth not many of them came mainly for political reasons.

Among the migrant loyalists were many of Scottish descent. Sir John Johnson, son of Sir William Johnson, who had planted so many Scottish Highlanders on his estates in the Mohawk Valley, was a loyalist, and in 1776 he led many of his people from Albany to Montreal, where he organized a loyalist force; he was followed to Canada by many of his tenants and employees. The loyalist Scots in North and South Carolina included Flora MacDonald's husband and her two sons, who had been commissioned in the North Carolina Highland Regiment, but Flora and her husband, after spending a winter near Halifax, Nova Scotia, returned to Scotland. Among the British regiments of regular soldiers which had fought during the war had been the Scots Guards, the Royal Scots, the Royal Scots Fusiliers, the Black Watch and also the Cameronians, who helped to defend Canada against the rebel colonists. When the war was over, some British soldiers were disbanded and settled in America, among them some from the Black Watch, who settled in Nova Scotia, and other Highlanders who, under Colonel MacDonnell, settled in Ontario. Two of the Royal Townships, running eastwards from the seigniory of Longueil, were allotted to Roman Catholic Highlanders and to lowland Presbyterians from Johnson's regiment. Glengarry County was formed in the extreme east of Upper Canada in 1792. Among the surnames which were common in Upper Canada were Grant, MacLean, MacKay, MacDonald or MacDonnell, McGillies, Macpherson and Cameron. The settlers, in their new homes, had to resume the pioneering way of life which they or their ancestors had earlier followed further south—felling trees, building their houses, clearing and ploughing rough ground and finally sowing their crops.

Until 1815, there was no steady emigration from the home country to Canada, though some important settlements were made by High-landers, especially about 1803,[1] and some Lowlanders went to

[1] Chapter 5.

Upper Canada both before and after 1800. After 1815, however, the
British government was anxious to foster the development of
Canada, for a variety of reasons. For one thing, it was a time of
economic difficulty, unemployment and poverty at home; for
another, Britain had just been at war with the United States (1812–
14), and therefore wanted to counteract possible American infiltration of Canada and to defend the frontier in case of further trouble.
(During the war, Ontario Highlanders, embodied as the Glengarry
Light Infantry Fencibles, had played their part in the defence of
Canada.) After the war, it seemed sound policy, in the interest of
defence, to demobilize some of the British regulars who had served
in America during the war and settle them, with their families, along
the frontier. Among the regiments who had so served were the Royal
Scots, who had defended Canada, and the Royal Scots Fusiliers,
who had been present at the capture of Washington and had taken
part in an expedition against New Orleans. But, besides this more
military policy, the British government made offers to 'industrious
families' who were prepared to emigrate from the home country to
Upper Canada; they received free passages, 100 acres of land, rations
of food for an initial period, and agricultural implements. Apart from
this official action, many books were published praising Upper
Canada in preference to the United States. The sharp increase in
the total emigration from Britain as a whole at this point—2,000 in
1815, 12,000 in 1816, 35,000 in 1819—made its mark on Canada.

The migration from Scotland at the time fitted into this general
pattern. With the resumption of emigration at the end of the wars,
about 250 people who were prepared to take advantage of the
government's favourable terms sailed from Greenock in 1815 and
settled on a range of townships west of the Rideau River which
became the enduring community of 'Perth', south-west of Ottawa,
and in 1818 300 Scots formed a group and settled in the Rice Lake
district of Upper Canada. The distress which required alleviation in
Scotland at this time was notably among the weavers, or at any rate
it was the weavers who had sufficient enterprise to make their case
heard. Already in 1819 distressed weavers had founded New Glasgow in Nova Scotia, and about the same time many petitions were
drawn up by weavers in Lanarkshire and Renfrewshire asking for
aid in emigration. In 1820 they were allotted lands in 'Dalhousie',
'Ramsay' and 'Lanark', all in Upper Canada, and between 1,200 and
2,000 people, mainly from Lanarkshire but also from Dunbartonshire, Clackmannanshire and West Lothian, were assisted to emi-

grate. The settlement at 'Dalhousie', made by people mostly from the Glasgow, Paisley or Hamilton areas, who sailed from the Firth of Clyde in April 1820, did not develop, nor did that at 'Ramsay', but 'Lanark' flourished and attracted other settlers from home, including a party from Blair-Atholl in 1834. The Glasgow Emigration Society also assisted weavers to settle at Grenville in Ontario. It was no doubt another incident in the same movement when eighty-four emigrants sailed from Greenock in 1825.

The history of certain settlements shows the different strands in Scottish emigration to Canada in this period, very often beginning with a nucleus formed by loyalists who had left the United States. One of the Scottish settlements in Lower Canada was a farming community on the Chateauguay River, which has its source in New York State and enters the St. Lawrence from the south, almost opposite Montreal. Among the settlers were two loyalists from the States—James Fisher, originally from Killin, and Andrew Gentle, who had gone from Dunblane to the States in 1784; others were William Ogilvie, James Wright, James Gilfillan, Archibald Muir, who was the miller of the community, and a smith called Dewar.[1] In Upper Canada, the township of 'Dumfries' owed its name to William Dickson (1769–1846), born in Dumfries, who emigrated to Canada in 1792, and practised as a lawyer. In 1816 he bought a block of nearly 100,000 acres and by the end of 1817 there were thirty-eight families settled, chiefly Scots who had previously lived in Genesee County, New York State. He also worked in Scotland for settlers, with considerable success. In Eldon, Ontario, there were by 1830 Highlanders straight from home, others from New York and yet others from Glengarry (Canada), and more came to Eldon from Mull and Islay and other parts of Argyll, so that it retained a markedly Highland character.[2] John Davidson, a native of Perthshire, had gone as a small boy to Dundee; on discharge from the army in 1817 he emigrated to Canada and started a store at a place called Dundee, in Lower Canada, where other Scots, largely Highlanders, arrived in later years. It must be kept in mind that for long after 1815 regiments of British regular soldiers were stationed in Canada, among them the Highland Light Infantry (1825–32), the Royal Scots (1838–9) and the Seaforth Highlanders (about 1850); as in the eighteenth century, the soldiers sometimes encouraged

[1] Robert Sellar, *The history of the county of Huntingdon and the seignories of Chateaugay and Beauharnois* (1888).
[2] *Ontario Hist. Soc. Papers and Records*, xxiv (1927), 462–71.

emigration and strengthened the associations between Scotland and the colonies. Later, when the Dominion of Canada acquired its own armed forces, several of the regiments bore Scottish names—the Queen's Own Cameron Highlanders of Canada (associated with Winnipeg), the Seaforth Highlanders of Canada (associated with Vancouver) and many more; and some Canadian regiments were affiliated with regiments at home—the Toronto Scottish regiment with the London Scottish, the Canadian Scottish Regiment with the Royal Scots and the Royal New Brunswick Regiment with the King's Own Scottish Borderers.

In the phase following the post-war emigration of weavers and Highlanders, the greatest single impact made on Upper Canada was an effort which owed a great deal to the Scottish novelist John Galt. Galt was a native of Greenock, a port from which emigrants had long been sailing to America, and it might be said that he had an hereditary interest in the New World, for a forebear of his had been banished to Carolina in 1684 for refusing to renounce the Covenants and condemn the rebels who had fought for the Covenants at Both-well Brig in 1679. Galt himself became the agent in London for the claims of the Canadians who had suffered losses in the war between Britain and the United States in 1812–14. He proposed to use the 'crown and clergy reserves' (that is, land not allotted to private settlers) for this purpose, and his Canada Company arose out of this proposal, but ultimately it was allotted 1,100,000 acres in the western part of the colony in place of the clergy reserves. One of Galt's associates was Dr. William Dunlop, who had served in the war of 1812–14, and another was William Dickson, already mentioned, who gave the name of 'Galt' to the chief place in his 'Dumfries' settlement. The Canada Company had an agent in Greenock. Galt was recalled from Canada in 1829, but he was soon associated with the British America Land Company, chartered in 1834 and concerned with a part of Upper Canada which had not previously received a substantial number of settlers. From the efforts of Galt and his friends came the colonization of a vast area in the peninsula lying between Lake Huron on the north-west and Lakes Erie and Ontario on the south. The settlement attracted some colonists from all parts of Scotland, including Shetland, which sent in 1838 the parents of William Bruce (1833–1927), who was to become a leading Canadian astronomer. The towns of Goderich and Guelph, as well as Galt, developed in this settlement, and there also are Dundas and Hamilton.

Many other place-names in Ontario recall the Scottish origins of the early settlers, among them Paisley, Arnprior, Athol, Dunvegan, Dunrobin, Perth, Douglas, Renfrew, Arran, Elderslie, Carrick, Glencoe, Crawford, Haliburton and Greenock. In Lanark County are rivers called the Tay and the Clyde, and both Orkney and Shetland are commemorated within the province. On the shores of Lake Huron are three villages called Leith, Annan and Johnstone. At first the people of all three worshipped together in the church at Annan, but when the majority in that congregation went over to the Free Church after the Disruption in 1843 the people of Leith decided to build a church of their own in connection with the Church of Scotland, and they did so in 1864. It seems that they modelled their building on a church in the original Leith, in Scotland, but oddly enough it was the old Free Church of North Leith which they took as their prototype.[1] Here as elsewhere schism ended in 1875, when the Presbyterian bodies came together to form the Presbyterian Church in Canada.

One weakness, which for a long time militated against the stability of the area of Galt's settlements and of other parts of Upper Canada, was the difficult communication with Lower Canada and the Atlantic seaboard. Consequently, there was a constant drain of disillusioned settlers westward through Detroit and ultimately into the Mississippi valley, and even in recent times Detroit attracted Canadian Scots over the frontier. The British government endeavoured from an early date to improve matters, with the Rideau Canal (1826–31) and, in 1833, the Welland Canal, which by-passed the Niagara Falls. Railways did not come until very much later, for it was cheaper to serve a scattered population by waterborne communications, and most of the places of importance were on or near lakes or navigable rivers. When the railways did come, they had the effect of facilitating movement in both directions, and there was a certain migration from Upper Canada to the western provinces.

While interest centred, in the first half of the century, mainly on Ontario or Upper Canada, a certain number of Scottish settlers had continued to join their fellow countrymen who had pioneered in earlier days in the maritime provinces. The Scots who had settled in Pictou, Nova Scotia, before 1770, were joined in 1783–4 by some disbanded soldiers, and others came out from Scotland, until in 1803 the population at Pictou numbered 500. The Cape Breton area attracted a very large number of Highlanders and islanders in the

[1] I owe this information to the Rev. J. S. Marshall.

early nineteenth century; between 1802 and 1827 the Scottish immigration to that area is estimated at 25,000, mainly highland. In the early stages, as the land was cleared by burning, seed was sown among the ashes of the trees, and ample crops were raised with little labour, but later on persistent work was necessary.

In Prince Edward Island, Scottish Roman Catholics founded Georgetown, Covehead, St. Peter's and Cavendish. Some Scottish Protestants were settled at the west side of Richmond Bay. By 1841, it is said, there were 4,500 persons of the surname MacDonald in the island. In New Brunswick, where a few Scottish colonists had settled at Athol Point in 1783 and two disbanded regiments of highland loyalists had been settled after the American War of Independence, colonization went on as immigrants came from Arran and other parts of Scotland in the early nineteenth century. Eastern New Brunswick, in particular, was settled largely from Scotland. William Davidson, from Inverness, who had settled at Wilson's Point as early as 1765, pioneered the timber industry of the area, and more Scots came later to Doaktown, Nipsiguit and Richibucto. James Glenie, a Scot who had been an officer in the Royal Engineers, became a member of the colonial assembly of New Brunswick in 1791 and showed 'talents and dash' which involved him in a duel with another member.[1] James Brown (1790–1870), a native of Angus, who emigrated to New Brunswick in 1808, became a member of the government in 1854 and surveyor-general of the province; as a special commissioner to advertise New Brunswick to immigrants he wrote a pamphlet, *New Brunswick as a home for immigrants*, and he was also known for his verse, including *The deil's reply to Robert Burns*.

In relation to the total figures for what became the Dominion of Canada, Scottish settlement in the maritime provinces was not substantial: after about 1828 the highland emigration to Nova Scotia declined, and from 1853 to 1860, over 25,000 Scots settled in Ontario and Quebec and less than 1,000 in the maritime provinces. But, in proportion to the area and total population of those provinces, the descendants of the original Scottish settlers and the persistent flow later—however slight at any particular period— made their mark, so that Prince Edward Island and Nova Scotia have the highest percentages, among all the Canadian provinces, of inhabitants of Scottish descent.

The maritime provinces, whatever their importance in earlier

[1] *Canada and its provinces*, xiii, 174.

times, were the merest fringe of Canada, and beyond even Quebec and Ontario lay regions which were to form far the greater part of the area of the future Dominion. The Hudson's Bay Company had been founded in 1670, with almost limitless rights over 'all countries which lie within the entrance of Hudson's Straits, in whatever latitude they may be, so far as not possessed by other Christian States'. The interest of the company, from first to last, was mainly in the fur trade, and through vast districts they established, for the purpose of trading with the natives, fortified posts, usually on navigable rivers. There were about a hundred such stations, scattered from the Labrador coast to the Pacific, manned in all by one or two thousand men, who represented the entire white population of this vast area, for it was not in the interests of fur traders to encourage colonization and diminish the sway of nature. The records of fur-trading in Canada contain the names of numerous Camerons, Campbells, MacDonalds, Stewarts and other Scots. The Company's staff, however, consisted very largely of Orcadians, who were recruited when the Company's ships touched at the Orkneys before beginning their transatlantic voyage. Sir George Simpson, one of the greatest governors of the Company, said, 'Two Orkney fisherman will do the duty of four such as we now have.' Orkneymen worked on the erection of Lower Fort Garry in Manitoba, 18½ miles north of Winnipeg, in the thirties and forties of last century. A National Historic Park has now been formed there, and a collection of Orkney furniture has been sent out to it to commemorate the old connection. It was Donald MacKay and John Sutherland, two servants of the Hudson's Bay Company whose names indicate an origin in the far north of the Scottish mainland, who first established posts of the Company in the Red River area.

In 1784 the North-West Company was formed as a rival to the older Company. Scots were prominent in its affairs too, and one of the early partners was William McGillivray (1764–1825), a native of Cloverdale in Inverness-shire.[1] The competition between the two companies was carried on, not infrequently even by bloodshed, until they were merged in 1821. It was against the background of this rivalry that Selkirk's Red River settlement was formed in 1812, and its early history has been recounted elsewhere.[2] The pioneering settlers found how fertile the soil was, but over decades it was only a few who came to join them. In the gradual development of what

[1] M. W. Campbell, *McGillivray, Lord of the Northwest* (Toronto, 1962).
[2] Chapter 5.

was to become the province of Manitoba, several Scots continued to play prominent parts. After the Red River settlement had recovered from its initial troubles, some Orkneymen from the service of the Hudson's Bay Company began to settle along the Assiniboine in 'Orkneytown'. Out of 419 people in the Red River area in 1821, 221 were Scots. The chief men among the Scots at Point Douglas were Robert Logan, James Bird, John Pritchard and Thomas Laidlaw. At Kildonan, on the Red River below Point Douglas, the Sutherland men predominated, and on their lots they reproduced the infield and outfield pattern of the agriculture of their homeland. With their Gaelic speech and their strong religious feeling they formed a close-knit community. They had hoped that Donald Sage would come out from Scotland as their minister, but he disappointed them and they did not obtain a minister until 1851, in the person of John Black. The Church Missionary Society had sent out a minister to the area much earlier, but he was not acceptable to the Sutherland Presbyterians.

Martin MacLeod (1813–60), born near Montreal of Scottish parents, took part in an overland expedition to the Red River in 1836–7, but went on from there to become a fur trader in the Minnesota area, where he became a member of the council and latterly its president. He advertised this area to Canadians, with some success, and gave his name to a county. James Sinclair, a trader, led a party from Red River to settle in Oregon in 1841, and in 1854 he led another party there. Of the Scots who remained in Manitoba, some played leading parts in affairs. In 1848 a petition by the free traders against the monopoly and rule of the Company was organized by Alexander Kennedy Isbister, who was obviously of Orcadian extraction (though with Indian blood in his veins), by James Sinclair and Donald Gunn, and in 1849 trade was freed from the monopoly of the Company. It was another Scot, Alexander Ross, who founded an Agricultural Improvement Society in 1850. John Norquay, prime minister of Manitoba from 1878 to 1887, was obviously of Orcadian origin, though his family had long been settled on Red River.

In 1869 the recently formed Dominion of Canada purchased the domains of the Hudson's Bay Company. This led to a rebellion by the French and half-breed population, led by Louis Riel, but it was suppressed in 1870 and British authority was firmly established. As yet the development of this area of surpassing fertility had continued to proceed very slowly: in 1871 the future town of Winnipeg had no more than 400 inhabitants, though a line of cultivated farms stretched for miles along the valleys of the Assiniboine and Red River, and the total white population was probably about 15,000. Transport and communications, both for ease of access by settlers and for facilities for the disposal of produce, were the great need, and this problem was soon solved, by both steamboat and railway. Winnipeg, linked by rail to St. Paul in Minnesota, to Lake Superior and to the western ocean, began to attract a considerable influx of settlers. By 1880 it had 12,000 inhabitants, and in the surrounding region some four millions of acres of land had been taken up by thousands of colonists, many of them from the United States, some from the older Canadian provinces, but some of them direct from Britain. In 1879 as many as 400 people might arrive in a single day. At this point, when capital was required, Scots did something to finance development, just as they did in the States, and among the large investors in Manitoba land was Lord Elphinstone, whose third son settled in Canada in 1890.

West beyond Winnipeg lay further tracts of country of similar character, and they were formed into the provinces of Alberta and Saskatchewan in 1905. Scots had appeared in Saskatchewan in the 1880s, when some highland crofters were assisted to settle near Wapella and Moosomin and at Saltcoats, as well as at Killarney in Manitoba. The excellent harvests of the beginning of the twentieth century were accompanied by vigorous propaganda in favour of emigration to all those provinces. As early as 1890 the government of Manitoba opened an office in Liverpool to publicize the attractions of the province in England and Scotland. The great period of expansion was from 1897 to 1912, when there were widening markets and rising prices for both wheat and cattle, and years of good crops. The population of Manitoba rose from 150,000 in 1891 to 450,000 in 1911. The fact that the yield of wheat per acre was appreciably higher in Manitoba than in any of the States of the Union goes far to explain the preference for emigration to Canada at this point.

In the extreme west of the future Dominion lay what was to become British Columbia, which offered not only tracts of fertile soil, but a far milder climate than the mid-western provinces and also riches in the shape of gold, coal, forests and fisheries. Gold was discovered in large quantities in 1858, bringing a large number of prospectors from the United States, Australia and New Zealand, as well as some from Great Britain, but not many of them remained permanently, and by 1870 the white population was only about 12,000. Yet there were many Scots in the area. The fact is that Scots had been involved here even from the outset, when the Hudson's Bay Company and its rival were opening up the area. Alexander Mackenzie (? 1755–1820) came from Stornoway in 1779 and entered the service of a firm which subsequently took part in founding the North-West Company. In 1789 he explored the area of the Great Slave Lake and then worked his way down a great river, named Mackenzie after him, to the Arctic Ocean; then, in 1792–3, he explored from Lake Athabasca up the Peace River, across the Rockies and down to the Pacific. A later explorer, Simon Fraser, born in New York of Scottish parents—his father was a captain in the British forces during the American War of Independence—gave his name to the river which flowed from the Rockies to the sea. Dr. James Hector, a native of Edinburgh, was surgeon and geologist to an expedition which explored the Rocky Mountains in 1857–60, and he discovered and named the Kicking Horse Pass. Later still, in 1865, it was John Rae, an Orcadian, who surveyed the route for a telegraph line from Winnipeg across the Rockies to the Pacific coast.

Apart from exploration, the influence of Scots in the trading companies, and in the civil governments when they were set up, helped to encourage emigration from Scotland. Dr. John McLoughlin, who had been born in the province of Quebec of an Irish father and a Scots mother, received his medical education in Scotland, returned to Canada and joined the North-West Company and then, after the merger of the companies in 1821, became chief factor of the Columbia post. In this capacity he virtually ruled, from his headquarters at Fort Vancouver, a large area on both sides of the later frontier. Later, James Douglas, who was governor of Vancouver Island in 1851 and of British Columbia when it became a colony in 1858,[1] encouraged Scottish settlers, and it is significant that the first Scottish Presbyterian minister appeared in British Columbia in 1861. Already in 1865 it was remarked of Vancouver: 'The Scotch, who are numerous in this city, are represented by a St. Andrew Society, established for affording relief to their needy countrymen, and the annual dinner connected with that institution is the most popular celebration of the sort in Vancouver'.[2] British Columbia did in fact become the Canadian province which, after the maritime provinces,

[1] In 1866 the colony of Vancouver Island was amalgamated with that of British Columbia.
[2] Matthew Macfie, *Vancouver Island and British Columbia* (1865), 80.

had the highest percentage of Scots in its population. A press report of 1910 makes it clear that in the period when the western provinces generally were making their maximum appeal, British Columbia still had a peculiar attraction for Scotsmen: 'Mr. Malcolm McIntyre, the Dominion Government emigration agent in the southern half of Scotland, . . . has pointed out that last year no fewer than 14,700 emigrated from "The Land O' Cakes" and that 30,000 is quite a conservative estimate for this year's total. Mr. McIntyre states that of late he has received a large number of inquiries with regard to agricultural, business and investment opportunities in Western Canada, and especially Vancouver Island and British Columbia. . . . The majority of letters written to him demand knowledge regarding the Far West. To go to Canada, and Western Canada in particular, is the ambition, he states, of those living in the agricultural districts of Scotland.'[1] It is significant of the figure which the Scots have continued to cut in the life of British Columbia that the Highland Games at Victoria are now one of the events of the British Columbia calendar and another of its events is a 'Summer Bonspiel', when kilted pipers parade and indoor curling is played by large numbers of men and women.

It was at the beginning and the end of the century between 1815 and 1914 that Canada played its most important part in the pattern of British emigration. Between 1815 and 1847 the number of British migrants to Canada was in some years greater than that to the United States, and over the twenty years between 1825 and 1846 Canada had a total of British immigrants almost equal to that of the United States—600,000 as against 710,000. After the later 1840s, however, the attractions of the United States gave that country unchallenged first place for the rest of the nineteenth century. In 1853–60, 61 per cent of British emigrants went to the United States, only 10 per cent to British North America, and between 1861 and 1870 the percentages were 72 and 8. It was only after 1900, as part of the general tendency now to emigrate to the Empire, that Canada came again within measurable distance of the United States. British immigrants to Canada increased from only 11,810 in 1901 to 120,152 in 1908 and, after lower figures in 1909 and 1910, to still higher figures, including a record of 150,542 in 1913. From 1905 to 1913 the net emigration from the British Isles to Canada exceeded that to the United States, except in 1909.

Apart from the competition of the United States, for the greater

[1] *The Scotsman*, 16th November 1910.

part of the nineteenth century Australia and New Zealand were also counter-attractions to Canada. There were, too, periods when Canada was peculiarly uninviting. Thus, in 1837, because of discontent at the failure of the British Government to grant responsible government to the two provinces of Lower and Upper Canada, rebellions were raised, a pro-French one led by Louis Papineau in Lower Canada and another, supported by the more radical advocates of constitutional change, in Upper Canada, led by William Lyon Mackenzie. Order was soon restored, but confidence had been shaken and there were few immigrants to Canada in 1838-9. Secondly, economic depression and financial difficulties in the 1850s caused some low figures for immigration. And, thirdly, there was a period of considerable unrest and uncertainty in the years before confederation was achieved in 1867. These facts partly explain why emigration to Australia and New Zealand surpassed the figures for Canada from 1851 until 1867—as it did again, briefly, in 1873-9 and 1883-5.

But the emigration, though thus subject to fluctuation, was massive, and the population of the British North American provinces, which had been less than 1½ millions in 1840, was nearly 3½ millions in 1867. The Scottish share in the British emigration was always a substantial one, though it was seldom seriously disproportionate to that of England until the later part of the nineteenth century. Between 1829 and 1859 the Scottish fraction of the total was seldom as high as a fifth, it was often very much less, and it was all but invariably much lower than the Irish figure. Yet, as a result of their long-continuing contribution to the peopling of the Dominion, men and women of Scottish descent make up a very substantial part of the population of Canada. The 1881 census estimated that, out of the English and Gaelic speaking people of Canada, about 30 per cent were English by ancestry, 25 per cent were Scottish and 33 per cent Irish. In the 1901 census, the Scottish proportion was similar—800,000 of Scottish origin, 988,000 of Irish origin and 1,260,899 of English origin. This census also shows that in terms of birth, and not descent, there were 83,631 Scots in Canada, 101,629 Irish and 201,285 English. Nearly 50,000 of those Scots were in Ontario, which had clearly continued to attract the great number of the emigrants, but there were 8,000 in Manitoba and 6,000 in British Columbia.

The 1951 census figures show that out of a Canadian population of 14,000,000, one and a half million were of Scottish origin and the inhabitants of Scottish origin now slightly exceeded the Irish. As to birth, there were now 226,343 Scots, 627,000 English and only 56,000 Irish. The Canadians of Scottish descent were distributed throughout the various provinces in a way which is certainly revealing as to the pattern of past Scottish emigration, and the figures are a commentary on a good deal of Scottish emigration history. The percentages are as follows:

Newfoundland	1%
Prince Edward Island	30%
Nova Scotia	25%
New Brunswick	12%
Quebec	2%
Ontario	12%
Manitoba	15%
Saskatchewan	12%
Alberta	13%
British Columbia	20%
Yukon	1%

The gold rushes of the 1890s to the Yukon which gave us two familiar words—bonanza and klondyke—stimulated a temporary interest in the remote north-west, but the Scots obviously took little part in it.

Individuals among the mass of Scottish colonists attained distinction, and some of them were associated with outstanding events in the main stream of the political life of the colonies, especially of Upper Canada, of which province it has been remarked that it happened 'to attract a number of fiery Scots who did much to enliven its history'.[1] One of them was Robert Gourlay. He had all along, even in Scotland before he emigrated, been involved in agitation, always with the best intentions. In 1817 he arrived in Upper Canada, where he had already purchased land and where he had kinsfolk. He visited the Perth settlement in the Genesee country in New York state, and decided to encourage to Upper Canada settlers of the type going there. He agitated about the absence of a vigorous official policy and the consequent lack of immigrants; in 1817 he accused the government of the province of corruption and was imprisoned and banished in consequence. Gourlay's struggle against abuses was taken up and pursued with even more determination by

[1]G. M. Craig, *Upper Canada: the formative years*, 93.

William Lyon Mackenzie, a native of Dundee, who arrived in Canada in 1820 at the age of twenty-five and became a partner in a general store at Dundas. He was described as 'a conceited red-haired fellow'.[1] In 1824 he started the *Colonial Advocate* newspaper to put forward a programme of political reform. Among his objects were the granting of responsible government, the sale of the clergy and crown reserves, vote by ballot, the amendment of the jury laws, the extinction of all monopolizing land companies, the disestablishment of the Church of England in Canada and the drawing up of a written constitution. As a member of the assembly of the province, Mackenzie was five times expelled from the house, but he was also mayor of Toronto (the name given to the former town of York in 1834). In 1837 he led the rebellion already mentioned, and fled to the United States.

As a consequence of the disturbances of 1837, in 1840 the two provinces of Upper and Lower Canada were united and responsible government was conceded. That the new system worked for a time was due partly to the Scot who was governor-general from 1847 to 1854—James Bruce, eighth earl of Elgin. But before long, tension grew between the two component parts of the union, especially as Upper Canada increased in population and wealth, for while the French feared that they might be swamped by the British, the British settlers in Ontario felt that they did not have the representation they deserved. The privileged position of the Roman Catholic Church in Lower Canada, and the refusal of the Roman Catholics to come into a national school system, caused further animosity. Deeply involved in the agitation was George Brown (1818–80), a native of Alloa who had migrated with his father first to New York, in 1838, and then to Toronto, where he founded the *Toronto Globe and Mail* in 1844.[2] The nature of his background in Scotland, where the evangelical party in the Church was fighting against the existing establishment and in favour of popular rights, determined his attitude. Brown's first paper, the *Banner* (1843–4), was a weekly for Presbyterians sympathetic to the cause of the Free Church, and the widespread support which that cause received in Canada helped Brown to establish his reputation both journalistically and politically. Brown was much opposed to 'the Establishment' in every sense of that term, and his anti-clericalism made him hostile to the provision of sectarian schools. He was the leader of the party known as the 'Clear

---

[1] *Ibid.*, 112.
[2] J. M. S. Careless, *Brown of the Globe* (2 vols., 1963).

Encampment of the Loyalists at Johnston, a new settlement, on the banks of the St. Lawrence River in Canada

'Log House near Blythe'

John Dunmore Lang

Grits', and in 1860 advocated the dissolution of the union of the two provinces.

The Scots were not, however, all on the same side in Canadian politics. One of Mackenzie's opponents was John Strachan (1778–1867). Born in Aberdeen, he studied at the university there and became a teacher. When he received the opportunity to become a teacher in a college projected at Kingston, Ontario, he went out there, on a four-months' journey, in 1799. The college did not materialize, and Strachan, after teaching privately for a time, decided to enter the ministry. Although his mother had been a Presbyterian, his father, like many Aberdeenshire folk, had been an Episcopalian, and Strachan decided to take orders in the Episcopal Church. He was ordained deacon in 1805 and priest in 1806, and ultimately became Bishop of Toronto—'the Fighting Bishop' as he was called. He was the first President of the Canadian Board of Education, in 1823, the founder of many schools and of McGill University. Strachan, standing in the conservative tradition, was inevitably at loggerheads with the radical agitators. He had already opposed, successfully, Galt's plan to acquire the clergy reserves for settlement, and he again and again fell foul of Mackenzie, who described him as 'a diminutive, paltry, insignificant Scotch turn-coat parish schoolmaster'.[1] For example, Strachan became a Director of the Bank of Upper Canada, which was started in 1819 and was opposed by Mackenzie, who denounced it as 'under the thumb of parson Strachan'.[2] More serious differences arose over the question of ecclesiastical establishment. The first Presbyterian ministers to arrive in Upper Canada direct from Scotland had been seceders, and Church of Scotland ministers did not arrive in any numbers until the later 1820s. There was considerable friction between the two, and the Church of Scotland was almost insignificant in point of numbers. Its claims to equality with the Church of England were therefore opposed by Strachan and by another Scot, Charles Stewart, the Anglican Bishop of Quebec. Strachan worked amicably with yet another Scottish bishop—MacDonnell, the Roman Catholic Bishop of Upper Canada.

George Brown's *Globe* was called 'the Scotsman's Bible', and it reflected both the radical opposition to privilege and the puritanical morality which were strong among the Scots. But among the Scots who did not agree with Brown was John Alexander MacDonald,

[1] *Craig*, op. cit., 113.
[2] *Ibid.*, 163.

who had been born in Glasgow in 1815, the son of an evicted Sutherland crofter, and had been taken to Kingston, Ontario, by his
parents in 1820. MacDonald became a member of the provincial
parliament and, as prime minister of the province, was an architect
of the Confederation which, in 1867, merged both 'the Canadas' in
the great Dominion, which ultimately embraced all the territories
stretching across the continent. Created a Knight Commander of
the Order of the Bath, MacDonald was first prime minister of the
Confederation.

Outside the political sphere, the two Scots whose names were best
known in Canada were Donald Alexander Smith (1820–1914) and
his cousin, George Stephen (1829–1921), who financed and directed
Canadian railways, including the great Canadian Pacific line, completed in 1885. Smith had become a clerk with the Hudson's Bay
Company in 1838 and was promoted to be a chief factor (1862) and
head of the Company's Montreal department (1868). He was a
member of the federal parliament from 1871 to 1879 and again for a
later period, and was created a baron, as Lord Strathcona and
Mount Royal, in 1897. Stephen had made his money as a cloth manufacturer in Montreal before going into railway direction; he was
created Lord Mountstephen.

By way of contrast to such men of note, an account may be given
of two much more typical families of neither fame nor distinction.
David Thomson, a thirty-one-year-old stonemason, and Mary
Glendinning, his wife, set out in 1795 with their four children from
Westerkirk, Dumfriesshire, to settle in Upper Canada, first at
Newark, then at York [Toronto] and finally at Scarborough town-
ship. A few years later David was followed by his brothers, Andrew
and Archibald, and the latter had eleven children and seventy-nine
grandchildren. To take another example, John Crawford, born in
Dalry, Ayrshire, in 1833, worked as a miner and married Mary
Cruickshanks. In 1865 they emigrated with their four children to
Pictou County, Nova Scotia, where John again worked as a miner.
In 1879 they moved on to Manitoba, where John took up 320 acres
of land north of Chester and his son, also named John, took another
320 acres, making up one square mile. John, senior, and his wife,
have had 447 descendants, and the historian of their family notes
that in 1961 there were ninety-eight Crawfords in the Winnipeg
City Directory.[1]

The impress of Scottish settlers, and the preservation of a Scottish

[1] J. H. Crawford, *Crawford, an historic Scottish family* (1963).

way of life, are perhaps most conspicuous in the maritime provinces of Canada. Most of the provinces of the Dominion can show their Scottish place-names, and some names appear many times, like Douglas in Nova Scotia, Manitoba, British Columbia, Ontario, New Brunswick and Prince Edward Island, and Dundee in Quebec, Nova Scotia, Manitoba, New Brunswick and Prince Edward Island. But it is in the maritime provinces especially that Scottish place-names abound. In Cape Breton Island, where the mountains and lakes recall the scenery of the Scottish Highlands, there is a county of Inverness, containing a village named Dunvegan and another named Glencoe. On the north coast of Prince Edward Island, there are little towns and villages named Scotchfort, Mount Stewart, St. Andrews, Douglas and Dundee; on its south coast place-names recall Caledonia, Iona, Glencoe and Culloden; and among the other names in the island are Dunstaffnage and Glengarry. New Brunswick has a Glencoe and a Ben Lomond. And in Prince Edward Island surnames such as MacLeod, MacDonald, MacNeill and Murray are common. The predominantly highland population of parts of the maritime provinces has been endowed with peculiar cohesion partly because of its possession of a distinctive language, Gaelic. It was significant of the enthusiasm for the ancient tongue that, from 1851 onwards, when a Gaelic magazine was started at Antigonish, several attempts were made to provide printed matter in Gaelic. A periodical called *The Casket*, first published at Antigonish in 1852, was for a long time partly in Gaelic and partly in English, and it still goes on, carrying a Gaelic column. The purely Gaelic *McTalla* ('The Echo') made its appearance at Sydney in Cape Breton in 1892, but it did not pay and ceased publication in 1904. In the twentieth century, the tendency of people to abandon the country and move to the towns, and conditions of modern life generally, with their emphasis on uniformity, have been detrimental to Gaelic. A mainly Gaelic community no longer has any hope of assimilating English speakers who join it, and Gaelic now flourishes only in areas where the influx of English speakers has not been marked. Yet in the 1941 census, 10,000 people in Cape Breton Island still gave Gaelic as their mother tongue. At St. Ann's, near Baddeck on Cape Breton Island, where Norman MacLeod settled his people from Sutherland in 1820, there is even a 'Gaelic College', founded by the Reverend A. W. R. MacKenzie, a native of Portree, Skye, in 1938, as a centre for the study of highland language, literature, history, folklore, music and dancing.

The Highlanders brought to the maritime provinces not only a language but a culture and a whole tradition. Clan rivalries, like those between Campbells and MacDonalds, persisted in the New World, and at present various 'Highland Societies' and 'Celtic Societies' keep alive the knowledge of the original home background. But, next to the language, the ecclesiastical life of the communities has perhaps done most to give them vitality. While a number of the immigrants were Roman Catholics, there was a large proportion of Presbyterians as well. As happened in the United States, the Presbyterian settlers in Nova Scotia did not find it easy to obtain ministers from Scotland, and their first minister came from Ireland. The first Church of Scotland minister in Nova Scotia was James Fraser, formerly chaplain to the 71st Regiment in the American War of Independence. The first Gaelic-speaking minister to come was James MacGregor, who arrived in Pictou in 1786. In 1787 Andrew Brown, who had been born at Biggar in 1763, was ordained as minister of Halifax; he returned to Scotland in 1795 and later became Professor of Rhetoric and Belles Lettres in Edinburgh University. These transatlantic Presbyterians were strong in schism and secession, and the controversies which had arisen in Scotland, irrevelant though they were to the situation in the American continent, were faithfully reproduced. Thus, there was an Associate or Burgher presbytery in Nova Scotia in 1786 and an Anti-Burgher presbytery in 1795; they united in 1817. A synod of the Church of Scotland was formed in 1833, but in 1844 it went over almost *en bloc* to the Free Church, leaving the Church of Scotland with only two ministers. In Cape Breton there was no resident minister before the famous and eccentric Norman MacLeod, in 1820. He was a 'Normanist', but a Church of Scotland presbytery was formed in 1836, only to go over solidly to the Free Church in 1844, though many of the people remained faithful to the Church of Scotland. In New Brunswick five ministers of the Church of Scotland formed a presbytery in 1836, and out of the thirteen ministers who were in the province in 1845 only three joined the Free Church. One of the most remarkable of the early ministers in the maritime provinces was Donald MacDonald, who had been born in Rannoch in 1783, ordained in 1816, and emigrated to Canada in 1824. For two years he served as a missionary in Cape Breton, where 'he braved the wild beasts of the forest, the almost arctic severity of the climate, and, above all, the indifference and degradation of the people. . . . He carried no scrip, and he had no money in his purse, nor would he take any reward for his labours except the primitive hospitality of the people'.[1] He then moved to Prince Edward Island, where he laboured for more than forty years, and before his death in 1867 he had erected thirteen churches.

In early days, when ministers were few, the people kept up their religion by family worship and by reading the Bible and theological tracts and books. In church services, the practices familiar at home were adhered to, often with a dogged conservatism, after they had been abandoned in Scotland. The practice of 'lining out' the psalms was one such practice, and the Nova Scotia Presbyterians were very reluctant to adopt organs or to introduce hymns as well as metrical psalms to public worship. The 'Communion Season' was another ecclesiastical fashion brought from Scotland; the rare celebrations of Communion were made the occasion for co-operation between parishes and were observed with the curious mixture of devotion and festivity which had become customary in eighteenth-century Scotland. The Presbyterian Church has perhaps retained its hold better than the Gaelic language has: at any rate, in 1936 the Church of Scotland claimed 60,000 members in Nova Scotia, New Brunswick and Prince Edward Island.

The best type of minister—and priest—might give valued leadership to his people, in their secular as well as their religious activities. We have seen how this might degenerate into tyranny, as it did with Norman MacLeod. But it was equally characteristic that it was the Reverend Duncan Ross of Pictou who founded the West River Agricultural Society, the first of its kind in Nova Scotia. This was a form of activity which appealed to many Scots, with their long experience at home of agricultural societies, and it was a Scot, John Young, who was responsible for the foundation in 1819 of the Central Agricultural Society of Nova Scotia and the formation of local societies throughout the province.

Apart from the maritime provinces, the Scottish community in Canada which has seemed most deserving of study is one on the north side of Lake Erie, where some Highlanders were settled on land granted to Colonel Talbot, a member of the Lieutenant-Governor's staff, in 1803 and were joined by others who came in the 1830s and 1840s. The predominant surnames—MacFarlane, MacCallum, MacPhail, Cameron, Galbraith, Campbell, MacDiarmid, Black, MacAlpine and MacColl—and the names they gave to places —Iona, Campbeltown, Crinan and Cowal, all in Elgin County,

[1] *Fasti Ecclesiae Scoticanae.* vii. 620.

Ontario—sufficiently indicate that they came mainly from Argyll, and they were, in consequence, Presbyterian. They formed what remained a conspicuously Scottish community, though it was less close-knit and less Highland in character than the society of the maritime provinces. It was essentially an agricultural and rural community, though there were some Scots in the towns as well, as tradesmen and professional men, and the farms were mainly of a size manageable by a family— 100 acres or so, very like a large number of farms in Argyll at the present day. Initially, conditions were different from those they had known at home, because they had to cope with forests, with a deep soil and with a more extreme climate, but they proved adaptable. The vagaries of the weather, at least, with late springs and wet summers from time to time, were not dissimilar to what they had been familiar with in Scotland, and were accepted with the same philosophy: 'You've got to take it as it comes.'[1] Their interest was especially in raising beef cattle, again as in Argyll. These colonists brought with them the peculiar Scottish combination of puritanical sexual morality and heavy drinking, and a description of their Sunday life would be applicable to many Scottish rural communities a few years back, if not even today: 'The Presbyterians had Sunday School, morning services which were attended by the entire family, evening services from which the elders were excused and at which religion was somewhat subordinate to the preliminary rituals of mating.'[2]

In other parts of Canada, the Presbyterians showed themselves somewhat less divisive than those in the maritime provinces. In Ontario and Quebec, for example, only twenty-three ministers out of about 100 declared in favour of the Free Church in 1844, and this was a lower proportion than seceded in Scotland. But in the 1920s, when the current had begun to run strongly in favour of reunion, Canadian Presbyterians split over the terms of union between their own church and the Methodists and Congregationalists, and many of them declined to enter into the union, not infrequently on grounds relating to church buildings and finance, which had proved a bone of contention in Scotland as well.

An interest in Gaelic is not unknown in other parts of Canada besides the maritime provinces. Toronto had a Gaelic periodical, *An Gaidheal*, for a few years from 1871 onwards, and at the present time there is a Gaelic Society in Toronto, while Vancouver boasts

[1] Galbraith, *Made to Last*, 43.
[2] *Ibid.*, 96.

both a Gaelic Society and 'an Comúnn Gaidhealach'. Canada is very well supplied with Scottish societies of every kind. There are St. Andrew's Societies in towns right across the continent, from St. John's (Newfoundland) to Vancouver, and some of them, as a development from their earlier charitable purposes, now grant scholarships to assist with university education. The 'Sons of Scotland Benevolent Association' has over 200 'Camps' or branches. As an example of a 'Scottish Club' with varied activities, the Edmonton Scottish Club will serve: it organizes a 'Scottish Day' in August, Country Dancing Classes, a Choir, a curling 'bonspiel', a Burns Supper, a St. Andrew's Day Banquet and a Hogmanay Ball. There are Burns Clubs in Canada, as in every country where Scots and their descendants live. There are clan societies, federated in the Order of Scottish Clans, and some of them ambitiously organized with local branches: the Clan McMillan Society of North America (Canada), for example, has a dozen branches, mostly in Ontario, and there is a 'National Council of Clan MacLeod Societies in Canada'. There are Scottish Country Dance Societies, for instance at Hamilton (Ontario), Toronto and Vancouver; a Highland Games Society in New Brunswick; and many Pipe bands. Some societies have very sensibly sought a territorial rather than a 'clan' basis, for instance the Stornoway Society at Sydney, Nova Scotia, and the Caithness Association of Toronto. There are over twenty curling clubs in Canada, a country eminently suited to this game of ice. Golf, introduced by Scots, has become a popular game, especially in British Columbia, the only Canadian province where it can be played throughout the year; that province has sixty-six golf courses, and, it is estimated, 32,000 golfers.

10

EMIGRATION TO AUSTRALIA

IF Canada was scarcely an area for British settlement before the American colonies became independent in 1783, Australia was at that time not such an area at all. In both Canada and Australia it was the loss of the American colonies which turned British attention to the development of new areas for settlement, but the interest in Australia was directed to its utility as a depository for the criminals who had previously been transported to America. The first fleet conveying convicts sailed in May 1787 and reached Botany Bay in the following January, but Governor Phillip, who was in charge, preferred to make his headquarters at Port Jackson or Sydney a few miles away. Between 1788 and 1820, 22,217 male and 3,661 female convicts were transported to New South Wales and Van Diemen's Land (the later Tasmania). Transportation to New South Wales was abolished in 1840, but a few years later transportation to the Swan River Colony (Western Australia) started, and it continued until so late as 1868.

The convicts, like the delinquents who had been shipped to America in the seventeenth and eighteenth centuries, were of very mixed character, and not all had been guilty of serious criminal offences. Some, indeed, were suffering, if not for their political opinions, at least for political activity which was regarded as subversive. The so-called 'Scottish political martyrs' of the 1790s had advocated constitutional reforms, but had prejudiced their case by entering into correspondence with the revolutionaries in France. One of them, Thomas Muir, an advocate, was sentenced to transportation for fourteen years; Thomas Fysshe Palmer, a Unitarian clergyman, was sentenced to seven years; the others were William Skirving and Joseph Gerrald, who both received a fourteen years' sentence, and Maurice Margarot. Muir escaped in 1796, leaving, however, the place-name Hunter's Hill, said to be derived from the name of his estate near Glasgow. Palmer died in Guam after his release, Skirving and Gerrald both died in Australia, and Margarot returned to Scotland. But among the early compulsory emigrants from Scotland to Australia even those who were criminals would not all seem today to deserve the heavy punishment they then received. The *Edinburgh Advertiser* of 19 January 1828 reported that 'On Saturday morning sixteen male convicts were shipped on board the smack *Ocean* at Leith on their way to the hulks, preparatory to being sent to Botany Bay. Most of them were under twenty years of age'. Modern treatment of such juvenile delinquents would be much more lenient.

It is right to say that all the convicts were not treated alike, and many were not set to the hard labour one associates with convict settlements. The Scottish political offenders were allowed to run farms of their own, with other convicts as their servants. Sometimes, too, a convict might be able to pursue his own trade in Australia. The first Australian newspaper was edited by a convict who had been employed on *The Times* and other London newspapers before being transported for theft. However, as long as transportation continued, few free settlers were likely to make their way to Australia, especially at a time when official policy favoured emigration to Canada, which was in any event so much easier and cheaper to reach. Of the population of New South Wales in 1820, only 1,307 had come to the colony as free settlers, whereas there were over 9,000 convicts. It is true that—besides 1,495 persons who had been born in the colony—there were some 4,000 freed convicts, but the latter were looked at askance by the free settlers and there was a prolonged controversy before the 'emancipists' or freed convicts, even although many of them were now leading perfectly respectable lives, were admitted to citizenship on terms of equality with those who had come voluntarily.

Yet the figures indicate that, even while transportation continued, there was a certain influx of free settlers. The number of people in New South Wales who had arrived freely rose from 1,307 in 1820 to 4,673 in 1828—as against 7,500 freed convicts and 15,600 still in bondage. The attraction of Australia was obviously increasing as the country came to be better known, but the growth in settlement was partly a consequence of the opening up of new areas of Australia. Until after 1813, nothing had been known of it save a coastal fringe, but when the exploration of the interior began it revealed plains ready for the growing of wheat or for pasture. The Cumberland Plain, inland from Sydney, and the Hunter Valley, some miles north of Sydney, were the only large valley areas with immediate access from the coast, and the latter was allocated for farming development in the 1820s. But with the discovery of routes inland from Sydney, over the Blue Mountains, in 1815, the prospects of New South Wales had changed, just at a time when emigration from Britain was showing a tendency to revive after the end of the wars with France. Some years later, between 1823 and 1836, exploration farther opened up the fertile pastoral lands of inland New South Wales. The business of settlement was very largely controlled and regulated, and a report about 1826 that 'the superabundant population and superabundant flocks and herds poured like a torrent over the dividing barrier ridge' was an exaggeration.[1] Yet it was true that many owners of cattle and sheep simply drove their flocks and herds over pastures in which rights of property were not yet clearly defined.

Scottish immigrants were associated in various ways with these developments, because from the earliest days there seem to have been some Scots among the small number of free settlers. Robert Campbell (1769–1846), a native of Greenock and a member of the Calcutta firm of Campbell, Clark and Company, was a merchant in Sydney as early as 1798; Archibald McKellup, a Scottish sailor, left his ship at Sydney in 1803, prospered as an inn-keeper and also owned a farm of eighty acres; and Alexander Barry (1781–1873), a native of Fife, was 'an eminent merchant' in Sydney by 1820. It was a Scot, John Hunter, who introduced sheep into Australia, but the best-known name in this connection is that of John MacArthur (1767–1834), who was born in England but had a Scottish father. He went to Australia as an army officer in 1790, but by 1795 he had acquired some land and was experimenting with the breeding of sheep, and in 1796 he obtained some of the merino sheep on which so much of Australia's prosperity was to be based. It is also true that Scots were all along much associated with the exploration of Australia, and have left their names plentifully on its mountains— Lindsay, Cunningham, Fraser, Aberdeen, Greenock, Dunsinane, Crawford, Murchison, MacDowall and Birnam. It was Allan Cun-

[1] T. M. Perry, *Australia's First Frontier: The Spread of Settlement in New South Wales, 1788–1829* (Melbourne, 1963), 94.

ningham, a botanist, who penetrated from Sydney to the Liverpool plains and, further north, to the Darley Downs behind Brisbane. Hamilton Hume explored in Victoria and Edmund Kennedy in the Cape York peninsula. John McDowall Stuart was on Sturt's expedition to the interior of the continent in 1845 and later he made his way to Lake Torrans and Lake Eyre; in 1860 he gave his name to Mount Stuart, in the centre of Australia, in 1861 he was within 250 miles of the north coast and in 1862 he at last reached Van Diemen's Gulf.

One can only speculate whether Scots were encouraged to go out to Australia in the early days of free settlement because the province had two successive Scottish Governors—Lachlan Macquarie (1809–1821) and Sir Thomas Brisbane. At any rate, the Australian Company of Edinburgh was founded in 1822 to operate ships from Leith to New South Wales and Van Diemen's Land and make a profit out of the emigration which had now commenced. Significantly, too, it was in 1823 that Australia got its first Presbyterian minister. There had been a church building since 1809, but it had been served only by catechists. However, John Dunmore Lang, born at Greenock in 1799, a minister of the Church of Scotland, arrived at Sydney in 1823, to join his brother George, who had emigrated there from Largs some time before. He prevailed on the governor to finance a Presbyterian church, of which he was minister until his death in 1878. J. D. Lang was a champion of emigration, and encouraged hundreds of emigrants to follow him. By 1832 there was a presbytery of New South Wales, and in 1842, as a result of the controversies which led to the Disruption, a new church, St. Stephen's, was founded in Sydney.

One Scottish pioneering venture of this early period is uncommonly well documented. In 1821, Patrick Wood, son of a merchant in Elie, Fife, and a captain in the service of the East India Company, joined with Philip Russell, the son of a Fife farmer, and Alexander Reid, son of a laird in the Lothians, in preparing for settlement in Australia. Reid took his wife, two children, a 'respectable person well acquainted with farming' and a sheep dog, while Russell took two stone-masons, a blacksmith, a ploughman and two female servants, enough to form 'a moderately large establishment'. The voyage from Leith took six months, but on the ship which carried Reid were seventy-six passengers, mainly Scots—'enterprising and intelligent Scotchmen who were carrying their families from the crowded walks of old world life to seek more elbow room in Australia'.[1] They settled in Van Diemen's Land, on a river already called the Clyde; at this time there were not many more than 1,000 people in the island who had come there voluntarily or had been born there, while there were about 6,000 convicts and ex-convicts. Other Scots came in later years to join this settlement: Archibald MacDowall, his wife and five children from Edinburgh in 1824, and in 1830 George Russell, son of a Fife farmer and a kinsman of Philip Russell. In 1836 the Clyde Company was formed. Five of the shareholders were associated with Glasgow and two of them were already settled on the River Clyde in Van Diemen's Land. The object was to develop pastoral farming, and with this end in view several of the Scots who had previously settled in Van Diemen's Land moved to Port Phillip, in what was to become the colony of Victoria. George Russell was the effective manager, and on a run extending to 20,000 acres he had 10,700 sheep and 300 cattle.

Among individual Scots who went out to Australia in the 1820s and 1830s were some who, unlike the Russell party, brought no capital, for one John Robertson landed at Hobart with a half-crown and a sixpence in his pocket. But many brought capital in the shape of acquired skills, like Robert Russell, of Kirkcaldy, who emigrated in 1832 as an engineer and ironfounder; John Rae (1813–1900), a native of Aberdeen, who went to Australia as an accountant in 1839; and Andrew Petrie (1798–1872), another native of Kirkcaldy, who emigrated to Sydney in 1831 to go into business as a builder, and left his name on the map in Petrie's Bight and Mount Petrie. There were the inevitable 'merchants', like James King (*c.* 1800–*c.* 1860), who was a merchant in Sydney early in 1827, and Thomas Walker (1804–66), a native of Leith, who arrived in Sydney in 1822 and so prospered as a merchant that he became Chairman of the Board of Directors of the Bank of New South Wales. James King, however, acquired interests in land as well as merchandise, and pioneered the cultivation of vines and the making of wine. Interest in the land, along pastoral lines, was shared by two emigrants from Aberdeen: Alexander Thomson (1800–1866), son of a shipowner at Aberdeen, settled in Tasmania in 1831, acquired land there and took part in the settlement of Port Phillip, afterwards becoming mayor of Geelong and developing interests in shipping and railways; and James Murray, who went out to Melbourne in 1839 and became a grazier. Hugh Dixson, who had been a tobacco manufacturer and retailer in Edinburgh, went to Sydney in 1839 to carry on a similar business

[1] *Clyde Company Papers* (O.U.P., 1941), i, 14; Margaret Kiddle, *Men of Yesterday*, 23.

and to become the real founder of the Australian tobacco industry. Scots were associated with the further expansion of Australian settlement in the 1830s. The Swan River Colony, in Western Australia, had been founded in 1829 by private enterprise as a 'free' colony, without convicts, and already in July 1830 the ship *Drummore*, of 500 tons, was advertised to leave Leith for the Swan River as well as Van Diemen's Land. But the western colony had a struggling existence for several years, and by 1849 had only 4,600 people. Then the inhabitants asked for the introduction of convicts, to provide labour, and after their arrival the colony made more progress, though it did not attract very high numbers of emigrants until gold was found at Coolgardie and Kalgoorlie in the 1890s. In the east, meantime, Angus MacMillan was sent out by a Scottish settler, Lachlan MacAlister, to look for new grazing areas and, following the valley of the Tambo, he reached Lake Victoria and discovered the Gippsland area, which proved excellent for grazing. The South Australian Association, to open up yet another area of Australia, was formed in 1833. Thomas Petrie, who had been taken to Australia as an infant in 1831, was a pioneer in opening up Queensland.

It was, however, pre-eminently with the colony of Victoria that Scots were connected, and a study has been made of their way of life and the lasting impress they made on that part of Australia.[1] Among those who sailed for Australia in 1839 was thirty-five-year-old Niel Black, son of a farmer in Argyll. He was managing partner of Niel Black and Company, a subsidiary of Gladstone, Serjeantson and Company of Liverpool, and was associated in partnership with William Steuart of Glenormiston (Peeblesshire), T. S. Gladstone of Gladstone, A. S. Finlay of Toward Castle (Argyll) and others. The company had a similar constitution to the Clyde Company, which had already acquired its interests in Victoria. Black settled at Melbourne and bought a run which he re-named Glenormiston and which extended to 44,000 acres. On Glenormiston the harvesting of crops was of little account compared with the raising of cattle and sheep, and Black latterly concentrated mainly on cattle, of which he had a fine herd. His employees and their wives were nearly all from the Scottish Highlands. Highlanders, accustomed at home to loneliness and wide open spaces, though of a different character from those in Australia, on the whole did well there. The employees of Black and others built miles of dykes out of the local stone, as they had been accustomed to do at home.

[1] Margaret Kiddle, *Men of Yesterday* (Melbourne U.P., 1961).

Another important holding in the same part of Australia was that of the Learmonths, which they named Ercildoun (the correct name of Earlston) to commemorate their legendary descent from the thirteenth-century Thomas the Rymer. This holding extended to 50,000 acres, and on them they soon had 300 cattle and 13,000 sheep. Thomas and Somerville Learmonth sold Ercildoun in 1873 and went back to Scotland.

Niel Black remarked in 1842 that 'all the men I brought out have stock of their own now, and will be masters in less than three years',[1] and there were many Scots who did well from small beginnings. Neil Campbell, who had come out from Mull in 1838, declared two years later that he was worth £1,000 a year. In 1842 a young Highlander, Robert McDougall, became a herd-manager in the employment of the Learmonths, but he soon began to build up a herd of his own and in the fifties and sixties became known as one of the leading breeders. Among other early migrants to Victoria from Scotland were George Mercer, from Edinburgh, Anne Drysdale, a spinster in her late forties who had farmed her own land in Scotland before settling in Victoria in 1840, Daniel Mackinnon, a native of Lagg in Arran, Charles MacLean, who acquired land in Gippsland in 1842, and Henry Monro, son of a famous Edinburgh professor.

Such a Scottish community was not likely to let many years pass before they organized their church. Services had been held in Victoria since 1837, and a presbytery was founded in 1842. In 1847 Niel Black and seven other Presbyterians agreed to guarantee a stipend of £220 a year to a minister who would itinerate in their district. They engaged William Hamilton, who had been in Australia since 1838 and—an unusual point of view—believed that the Australian Presbyterians should not become involved in the disputes going on in Scotland. He arranged to conduct services in the various homesteads in rotation. These Australian Presbyterians were somewhat lax by Scottish standards in such matters as Sunday observance, and the Learmonths, though themselves Presbyterians, were so liberal in their outlook that in 1848 they arranged for an Anglican bishop to hold a service on their premises. Victoria had rather a different record in this respect from New South Wales, where the presbytery had split even before the Disruption of 1843, when, however, sixteen of its members adhered to the Church of Scotland and only six joined the Free Church. In Victoria, a Free Church was formed only

[1] Kiddle, *op. cit.*, 141.

belatedly, in 1847, and a United Presbyterian Church in 1850, but the two united in 1859.

Melbourne was described in 1839 as 'a Scotch colony. Two-thirds of the inhabitants are Scotch'.[1] A Highland Society was established quite early: at Geelong the Fingal Society held its first meeting in 1857 and held Highland Games annually thereafter; Warrnambool and Ballarat also had early Caledonian Societies. The Scots Church in Collins Street, Melbourne, was the place of worship for a large, fashionable congregation: 'Here are men whose yearly income is reckoned by the thousand up to hundreds of thousands; squatters, whose flocks and herds are greater than those of Abraham; merchants, bankers, lawyers, men of the first repute on the mart and in the forum'.[2]

In the 1830s the Wakefield movement led to a new emphasis on Australia, as well as New Zealand, because in the operation of that system assistance could be given towards the passage money, and for most emigrants the cost of going to Australia without assistance made it unattractive as compared with North America. However, relatively few Scots benefitted by the assisted immigration schemes at this stage; nearly half of the people sent out to Australia under them were Irish, and a slightly smaller number were English. But in the later 1830s another stimulus to emigration to Australia arose with the disturbances in Canada in 1837, which temporarily checked the movement to that country, and in 1840 the cessation of transportation to New South Wales helped to make Australia more attractive. Emigrants from Britain to Australia numbered 14,000 in 1838, 16,000 in 1839 and 1840, and 33,000 in 1841, making this phase the first in which emigration to Australia had been very significant numerically. In 1839 several ships were advertising their readiness to carry emigrants from Scottish ports to Australia.

From 1842 to 1848 there was something of a lull, but soon afterwards came the episode which transformed the whole outlook on Australia, namely the discovery, in 1851, of gold in New South Wales and Victoria (which had become a separate colony in 1850). It so happened that the beginning of 1851 was a disastrous season for the graziers, owing to a great fire, driven by a gale, and a drought which followed the fire, so that the gold discoveries saved many an immigrant from catastrophe. But the more important result was to encourage new immigrants. It took months for the news to reach

[1] Kiddle, *op. cit.*, 517–8.
[2] *Ibid.*, 343.

Britain, and months more for immigrants to arrive, but in September 1852 more than 19,000 persons landed at Melbourne, the port of access to the Victoria mines, which proved the most remunerative, and in the year the total immigration to Victoria was nearly 100,000, mostly from Britain—seven times the total for 1851. From the gold discoveries until 1867 Australia proved more attractive to emigrants than any other part of the British Empire. Apart from the intrinsic value of gold, it proved a great advertisement for the colonies and made them known as they would not otherwise have been. After the first pioneering days, of course, gold operations required substantial capital, but also provided steady employment for labourers at good wages. Between 1840 and 1850 the population of Australia had increased by 215,000; in the next decade the figure was 740,000. Even in Victoria, the economy was based on far more than gold: between 1854 and 1857 the number of persons employed in farming there rose from 7,600 to 26,800.

All these developments were reflected in the movements from Scotland. Some of the heavy emigration from both Highlands and Lowlands in the 1840s was diverted to Australia, and in the early 1850s, at the very time when the gold discoveries were themselves sufficient propaganda, the Highlands and Islands Emigration Society encouraged emigration to Australia rather than to Canada—partly on the argument that the former, being a pastoral country, was peculiarly suited to Highlanders. From 1852 to 1857 the Society sent out a total of 4,910 people—537 to New South Wales, 3,134 to Victoria, 848 to South Australia and 391 to Van Diemen's Land. The heavy preponderance of Victoria indicates the importance of its goldfield, but it was not, of course, the intention or the achievement of the Society to ship starving Highlanders to Australia so that they could join the gold rush: the point was that the gold rush denuded the sheep farms of workers and gave the Society's emigrants a favourable opportunity to find profitable employment. At the same time, Scots who were already in Australia, as well as Scots from home, were not backward in making for the diggings. Nor were they averse from making money out of the diggers: it was remarked, 'Ten times Scotch . . . are all the Highlanders. . . . Poor as rats at home they are as rapacious as rats abroad.'[1] No doubt they contributed to raise the costs of optimistic gold-seekers, who sometimes found that they could not pay their expenses between landing in Australia and reaching the goldfields. One of the medical men who practised among the

[1]Kiddle, *op. cit.*, 189.

diggers was Dr. Preshaw, an Edinburgh surgeon with twenty-three years' experience in general practice; the ensign above his tent bore a Scots thistle. Of the immigrants from the British Isles to the gold-fields, those from Scotland and Ireland together outnumbered those from England.

Typical of the Scottish emigrants of this period were William Crawford, who had been born in Edinburgh in 1817 and emigrated to Melbourne in 1853, and Neil MacDonald, who exchanged his work as a ferryman across the narrow sound between Mull and Iona for a twelve-thousand-mile voyage to Australia in 1852. Duncan Gillies (1834–1903), a future prime minister of Victoria, was born near Glasgow and emigrated to Australia in 1852 as a gold-prospector. Robert Christison (1837–1915), son of the minister of Foulden in Berwickshire, was packed off to Melbourne in 1852, with his brother, a year older than himself, and no resources; after trying his hand at various occupations he became a pioneer pastoralist in a new area, in Queensland, which he called Lammermoor. He carried on the work already done by Scots in Victoria: all over eastern Australia Scots played a large part in covering the scrub with homesteads and sheep stations. Thomas McIlwraith (1835–1900), afterwards premier of Queensland, was a native of Ayr who emigrated in 1854 as a civil engineer. James Service (1823–99), a future premier of Victoria, was a native of Kilwinning who went to Australia in 1853 to represent his commercial firm. William Guthrie Spence (1846–1926) emigrated with his family from Orkney in 1853, and became a miner, later a leader in the Labour party.

Once the lure of gold lost its early attractions, emigration to Australia fell off, and, whereas between 1853 and 1860 28 per cent of British emigrants had gone to Australia and New Zealand, between 1861 and 1870 the percentage was only 17. Yet Australia and New Zealand attracted more emigrants than British North America from 1852 until 1867 and again from 1873 to 1880 and from 1883 to 1887. From about 1860 the Australian government began to aid immigration from Britain, and in 1862 there were meetings in Scottish towns like Paisley, Greenock, Dumbarton and Stirling, presided over usually by the local provost and addressed by Sir Henry Parkes as Emigration Commissioner, where the case for emigration to Australia was put before the public. The Australian policy of aiding immigration continued until nearly the end of the century. Then, owing to the attitude of the Australian Labour movement, which feared the competition of additional manpower, immigration was restricted. It also happened that about this time Australia suffered severely from drought. From 1905, however, there was again encouragement by the Australian authorities, who were now resolved to foster the white population of the continent to counter the possible menace from China and Japan, and emigration increased once more.

Among the British immigrants, Scots had not at first formed a high percentage: in 1841, out of 19,523 emigrants from the United Kingdom to Sydney, only 1,616 were Scots, whereas no less than 13,344 were Irish. In 1860 the Scots made up only 5 per cent of the population of Australia, as against 25 per cent English and 15 per cent Irish. But later on the Scots immigrants nearly equalled the Irish and, in proportion to the respective populations of the two countries, made a higher contribution to peopling Australia than did the English. The number of persons in Australia who had been born in Scotland was recorded in 1891, 1901, 1911 and 1921 as in the region of 100,000—showing how steadily the migration was maintained over the decades: in 1911, by comparison, the Irish figure was 141,000 and the English 350,000, at a time when the population of England was about eight times that of Scotland.

It is significant of Scottish interest in Australia that that country, besides being an objective for Scottish emigrants, was an important field for Scottish investment.[1] The Scottish Australian Company, founded in Aberdeen in 1840, engaged in the mortgage business in New South Wales, and the City of Glasgow Bank, remembered for its disastrous collapse in 1878, had large property interests in Australia and New Zealand.

In the course of the decades during which emigration to Australia went on, Scots made their way into all of the colonies which were in the end to be joined together to form the Commonwealth. The two brothers Elder, from Kirkcaldy, for instance, went to Adelaide, in South Australia, and the younger of them, later Sir Thomas (1818–97), became a pastoralist and at one time was said to own an area exceeding that of Scotland. Andrew Fisher, to take another example, born in Ayrshire in 1862, was a miner before emigrating to Queensland in 1885, where again he worked as a miner, before making his way into politics as a trade union leader. George Henderson, the son of a well-known Edinburgh architect, arrived in Victoria in the later 1860s, and, taking up his father's profession, designed many homesteads and churches. It was remarked that 'In all parts

[1] D. S. Macmillan, *The Debtors' War* (Melbourne, 1960) deals with Scottish investment in Australia.

of the country, in many towns and conspicuously in Melbourne and Adelaide, they [the Scots] controlled affairs and gave the prevalent tone to the community'.[1] However, the colonies which had the highest proportion of Scottish settlers were New South Wales (where there are counties called Argyll and Roxburgh), followed closely by Victoria and Queensland (which has an Aberdeen and an Ayrshire). Western Australia, though it has place-names like Stirling and Lanark, did not become the home of so many Scots, and its capital, Perth, is not named directly after the Scottish city but commemorates a secretary of state of 1831 who happened to be M.P. for Perth.

The strength of the Scots in the various provinces is shown by the distribution of the Scottish societies. They are far and away most numerous in Victoria and New South Wales. In their character, or at any rate their nomenclature, they show some significant differences from the Scottish societies in the United States and Canada. Presumably because of the later development and the absence of a pre-nineteenth-century tradition, Australian Scots faithfully followed Presbyterian practice and avoided the name of the Scottish patron saint, for St. Andrew's Societies are rare. The popular names are Caledonian Society (which reflects the romantic tastes of the Victorian era) and the commonsense Scottish Society or Association. 'Clan' organizations, too, are rarer than in America, but there is an abundance of Pipe Bands—thirty in New South Wales, fifteen in Queensland and as many in Western Australia—and a good sprinkling of Highland Dancing Societies or Scottish Country Dance Associations. Gaelic Societies, too, are rare, for on the whole there was a weaker highland element in Australia, and the Highlanders who went there went later, after Gaelic was becoming less prevalent in the home country. Few of the Australian Scots show much sign of wanting to get together on the basis of their local origins in Scotland but there is an Orkney and Shetland Association of Australia—fittingly enough, for many people from those islands found new homes in Australia, not infrequently by way of service in the merchant navy: from a British shipping line they transferred to an Australian line and then settled in the southern continent. Scots, indeed, played a great part in Australian shipping, for it was Scottish-built ships, with Scottish captains, that led in the races for cargoes of wool and gold from Melbourne and Sydney, and Scots were pioneers, too, in the refrigeration of meat for the long voyage. James Harrison

[1] Quoted in A. Wyatt Tilby, *The English people overseas: Australasia*, 178–9.

patented a refrigerating apparatus in 1856, but his first cargo of frozen meat, in 1873, was a failure and he was ruined. Complete success in refrigeration was not achieved until the late 1870s. Archibald Mosman, who gave his name to Mosman's Bay, was a Lanarkshire man who started a whaling station in New South Wales in 1829, and Ben Boyd was another Scot who was in the whaling business. John Piper had been harbour-master of Sydney as early as 1814.

Another indication of the distribution of the Scots is, of course, given by the organization of the Presbyterian churches, especially as there were very few highland Roman Catholics among the emigrants to Australia apart from those who went out under the auspices of the Highlands and Islands Emigration Society: of the Scots in New South Wales in 1911, for example, 67,705 were recorded as Presbyterian and only 3,947 as Roman Catholic. Some account was given earlier of the establishment of Presbyterian churches in New South Wales and Victoria. South Australia was not far behind Victoria, for a Presbyterian church existed at Adelaide in 1839. In Queensland, where settlement was in the main rather later, services began to be held (at Brisbane) in 1849 and a synod was organized in 1866. It is significant of the relative unimportance of Western Australia in the pattern of Scottish settlement that the first Presbyterian church did not appear there until 1878 and a presbytery was formed only in 1892. Scottish influence extended beyond the Presbyterian churches, for it was Governor Macquarie who arranged that the Anglican cathedral in Sydney should be dedicated to Scotland's patron, St. Andrew. It was in Australia that James Alexander Dowie, later founder of the 'Christian Catholic Church in Zion', began the remarkable career which was mentioned in chapter 8. His parents took him out from Edinburgh to Adelaide in 1860, when he was twelve, and after a few years he returned to Edinburgh to study for the ministry. He became a Congregationalist pastor in Australia in 1870 and founded an independent tabernacle in 1882.

In areas where the Scots were strong, they were usually associated with educational, as well as ecclesiastical, effort. Presbyterian support for Melbourne Academy, founded by James Forbes (1813–51), a native of Aberdeenshire, was so conspicuous that it became known as 'the Scotch College'; it had been opened in 1851 and gave the traditional classical education of Scottish high schools. A Presbyterian Ladies' College was founded at Melbourne in 1875. Sir

Charles Nicholson (1834–1903), trained as a physician in Edinburgh, arrived in Sydney in 1834 and was prominent in the foundation of the University of Sydney in 1851. As Australian education developed at university level, Scottish contributions continued: a recent illustration is the career of Sir Robert Dickie Watt (1881–1965), a native of Ayrshire who graduated in Agriculture at Glasgow and was the first occupant of the Chair of Agriculture at Sydney, which he held from 1910 to 1946.

As in other lands, Australian Scots were associated with those fields of activity so closely connected with education—printing, publishing and journalism. David Syme, who had begun life in Scotland as a printer's reader, emigrated first to the Californian goldfield and then to Victoria, where he arrived in 1852. By 1860 he was in control of the *Age* (Melbourne) which he made a radical organ, and he was for a time the most influential man in the state of Victoria. An early newspaper in Western Australia had a Graham, a Yule and a Johnstone on its staff. James Harrison (1816–93), born near Glasgow, emigrated to Australia in 1837 and worked as a journalist before developing the interest in refrigeration already mentioned. James Munro (1832–1908), afterwards premier of Victoria, was a native of Sutherland who emigrated to Australia as a printer in 1858. George Robertson (1825–98), a native of Glasgow, emigrated as a bookseller, taking his stock to Australia with him. The bookselling and publishing firm of Angus and Robertson bears a name which sufficiently indicates its origin in the partnership of two Scots.

But it was perhaps in politics that Scots made their greatest mark on Australian life, and in proportion to their numbers perhaps played a more conspicuous part in politics in Australia than in any other area where they settled. Many of them represented a radical element. 'Of all the Scots' farmers' sons who settled in the Australian colonies and burdened the lives of Governors, John Dunmore Lang was the most outstanding. In him, stiff-necked pride, independence, self-righteousness, pig-headed persistence and the will to succeed were almost caricatured.' We have met him already as the minister of the Presbyterian Church in Sydney in 1823. Almost from his arrival, 'he was in the thick of every colonial controversy, the embarrassment, as well as the valiant champion, of his church'.[1] He was editor of *The Colonist*, author of many pamphlets, and a member of parliament. He supported the separation of Victoria from New

[1] Kiddle, *op. cit.*, 150.

South Wales. The connection of Scots with agitation is indicated by an incident in 1844: in the course of protests by the 'squatters' on Victorian pastures against new regulations, there was a great assembly of people at Melbourne, when 'the banners which had been prepared for the occasion made their appearance preceded by a highland piper in full costume followed by the town band'.[1] Some of the Scots who became famous in Australian politics have been mentioned already, like Duncan Gillies, James Munro and James Service, premiers of Victoria, and Sir Thomas McIlwraith, premier of Queensland. Among others who attained the office of premier of Victoria were William Neal Gillies (1868–1928), born in Australia of Scottish parents, while Scottish premiers of New South Wales included Sir Stuart Donaldson, George Houston Reid and Arthur MacAlister (1818–83), a native of Glasgow who emigrated in 1850 and practised as a solicitor. Sir James McCulloch (1819–93), four times premier of Victoria, was a native of Glasgow who went out as a business man in 1853; one of his ministers was J. M. Grant, who had come to Australia in 1836 as a boy of fourteen. Sir John Cockburn (1850–1939), a native of Berwickshire who qualified in medicine and emigrated to Australia in 1875, became premier of South Australia; Sir Robert Philp (1851–1922), born in Glasgow, emigrated with his father in 1862 and became premier of Queensland; Sir James Milne Watson (1812–80), born at Banff, the son of a shipowner, became manager of a brewery in Tasmania and finished up as premier of that colony. Andrew Fisher was prime minister of Australia in 1908–9 and 1910–13. Sir Robert Gordon Menzies, prime minister of Australia from 1939 to 1941 and again since 1949, was born in Victoria, but bears a name which points unmistakably to the Scottish origin of his family; his ancestor came from Weem, in Perthshire, in 1850, and settled at Ballarat.

[1] *Ibid.*, 166.

11

EMIGRATION TO NEW ZEALAND

THE earliest systematic British interest in New Zealand was along the lines of missionary effort. In 1814 the Church Missionary Society began to operate in New Zealand, and it was followed by others. By 1837 these societies had acquired wide influence. However—rather like the Trading Companies in North-West Canada, though for different reasons—the missionaries were opposed to colonization or to the annexation of the islands by Great Britain. They were thinking in terms of their ascendancy over the natives, and they feared rival influences, which might indeed corrupt the natives and undo some of the work of the missionaries. However, while the missionaries would not co-operate in any systematic scheme of colonization, they could not prevent irregular settlement, and by about 1830 there were some 2,000 whites in New Zealand, mainly round the Bay of Islands in the north, living without any official organization or supervision.

In 1825, and again in 1837, New Zealand Associations were formed under the leadership of Wakefield for the purpose of planting a colony in New Zealand. Some Scottish artisans were sent out in 1827 to Hokianga, but they had no success there and moved to Kororareka, which had for some time been a centre for traders and whalers. On the whole the first Association was a failure, but the second was in 1838 converted into a colonization company to buy land, and in 1839 the New Zealand Land Company was formed by an amalgamation of the existing Associations. It was responsible for purchasing 20,000,000 acres of land from Maori chiefs and—still in anticipation of any action by the British Colonial Office—settlements were formed, mainly in the North Island but one of them, Nelson, at the extreme north of South Island. Fears lest the French might lay claim to New Zealand had stimulated the British government to send a resident in 1832; in 1839 a governor was sent from Britain to negotiate a treaty with the Maoris; and in 1840 New Zealand became organized as a colony, with a constitution. The Wakefield settlers were brought within the new framework.

Although, out of sixty-three ships despatched to New Zealand between 1839 and 1844, only three sailed from Scottish ports, many Scots must have left from English ports, for it is evident that New Zealand made its appeal to Scots from an early date. By 1839 there was a New Zealand Emigration Society in Paisley, and a considerable number of Scots went out between 1839 and 1842. In 1839 over 150 Scots landed at Port Nicholson, in the southern part of North Island. Among them was Archibald Anderson, who had been born in Stirling in 1817; he was persuaded by the New Zealand Company to buy a lot of 100 acres at Port Nicholson, and he took a ploughman out with him. The emigrants were accompanied by John MacFarlane, a Paisley minister, who became the first Presbyterian pastor in New Zealand and preached in both Gaelic and English. On the heels of the pioneers followed a number of other Scots who also settled in the southern part of North Island: James Alexander, for example, who arrived in 1840 and settled at Wanganui, where he soon had as a neighbour Moses Campbell, who came out from Auch, in Perthshire, with his wife and family. But Scots found their way to other areas as well. William Brown, born near Dundee in 1809, came to New Zealand after spending some time at Adelaide and Sydney and was a founder of a settlement on the site of the future town of Auckland in 1841. John Gebbie, a native of Ayrshire, settled in Wellington in 1840. Among Scots settlers at Nelson, another settlement of the New Zealand Land Company, were William and John Deans, two brothers from Ayrshire, and the Allan family from Irvine, also in Ayrshire, who all arrived in 1842. The appeal which New Zealand made to the emigrants of this period (most of whom came out under the auspices of the New Zealand Land Company) was its possibilities for farming and stock-rearing, and it is significant that a man like James Allison, who had graduated in medicine at Edinburgh, settled in New Zealand as a farmer in 1840 and did not practise his profession, and that Donald Gollan, born at Culloden in 1811, was trained as an engineer and surveyor but became a successful sheep farmer in New Zealand. Dr. David Monro, born in 1813, a member of a remarkable medical dynasty, paid £1,200 to the New Zealand

Company for four allotments of land near Nelson, where he arrived in 1842. He introduced sheep from Australia, and in less than twenty years he had 13,000 acres and 14,000 sheep. He did, however, practise his profession occasionally, and some of his descendants followed careers in medicine. One of the few Scots of this period who did not go on the land was Robert Graham (1820–85), who was born near Glasgow and who, at once on his arrival in Auckland in 1842, chartered a cutter and loaded her for the Bay of Islands—the first step in a successful mercantile business which he carried on with his brother David. When the 'original extraction' of the population of the New Zealand Company's southern province was investigated in 1848, it was found that 12.16 per cent of them were Scots.

It was in 1842 that the concept of planting a 'New Edinburgh' in New Zealand originated in the mind of George Rennie, a sculptor. According to his ideas, the colony, as befitted a Scottish one, was to be Presbyterian, but there was no notion at this stage of making it narrowly sectarian. In 1843, however, came the Disruption and the formation of the Free Church of Scotland, and the plan for a 'New Edinburgh' fell into the hands of men who set aside Rennie's broader views in favour of a strictly Free Church settlement. Otago was selected as the objective in 1844, and the Lay Association of the Free Church of Scotland arranged to buy from the New Zealand Company 2,400 lots, each of 60 acres, or 144,000 acres in all. These lots were to be sold to emigrants at £2 an acre.

Active leadership passed to the Reverend Thomas Burns (1796–1871) and Captain William Cargill (1784–1860). Burns, a nephew of the poet Robert Burns, had withdrawn from the Church of Scotland in 1843 to join the Free Church; Cargill was a veteran of the Peninsular War who characteristically claimed descent from the covenanting 'martyr' Donald Cargill, although the martyr had no recorded legitimate descendants. Burns sailed, with 247 persons, in the *Philip Laing* from the Clyde on 27th November 1847 and had a voyage of 117 days, arriving on 15th April 1848. Life during the voyage was carefully regulated, to provide for public worship, the education of the children, sound feeding and medical attention, but inevitably there was a good deal of misery when stormy conditions prevailed. Captain Cargill sailed, with ninety-seven persons, on the *John Wickliffe* from the Thames on 24th November 1847, and had a slightly shorter voyage, arriving on 22nd March 1848. On the *John Wickliffe*, as on the *Philip Laing*, careful provision was made for the health of the emigrants—the surgeons were each to receive a gratuity of £25, less £1 in respect of each death which took place on the voyage—and the *John Wickliffe* had, among the stores for the colony, a considerable quantity of religious and informative books; but the *John Wickliffe*'s passengers were so mixed that the religious and moral standards of the *Philip Laing* could not be maintained on board her.

There were already a very few white settlers in the Otago area, and with the new arrivals they made a total of 444 in October 1848; another 159 arrived before the end of the year. The Maori population, which was very small, had already been largely converted to Christianity and were peaceful in their habits. The land for the settlement had been bought from the local Maoris, amicably, in 1844, and they brought food and other articles for sale to the colonists. The Otago settlers were much more fortunate than the whites in North Island, where the Maoris had become resentful and suspicious; although there was one outbreak of violence, in the extreme north end of South Island, in 1843, when some settlers had been killed by Maoris at Wairau, yet when the Maori wars broke out in 1860—to last for ten years—they were confined entirely to North Island.

The Otago settlers had in the main no enemy but nature to contend with. On their arrival, in March and April, winter was approaching in those latitudes, and cottages had to be thrown up hastily, built of turf or of wattle and daub. The surroundings of Dunedin were very thickly wooded, and much clearing had to be done before cultivation could start. However, once crops began to grow it was found that there were enormous returns from the hitherto uncultivated soil: the colonists rejoiced to find cabbages exceeding 40 pounds or even 50 pounds in weight, a beetroot weighing 21 pounds, and potatoes to the weight of 18 pounds from a single plant.

The character of the settlement was intended to be Scottish, and perhaps aggressively so—Cargill is shown in cartoons dressed in the traditional lowland Scottish bonnet and plaid—and the colony was to be a branch of the Free Church of Scotland, governed 'according to its doctrines, policy and discipline'. Of the sum raised by the sale of land to settlers, 12½ per cent was to be devoted to the causes of religion and education. It is true that right from the outset there were non-Presbyterians in the colony, for those who had sailed on the *John Wickliffe* were very largely Church of England people and in 1849 the Presbyterians were only 64 per cent of the European population; Anglican services were held from 1852, but this element was known to the unyielding Free Churchmen as 'the little enemy' and considerable strain was caused by the determination of the Presbyterians to make their system prevail. The festivals of Christmas and Easter were not holidays, and were publicly ignored; in the schools the Presbyterian *Shorter Catechism* was a piece of compulrory instruction; funeral services were forbidden; and the musical part of public worship was led by a precentor. It was more laudable that, at a time when the Free Church at home was raising vast sums of money for the erection of schools where its own tenets could be taught, the Otago settlers brought with them the devotion to education which had long characterized Scottish public policy. The editor of the *Otago News* remarked, 'as a Scotch settlement, we have greater cause for exertion in the cause of education than any of the sister settlements'. It was also characteristic that in 1849, the first full year of the settlement, a subscription library was formed in association with the church. The grandiose ambitions for a 'college' were, however, over-publicized, and brought disappointment to at least one family which arrived in 1849: 'The only school,' wrote the mother, 'is a sort of national affair, by a master, girls and boys all together, and of all grades; they come in their bare feet for miles around (the Scotch are not fond of shoe leather). The pupils number more than fifty. . . . It was a gross deception, advertising the college with its headmaster and under-masters. Nothing of the sort exists. The minister could only say it was a thing in perspective . . . but however I told the old rascal we . . . should very soon toddle to something more civilized, as the rest of the English appear to be doing.'[1]

Propaganda on behalf of the Otago settlement was conducted not only before the first colonists went out but also for some years afterwards. John MacGlashan (1802–64), an Edinburgh solicitor, became secretary of the Otago Association and was perhaps the chief propagandist for the settlement in the early stages, especially through the issue of pamphlets and the publication of the *Otago Journal*, though he did not himself go out to the colony until 1853. James Adam, on the other hand, a shipwright in Aberdeen and precentor in the Free Church there, was one of the original emigrants on the *Philip Laing* but was sent back to Scotland by the Otago Provincial Council to act as an emigration agent. Under his auspices, 2,000 people sailed in eight ships in 1857, and much later, in 1876, he wrote *Twenty-five Years of an Emigrant's Life in New Zealand*.

[1] A. H. Reed, *Story of Early Dunedin*, 82.

Thomas Birch (1825–80) was another of Otago's publicists. A native of Fortrose, he became a cabinet-maker in Aberdeen and emigrated to Otago in 1852. On a visit to Scotland in 1858 he lectured to promote emigration, and in 1873 he paid another visit home as an emigration agent for Otago. It is hardly necessary to say that the Free Church composition of the emigrants, which had not been uniform even initially, became increasingly diluted with the passage of years.

Although growth in Otago was at first slow, and in 1854 the total population was only 2,400, of whom 700 were in Dunedin, the area continued, thanks to the propagandists, to attract a certain flow of emigrants direct from Scotland, before as well as after a fresh attraction arose with the discovery of gold in Otago in 1861. Individual examples of colonists are—James Barr, from Glasgow, 1849; James Macandrew, from Aberdeen, 1850; John Barr, from Paisley, 1852; Alexander Begg, from Edinburgh, 1859; William Barron, from Edinburgh, 1861; Alexander and John Bathgate, from Edinburgh, 1863. But, in addition to Scots direct from home, such a peculiarly Scottish settlement as Otago drew a certain number of Scots from other parts of New Zealand: James Allan, for instance, who had settled with his parents at Nelson in 1842, when he was eighteen, subsequently became a successful farmer and stockbreeder in Otago; and Archibald Anderson, one of the 1839 immigrants to Port Nicholson, moved to Otago in 1845 and took land at Inch Clutha and Stirling. Some came even from outside New Zealand: Arthur Beverley had emigrated from Aberdeen to Melbourne in 1852 and came on to Dunedin in 1856; Edward McGlashan was in Adelaide, Melbourne and Sydney before he reached Dunedin in 1850; Donald Ferguson, from Argyll, joined his uncle on a sheep farm in Australia in 1851 and in 1862 went on to Otago, where he was a successful cattle-breeder. Fewer colonists seem to have left Otago, but George Thomson Chapman, after being a missionary teacher in Otago, went off to the Victoria goldfield and finished up in Auckland.

The peculiar appeal of the Dunedin area did not, however, mean that no Scots went to other parts of New Zealand in the middle of the nineteenth century. In the extreme south end of South Island, in what came to be the separate province of Southland, there was a Scottish settlement at Invercargill, formed in 1857. And in the far north of North Island, the Nova Scotian Highlanders, under the leadership of Norman MacLeod, settled at Waipu, north of Auckland, where by 1860 there was a community about a thousand strong. Apart from such settlements, individual Scots made their way to a variety of places. David Burns (1811–87), trained as a builder in Scotland, settled at Nelson about 1848 and worked as a builder there. The Deans brothers, William and John, who had taken up land in Nelson in 1842, later transferred to Canterbury, where they were the first settlers at Riccarton, Christchurch, years before the substantial settlement of English people started there. Another early Scots settler in that area was John Anderson, who arrived at Lyttelton, near Christchurch, in 1850. It was partly his doing that Charles Fraser, an M.A. of Aberdeen, arrived in Canterbury in 1856; in 1857 Fraser opened St. Andrew's Church, the first Presbyterian church in Christchurch, and he also founded the Christchurch Boys' High School. An early comer to Lyttelton was Charles Hunter Brown, a native of Scotland who had been in Australia for a time and in 1850 brought his own sheep and cattle to New Zealand. Walter Charles Buchanan (1838–1924), son of an Argyll farmer, had been employed by Niel Black at Glenormiston in Victoria, but in 1862 crossed to the New Zealand goldfields, where he made money which enabled him to set up in North Island, with his brother Donald, and become a famous breeder of cattle and sheep. Another Scot who came to New Zealand for gold and remained to farm was James Bennet (1830–1908): he had been brought up to farming in Angus, but came to Victoria in 1853 and was a carter in the goldfields there, then in 1865 he moved on to New Zealand where he was a carter first before buying land. It was perhaps rarer for a gold-miner to use his gains to pay for his further education, but this was done by James Chisholm (1843–1916), a native of Scotlandwell, who came to New Zealand as a carpenter in 1858 and in 1861 made enough money in the goldfield to enable him to return home and study for the ministry; he returned to New Zealand as a minister in 1870. A remarkable illustration of the attraction of New Zealand is provided by the career of James Meiklejohn. He was an Edinburgh sea-captain who for years had been engaged in building ships in Prince Edward Island and sailing them to Great Britain, where he sold them. In 1856 he embarked his family on a ship he had built and put to sea, determined to cruise until he found a place which specially appealed to him. After a year or more he came to New Zealand, where he decided to settle, and acquired land at Big Omaha in North Island, where he resumed ship-building. It is significant of the extent of Scottish settlement in

North Island that a presbytery of Auckland came into existence in 1856, only two years after the presbytery of Otago.

The persistent appeal of New Zealand was to those who were minded to go in for farming and stock-raising, sometimes although they had little or no previous experience of that kind of life. Robert C. Bruce, for example, born at Kelso in 1843, spent twenty years of his life mainly at sea, with spells on the goldfields in California, Australia and New Zealand, before settling in New Zealand as a farmer in 1877. Cuthbert Cowan (1835–1927), a native of Ayr, was a bank clerk in Scotland but after emigrating to New Zealand in 1857 he took up agriculture and sheep breeding, and R. F. Cuthbertson (1840–1913), a native of Glasgow, trained as an accountant but in 1860 joined his brother on a sheep farm in New Zealand. David Buddo (1856–1917) trained as an engineer in Scotland but became a farmer soon after he arrived in New Zealand. Nathaniel Chalmers, born at Rothesay in 1830, served in a shipbroker's office and a London bank before sailing in 1846 for Otago, where he took up sheep-farming. Unusual enterprise was shown by Peter Dalrymple (1813–1901), a native of Galloway: he was for a time a draper in Manchester, but in 1853 he bought sixty portable houses, shipped them to Melbourne where he sold them at a good profit, and in 1856 he took up land near Bluff which he called Appleby, and farmed there for the rest of his life. One of the many notable success stories was that of Thomas Whillians Bruce (1832–1908), a native of Jedburgh who came to New Zealand in 1859 and on his land at Cora Lynn and Riversdale ultimately had 17,000 sheep. Some of the Scottish immigrants were led on to take an interest in industries associated with the exploitation of New Zealand's products: Walter Clarke Buchanan, a famous breeder of cattle and sheep, went on to an interest in refrigeration, and Thomas Brydone (1837–1904), a native of West Linton, was a pioneer in both the frozen meat and the dairy industry: Brydone was a partner with another Scot, Davidson, in the New Zealand and Australian Land Company, and loaded the first cargo of frozen meat sent from New Zealand to Britain in 1882, shipped from Port Chalmers to London on a ship called the *Dunedin*. Colonists who had served as soldiers in the Maori war were entitled to 200 acres of land, and some Scots who were among them took up such allotments.

Those Scots, and many others who, like them, were engaged in farming and similar occupations, were employed in an industry which enjoyed a spectacular expansion in the second half of the nineteenth century. In 1858 New Zealand had 1,500,000 sheep, 130,000 cattle and 40,000 pigs; in 1909 the figures were 23,500,000, 1,773,300 and 245,000. The exports of frozen meat, worth £28,339 when this industry was in its infancy in 1882, were worth £3,500,000 in 1909. Quite apart from the emigrants who were able to acquire land of their own and set up in business on their own account, there were many Scots who learned that, even for employees, hours were shorter and wages were higher in New Zealand than at home and that there was a conspicuous lack of poverty in the colony. The general pattern of emigration to New Zealand showed considerable fluctuation: the gold rush resulted in a net immigration figure of 93,169 for the five years 1861–5, and an awakening to the other attractions of the country led to the settlement of 82,000 people there in 1871–5, but the years 1886–90 actually showed a small adverse balance, and in 1896–1900 the credit balance was only 10,638. For Scots, however, the appeal of New Zealand was fairly steady, and in the late nineteenth century it enjoyed outstanding popularity among British dominions: in 1882 an Australian visitor to Scotland learned that 'in this country New Zealand is everything. . . . In Scotland, going to the Colonies always means going to New Zealand.'[1]

Despite the attractions of farming, in New Zealand as elsewhere there were Scots who made their careers by following up the trades or professions on which they had entered before emigrating. Arthur Beverley (1822–1907), son of a farmer, became a watchmaker in Aberdeen, but in New Zealand he blossomed out as something of a polymath—geologist, botanist, mathematician and designer of optical and meteorological apparatus. Thomas Forrester (1838–1907), after studying at the Glasgow School of Art, went in 1840 to Otago, where he was an architect and surveyor. John Gillies (1802–71), already an experienced solicitor in Rothesay, went to Dunedin in 1849 and became a solicitor there. John Ewart (1858–1939), trained in medicine and surgery at Edinburgh, pursued a professional career in New Zealand from 1887 onwards. Henry Clark (1821–1905) was a carpenter in Edinburgh and after reaching New Zealand in 1848 was a builder and contractor. John Guthrie Wood Aitken (1849–1921), son of a farmer in Kintyre, had learned the carpet manufacturing craft in Templeton's factory in Glasgow, and established a business at Wellington in 1882. John Anderson (1820–97), trained as a blacksmith and engineer in Edinburgh, founded the Canterbury ironworks, which made boilers, engines, bridges, milling machinery,

[1] Margaret Kiddle, *Men of Yesterday*, 492.

railway lines and ships. Three notable engineers in Otago were James Melville Balfour (1831–69), a cousin of Robert Louis Stevenson and consequently connected with the 'Family of Engineers' of which that author wrote, George Morrison Barr (1837–1907), a native of Glasgow, and William Newsham Blair (1840–91), a native of Islay, who had trained as a surveyor in Oban before going to Otago in 1863; they were employed by the Otago government in public works, including harbours and lighthouses.

For many Scots, the profession was teaching. The ideals of the founders of Otago were never lost sight of: by 1871 there were over a hundred schools in the province, and a university—the first in New Zealand—had been founded, with Dr. Burns as its chancellor. James M. Brown (1846–1935), a native of Irvine, had a distinguished university career at Edinburgh, Glasgow and Oxford before being appointed Professor of Classics and English when Canterbury College was founded in 1875. The novelist Ian Maclaren's *Days of Auld Lang Syne* has as one of its characters an Australian professor, of whom James Gow Black (1835–1914) is believed to be the original; Black went in 1871 to be Professor of Natural Science at Otago. William MacDonald (1840–90) went from the staff of the Royal High School of Edinburgh to be Rector of Otago Boys' High School in 1877. Alexander Fleming (1843–73) taught at Helensburgh Academy before emigrating to Southland, where he became the first headmaster of Invercargill Grammar School. Margaret Gordon Huie (1825–1918), a native of Edinburgh, had a private school at Geelong for a time and in 1857 married Andrew Burn, a master of the Scots College and later head of the Presbyterian school at Geelong; in 1870 she became head of the Otago Girls' High School. Some Scots who did not themselves teach were nonetheless enthusiasts for education. James Macandrew (1820–87), a native of Aberdeen, was an early emigrant to Otago (1850) and his business interests lay in the development of shipping, both on the New Zealand coast and with Great Britain, but as a member of parliament and a minister he did much to foster the foundation of the university at Dunedin and to found training colleges and schools. Thomas Reid Fleming, born at Edinburgh in 1863, emigrated with his parents in 1868; he became an inspector of schools, was a founder of Victoria University College and advanced further education through the Workers' Educational Association and similar movements. Dr. David Monro was a foundation member of the Company of Governors of Nelson College and Sir James Hector, Director of the Geological Survey of New Zealand, became first Chancellor of the University of New Zealand. New Zealand also had its quota of Scottish newspaper men, among them two emigrants who went out in the same year, 1858. Henry Anderson (1838–88), born in Glasgow, trained as an analytical chemist, but after he went to New Zealand he entered journalism and became editor of the *Wellington Independent* and other journals; and James Walter Bain (1841–99), a native of Edinburgh, trained at home as a compositor and after he emigrated entered the newspaper business and became proprietor of the *Southland News* and the *Southland Times* (of which Thomas Denniston, a native of Greenock, was editor from 1879 to 1885). David T. Fleming (1861–1938), who was taken by his father to New Zealand when he was a child, became editor and part-proprietor of the *Leader* and the *Bruce Herald*. William Berry (1839–1903) was an apprentice on the staff of *The Scotsman* in Edinburgh before he emigrated in 1864 to join the *Southern Cross*, and he was later editor of the *New Zealand Herald*. Walter Clarke Buchanan (1838–1924), who became a member of parliament and founded the *Dominion* newspaper, was knighted in 1913. David Bell (1863–1937), born in Dunfermline, emigrated to Queensland in 1883 and was sub-manager of a newspaper there before moving on to New Zealand, where he had an eminent career, as manager ultimately of the *Lyttelton Times* and chairman of the *Timaru Post*. Gilbert Carson, born on a voyage between Scotland and Auckland in 1842, became proprietor of the *Wanganui Chronicle*.

The enterprising career of Edward McGlashan (1817–89), a native of Edinburgh, was connected with an industry allied to journalism. In 1848 he bought up the surplus stock of Chambers and Sons, the Edinburgh publishers, and sailed with it for Australia, where he sold it off in Adelaide, Melbourne and Sydney; then, in 1850, he bought other merchandise for disposal in Dunedin, where he turned for a time to milling and dealing in stock but ultimately went in for paper-making and produced the first paper manufactured in Otago. Another example of enterprise and versatility was George Thomson Chapman (1824–91), a native of Stonehaven; he was a storekeeper in Scotland, a missionary-teacher in Otago in 1849, a merchant, a gold miner in Victoria and finally a bookseller and publisher in Auckland.

One of the first Scots to become prominent in New Zealand political life was David Monro, the doctor and farmer. He was elected to the House of Representatives in 1853, was Speaker from 1861 to 1870 and was knighted in 1866. He died in 1877. Radical politicians and agitators of Scottish origin were perhaps less numerous in New Zealand than in Canada or Australia, but the breed was not unknown. John Barr (1867–1930), a native of that hotbed of radicalism, Paisley, was involved in industrial disputes there while he was a weaver, and subsequently he became a stone-mason; he emigrated first to Winnipeg, and was engaged as a telegraph linesman in both Canada and the United States; after he arrived in Christchurch in 1902 he was prominent in the Labour movement there. Sir Robert Stout (1844–1930), born at Lerwick in Shetland, trained as a teacher under the pupil-teacher system and went out to New Zealand in 1864 to become a teacher there, but he studied law and for a time was a lecturer in law in Otago University. As an M.P. from 1875 he was a left-wing Liberal; he was a free-thinker and an enthusiast for the Temperance movement. He was prime minister of New Zealand from 1884 to 1887 and Chief Justice from 1899 until 1926. One of Stout's more radical supporters was John McKenzie, who was born near Tain in 1838 and carried to New Zealand in 1860 a hatred of landlords which coloured his whole attitude to public affairs; he became Minister of Lands in 1891. On the other hand Mackay John Scobie Mackenzie, who was born at Tain in 1845, was on the conservative side in New Zealand politics. Peter Fraser, like the former of the two Mackenzies, was a left-winger from Easter Ross. Born at Fearn in 1884, he was secretary of the local branch of the Liberal party at the age of sixteen. In London, in 1908, he joined the Independent Labour Party. On emigration to New Zealand in 1910 he worked as a labourer, and became prominent in the Socialist movement. He became an M.P. in 1918 and was Prime Minister from 1940 to 1949.

A great many of the Scottish settlers in New Zealand, especially the Highlanders in North Island, were seafarers and shipbuilders, but it is also true that a certain number of Scots have always made their way to settlement in New Zealand through service in the merchant navy: from employment in ships trading to and from New Zealand, they transferred to ships trading on the New Zealand coast, and then, perhaps after marrying, they took up a job ashore. Scots from some of the Scottish islands were especially apt to follow this pattern, because at home they had been brought up to a life consisting partly of crofting and partly of fishing and were often, besides, clever handymen, able to turn their attention to crafts for which there was a demand in a new colony. William Mowat Bolt (1838–1907), a native of Lerwick, in Shetland, who settled in New Zealand in 1863 after being at sea for years, was only one of many Shetlanders who have done so. James Davidson (1829–98), a native of Aberdeen, was one of many seafaring men who left their ships to make money in the Victoria goldfield in 1852; in 1857 he crossed to New Zealand, where he became a ship-owner and trader. William Black (1815–94), born in Stirlingshire, trained as a baker at home and then became a steward on passenger ships; in 1841 he married and settled in New Zealand, where he resumed his old trade of baking.

Apart from the many other attractions of New Zealand, gold was a magnet too. There had been a few sporadic and small discoveries of gold in New Zealand earlier, but the discoveries in Otago in 1861 led to the first 'gold rush'. Between July and October, the community of some 13,000, relying for their livelihood mainly on their flocks of sheep, was suddenly doubled, largely by migrants from the Victoria field. The rush went on in 1862 and 1863; in March 1863, 14,000 persons landed at Dunedin. Gold production continued to be important for a long time, but of course the feverish and amateurish phase soon passed. More solid foundations for New Zealand's economy lay in the farming on which emphasis has already been laid. It is also true that after the end of the Maori wars, in 1870, there was a rapid development of roads, bridges and railways, and the opportunities for employment which thus opened up attracted so many immigrants that the population nearly doubled between 1871 and 1881. The New Zealand government assisted immigration for several years before 1891 and again from 1904 onwards, giving preference to the friends and kinsfolk of people already settled in the country. In this pattern, the Scottish element, even in areas like Dunedin, was inevitably diluted, but it remained conspicuous, and Scots continued to colonize New Zealand to an extent out of all proportion to their own country's population: in 1901, nearly 48,000 of the people of New Zealand had been born in Scotland, as against 111,000 born in England and 43,000 born in Ireland.

In the whole history of Scottish colonization, the town of Dunedin presents perhaps the best known and most elaborate attempt at deliberate imitation of a Scottish prototype, for the names of its streets, of its physical features and of its environs are copied from Edinburgh: thus we have Princes Street, George Street, Moray Place, Cumberland Street, Great King Street, the Canongate and the Water of Leith. Port Chalmers commemorates, fittingly, the divine who led the Free Church out from the Church of Scotland in 1843. Little Paisley was appropriately chosen as the name of the place where the first weaving loom was set up. And throughout South Island there are many more Scottish names—Bruce, Ettrick, Campbelltown, Oban, Wallace, Roxburgh, Stirling, Fortrose, Ben Nevis, Ben Lomond and Ben More.

The Highlanders at Waipu, however, presented a more clearly defined picture of a community than the Otago settlers, partly because they had inherited a tradition which had been preserved in their travels from Scotland to Cape Breton and then to Australia and New Zealand, and partly, no doubt, because of the imprint made on them by Norman MacLeod. Among them the ritual of eighteenth-century Scottish church services persisted for a long time—standing for prayer, sitting for the praise (which was restricted to the metrical psalms and paraphrases and was led by a precentor). As long as services were conducted in Gaelic, the practice of 'lining-out' the psalms went on, but knowledge of Gaelic was gradually extinguished after the original settlers and their children had died off. There was the same punctilious adherence to the fourth commandment as there had been in Cape Breton: even shaving on Sunday was forbidden (we are not told about washing) and some thought it hard that they could not even go to a clear running stream for a drink of fresh water. On the other hand, it is to the credit of these people that, as is still the practice in some of the more remote parts of Scotland, property was so secure that doors were never locked and articles of utility and value could be left in safety anywhere.

Generally throughout New Zealand, the Scots have adopted their customary methods of ensuring some cohesion. The general pattern of their associations is very much as in Australia, with a preference for 'Caledonian' and 'Scottish' societies; but New Zealand surely outdoes most countries in its devotion to pipe bands, for it has over a hundred and twenty of them. The objects of the Caledonian Society of Waipu, which has held a gathering every New Year's Day since 1871, are representative of those of innumerable societies throughout the world and throughout the generations: 'To keep up the customs, traditions and language of the Mother country, Highland dancing, music, games, etc., and to assist any immigrants from the Highlands of Scotland or from Nova Scotia who settle in Waipu and are in need of help.'[1]

---

[1] N. R. McKenzie, *The Gael Fares Forth* (Wellington, 1935, 2nd edn. 1942), 238–9.

12

THE SCOTS IN AFRICA

AFRICA has been so emphatically the continent in which Scots made their names as explorers and missionaries, while it has been only secondarily a continent for colonization, that a book on Scottish emigration must say something of the Scots who did so much to open up the continent to trade and to European civilization. Some Scots were playing their parts as explorers in Africa long before Britain had any substantial possessions there and before South Africa—the one area in which Britons were likely to settle—had passed into British hands. Indeed Robert Jacob Gordon was actually in the service of the Dutch, then the owners of South Africa, when he discovered the Orange River and named it, in 1779.

The first famous name in the history of exploration is that of James Bruce, 'the Abyssinian' (1730–94). He became consul at Algiers in 1763 and pursued his archaeological interests on various tours in the Near East before starting explorations of unknown territory. In 1768 he sailed up the Nile to Assouan and crossed the desert to the Red Sea; in 1770–71 he explored Abyssinia and the sources of the Blue Nile. His pioneering work was so completely novel that many contemporaries simply declined to regard his accounts of his travels as fact.

As well known as Bruce is Mungo Park. He was born near Selkirk in 1771, and became a successful surgeon, but the mysteries of the interior of Africa fascinated him. In 1795 he was commissioned by the African Association to explore the Niger, and on his first expedition, approaching the interior through Gambia, he made his way some distance down river. A second expedition was commissioned by the government in 1804, and Park died on the Niger, near Timbuctoo, in 1806. Hugh Clapperton (1788–1827), a native of Annan, also lost his life exploring the Niger. MacGregor Laird (1808–61), a brother of a shipbuilder, and William Baikie (1825–64), were concerned in the further exploration of the Niger and in the opening up of it to navigation. Dr. Andrew Smith (1797–1872), a native of Roxburghshire, spent the years 1820–37 in Africa and in the 1830s was director of an 'Expedition for exploring Central Africa'; later, in 1853, he became Director General of the Medical Department of the British Army. James Augustus Grant, born at Nairn in 1827, was associated with John H. Speke in the exploration of the sources of the Nile in 1860–63. They were the first Europeans to cross equatorial Africa, and the title of Grant's account of his travels, published in 1864, is a classical understatement—*A Walk across Africa*. Joseph Thomson (1858–94), a Dumfriesshire man, explored Tanganyika and Kenya.

The Scots were also early in the field in missionary work in Africa, and this enterprise was one in which the zeal of individual Scots outstripped the official undertakings of Scottish organization. The Edinburgh and Glasgow Missionary Society was indeed founded in 1796, but it did not start work in Africa until 1821, and the Church of Scotland sent out no missionaries at all until 1829, when Alexander Duff was sent to Calcutta, to initiate work in a region which in the end was second only to Africa as a field of Scottish missionary endeavour. However, Scots were associated with African missions before any Scottish organization was operating in Africa, and they began under the auspices of the London Missionary Society, which had been founded in 1795 and started to work in Africa in 1799. William Anderson, son of an Aberdonian settled in London, was sent out by the London Society to South Africa in 1800 and laboured among the Griquas until 1818. John Campbell, a travelling director for the London Society, initiated the mission to the Bantu in 1813; he was 'a dumpy Scottish minister who traversed the African wastes with a black umbrella to ward off the sun'.[1] Much better known is Robert Moffat, who was born at Ormiston in East Lothian in 1799. He went out as a missionary for the London Society in 1816 and worked for fifty-four years in Bechuanaland and adjacent territories: he had to retire in 1870, but lived until 1883. John Brownlee, another Scot, went as a missionary to Kingwilliamstown in 1820. In direct

[1] John Bond, *They were South Africans* (O.U.P., 1956), 80.

succession to Moffat was the most famous of all Scottish missionaries and explorers, David Livingstone (1813–73), who married Moffat's daughter and was influenced by his father-in-law to go out to Africa under the auspices of the London Missionary Society. Livingstone's explorations were designed to find routes through the continent and to make possible the suppression of the slave trade. He was the discoverer of many parts of the interior, especially in the south central area, which subsequently attracted a great deal of British investment and even settlement. John Mackenzie, born on Speyside in 1835, served under Moffat and afterwards became British commissioner in Bechuanaland. A later Scottish missionary is another of those heroic figures which were always held up as examples to the older generation of Scottish children—Mary Slessor, the Dundee mill-girl, who educated herself so that she might be fitted to go out to Old Calabar under the auspices of the United Presbyterian Church in 1876. After Nigeria became a colony, Mary exercised considerable influence and held office as an administrator. She died in 1921. All in all, Africa was perhaps the greatest of all Scottish mission fields: the Free Church, besides being active in Zululand, founded the first mission station on Lake Nyasa in 1875 and named it Livingstonia; the Church of Scotland soon afterwards established a station in the Shiré Highlands, 350 miles south of Livingstonia, and called it Blantyre, after Livingstone's birthplace; the United Presbyterian Church, as already mentioned, was active in Nigeria; and the Scottish Episcopal Church chose as its field Kaffraria. These were by no means the limits of Scottish missionary operations, and Scotland played its part in the conversion of the many millions of the natives of all parts of Africa who now profess Christianity. According to a recent estimate, there are 150,000 Presbyterians in Nyasaland and Northern Rhodesia, 80,000 in the Congo, 53,000 in Ghana, 25,000 in Kenya and 15,000 in Nigeria.

Glasgow merchants had long been alive to the possibilities of expanding their commerce as Africa was opened up by exploration, for in 1820 they were talking of schemes for trade in northern Africa as the Niger was explored.[1] Then, as early as 1840, the dual concept of missionary and commercial enterprise in Africa had taken shape in the minds of men in Glasgow: 'Instead of forest depths . . . may the thronged city, the busy wharf, the crowded street be hereafter seen . . .; instead of . . . the clank of chains . . . there may be heard the voice of prayer, the sound of praise and the sweet music of the

[1] Melville Castle Muniments in Register House, 2/619.

"church-going bell" '.[1] Livingstone's own belief was that Christianity and commerce would together introduce civilization to Africa and its peoples. Consequently, many of Livingstone's fellow-countrymen were ready to follow up the more secular aspects of his work. The African Lakes Company was founded in 1878 by Glasgow commercial magnates, some of them associated with the Free Church. Its motto was 'to advance the kingdom of God by honest trade', and the community which developed under its auspices, with commercial and missionary work running parallel, has been compared to the state organized by the Jesuits in Paraguay. Somewhat similarly, Sir William Mackinnon (1823–93) and other Scots founded the British East Africa Company.

[However, apart from exploration and missionary work, there were enterprising Scots who were ready to settle in South Africa as soon as it passed into British hands. Indeed, some who were in the ranks of the army which conquered it from the Dutch themselves remained as colonists. Robert Hart, a native of Glasgow, was an eighteen-year-old private in the British force which occupied Cape Town in 1795. After seven years there, he served elsewhere for a time, but returned in 1807 as an officer, with his wife and child, and settled in the colony, where he pioneered the breeding of merino sheep. He lived until 1867. Other Scots besides Hart settled in South Africa after campaigning there, just as they had done in the United States and Canada. Among them was G. A. Lucas, a survivor of the *Birkenhead* disaster of 1852; he became chief magistrate of Durban.

It appears, however, that the ubiquitous Scottish trader or 'merchant' was ready to set up business in South Africa, as in so many other parts of the world, as soon as it passed under the British flag, for one John Murray had a store at Mossel Bay as early as 1803 and David Hume was one of the first traders to venture far beyond the borders of the Colony. The first suggestion for organized emigration from Scotland to South Africa seems to have come from John Graham, a cousin of Lord Lynedoch, who had himself become acquainted with the territory in his military career. Graham landed at Cape Town as an officer in 1806, but he married a descendant of one of the original Dutch settlers and, although he himself died early, in 1821, his descendants played prominent parts as officials in South Africa. It was in 1812 that Graham suggested the settlement of five hundred highland crofters in South Africa.

After the end of the war with France, in 1815, South Africa shared

[1] Saunders, *Scottish Democracy*, 393.

to a small extent in the wave of emigration which at that time carried so many Scots to Canada and Australia. Benjamin Moodie, of Melsetter in Orkney, had been an early British settler and had acquired a large estate in the Swellendam district. When he was in Scotland in 1817 he conceived the idea of bringing out a labour force from Scotland, partly at his own expense, on condition that the men would indenture themselves to him for three years, and he took back with him to the Cape about 200 young lowland Scots under these conditions. In 1818 two other Scotsmen, Tait and Goslin, organized a similar venture. These first Scottish labourers and artisans did well, and wrote home favourable accounts which stimulated Scots to join in the larger movement which was organized by the government in 1820. The motives which prompted government interest at this point were similar to those which prompted its similar interest in Canada in the same period: that is, there was an alien white population, in this case the Dutch, whom it was desirable to counterbalance by British settlers, and there was a frontier to be defended against possible attacks, in this case from the natives. In 1819, therefore, parliament voted £50,000 to aid emigration to South Africa, and it was provided that settlers would have 100 acres of land, free of rent for ten years. Newspaper advertisements brought twenty times as many applicants as there were places. Some 3,000 to 4,000 settlers were sent out, mainly to the present Albany district, where they were intended to act as a defence against native attacks, but they encountered so many difficulties and discouragements that many of them subsequently withdrew to Cape Town. It was intended that a substantial number of Scots should be included in this settlement—one Captain Grant was supposed to be bringing 400 families from the Highlands—but in the end not many were. For one thing, the *Alcoma* (320 tons), which sailed from the Firth of Clyde in October 1820, with about 200 persons on board, caught fire when near the Equator and was burned out with heavy loss of life. It says much for the determination of some of the emigrants that five men and one woman among the survivors did make their way to South Africa later; the persistent five were John McLaren, joiner, John McLean, turner, James Clark, merchant, Robert Thomson, bricklayer, and Thomas Reid, lawyer. Other Scots who were designated for the settlement withdrew, and it was only a small party of just over twenty persons which actually landed at Simon's Bay from the *Brilliant* on 30th April 1820 and settled in the present Bedford district, north of Albany. Among those 1820 settlers from Scotland were Robert Pringle and his four sons, one of whom was Thomas Pringle, a poet and author of a *Narrative of a Residence in South Africa*. The Pringles and others gave names to their farms like 'Glen Lynden', 'Haining' and 'Eildon'.[1]

After these beginnings, South Africa was always the objective of a certain number of emigrants, but for a long time the movement was no more than a trickle, and an intermittent one at that. In 1824 a handful of British colonists established themselves in Natal, which was proclaimed a British colony in 1843 and declared independent of the Cape in 1856. When an interest in Natal first began seriously, in 1848, among the Scots who were involved were Hugh MacLean, proprietor of the island of Coll, who sent his eldest son out to prospect, Patrick Maxwell, who had estates in Hampshire, and William Schaw Lindsay, a native of Ayrshire who had become a shipbuilder in London. A party of 127 emigrants sailed from Glasgow in 1849. They found that they were not quite the first Scots to arrive, because Hugh MacDonald was already in charge of a hotel in Durban, and inland there was John Anderson, who had come from Auchterarder some years earlier. Most of the Scots who went to Natal about 1849 were from the Clydeside area, but there was a sprinkling from the east of Scotland as well. John Smith came from Montrose, William Taylor from Kincardineshire and W. M. Collins from Edinburgh. William Mackenzie, the son of an Edinburgh lawyer, arrived in Natal in 1850 and married Isabella Trotter, the daughter of a West Lothian farmer who had taken his family out to the colony; they settled at 'Cramond'. There were a few colonists from the Highlands — Donald MacArthur from Argyll and Duncan Mackenzie from Loch Awe, William Campbell, born in Ireland of Scottish stock, was a pioneer of the sugar-beet industry. As in New Zealand about the same time, there was a certain Free Church element in the movement. Charles Scott, minister of Peterhead, had joined the Free Church and lost his charge, and when he emigrated to Natal in the *Unicorn* in 1850 there were other Free Church people with him, including William Campbell, who had been Free Church minister at Alexandria.

In the 1840s the operation of the Wakefield system benefited South Africa to some extent by bringing out labourers, mechanics and servants: in 1841 there were only fifty-five immigrants from Great Britain, but there were 1,342 in 1849 and 1,037 in 1850, and

[1] Colin T. Campbell, *British South Africa* (1897), gives the names of the 1820 settlers and has a biographical note on Thomas Pringle.

from 1846 to 1851 over 4,000 persons in all went out. Further provision was made in 1857, and in 1858 Cape Colony voted funds to assist immigrants; as a result a further 10,000 persons were introduced over a period. In 1858 the *Gipsey Bride* brought to Cape Town 515 people, men, women and children, chiefly from Dumfriesshire. The year 1859 saw a record number of immigrants to the Cape, and government aid continued until 1862. But on the whole the appeal of South Africa was limited, partly because there was little scope there for the unskilled labourer or for anyone intending to farm on his own account on a small scale: the demand was for settlers with capital, who could employ native labour on farms of substantial size.

It was, therefore, not until late in the nineteenth century that South Africa became a significant field for British colonization, in comparison with other parts of the world. But between 1893 and 1907 it surpassed Australia and New Zealand and between 1895 and 1898 it even surpassed Canada. One reason for the sudden influx of Britons was the discovery of mineral wealth: diamonds were first discovered in 1866, in the Hopetown district, not far from Kimberley, and the gold rush to the Rand, in the Transvaal, was at its height in 1886. Johannesburg originated with the gold rush, and one of the earliest settlers there, when the place was no more than a site, with posts and pegs marking out where streets were to be, was a Scot named Marshall. And among the earliest gold-miners in the Transvaal were two Scots—James Sutherland, who had previous experience in California and Australia, and Thomas MacLachlan. The discovery of gold in the Transvaal happened to coincide with a depression in Australia and the United States. The end of the South African War (1899–1902), which made the whole of South Africa British, further encouraged immigration from Britain, and there were plans to encourage British migration to counterbalance the Dutch, but they were not very successful and there was a depression from 1904 to 1910.

Consequently, the English-speaking South Africans never numbered much more than 1,000,000, so that they formed the smallest English-speaking community in any British Dominion—smaller even than that in New Zealand. The Scottish element was, however, proportionately conspicuous here as elsewhere. The population of Scottish birth in 1904 was 41,227 and in 1921 it was 35,867—more than twice that from Ireland and nearly a third that from England. Yet the total number of Scottish settlers, among Dutch as well as English and Irish, was too small to make a very marked impression as a community. Thus there are not many Scottish place-names, except for one group (Lovedale, Balfour, Burnshill and Pirie) deriving from the names of founders and officials of the Glasgow Missionary Society, and another group (Murraysburg, Sutherland, Fraserburg, Robertson and McGregor) deriving from the names of ministers. Bains Kloof commemorates a Scottish road-builder. Caledon is not of Scottish origin, but is named after the Earl of Caledon, an Irish peer who was governor of Cape Colony from 1807 to 1811. Equally, South Africa can show nothing like the number of Scottish societies which appear in other regions which have been colonized. Like the societies in Australia, which originated in the same period, they favour the designation 'Caledonian'. They do extend beyond the provinces which formed the Union of South Africa, into the Rhodesias and other parts of the continent, but they are strongest in Johannesburg.

The pattern of Scottish achievement differed little from that in other areas. There was an unusual ecclesiastical situation, in that the Dutch Reformed Church in South Africa had theological affinities with the Scottish Presbyterian churches and after 1816 it received ministers from Scotland for a couple of generations. Dr. George Thom was the first Scottish pastor in the Dutch Church (1812) and soon he was followed by others—Andrew Murray, Alexander Smith, John Taylor, George Morgan, Henry Sutherland and Colin Fraser. The first Scottish Presbyterian church in Cape Town was opened in 1829, under the ministry of James Adamson, who had been sent out from Scotland in 1827. In 1850 churches were established in Natal and subsequently in the Orange Free State and the Transvaal, and in 1890 work was begun in Rhodesia. In 1897 all these congregations were united to form the Presbyterian Church of South Africa, with seven presbyteries. There are now over 250,000 Presbyterians in the Union of South Africa, more than half of them coloured.

The Scottish contribution in the field of education, stemming from missionary zeal on one hand and the alliance with the Dutch Church on the other, was conspicuous. One of Pringle's 1820 party, William Elliot, started a school in Cape Town in association with A. Duncan, very soon after he arrived in South Africa. James Rose Innes, son of a farmer in the shire of Banff and a graduate of Aberdeen University, was appointed the first Superintendent General of Education in Cape Colony in 1821 and arrived in 1822 in company with other Scots—Archibald Brown, also an Aberdeen graduate, William Robertson, an Aberdeen undergraduate, William Dawson, an elementary teacher, Robert Blair, another teacher from Glasgow, John Tudhope, also a teacher, and one Rattray from Dundee. In 1841 Innes brought out another seven teachers from Scotland. He worked as Superintendent until 1859. The South African College was founded at the Cape in 1830 by the Reverend James Adamson, already mentioned, and James Fairbairn, another Scot, born at Legerwood in 1794. J. R. Innes was associated with them too. A schoolmaster named MacDonald was one of the victims of a massacre by the Matabele in 1836.

The Scottish contribution to South African education has continued in later times in a variety of ways. There were individual teachers, like John C. Rae, who was born at Dundee in 1874 and emigrated to South Africa in 1899 to pursue a career of remarkable versatility, as artisan, teacher, farmer and journalist and in the end to become mayor of Albany, and James McLean, who was born in Stranraer in 1878 and went to South Africa in 1907 to serve for twenty-five years as a schoolmaster and to finish up as a member of a city council and a member of parliament. There was also significant Scottish interest in the education of the coloured population. Dr. James Stewart took an early lead in the campaign to provide opportunities of higher education for the Bantu. As a result of his representations, it was recommended in 1905 that a college be established, and the United Free Church offered a site at Fort Hare, where a university college developed. Lovedale, eighty miles inland from East London, was the site of a station founded by the Glasgow Missionary Society in 1824 and became a great Presbyterian theological college. In recent times, several Scots have attained distinction in South African universities: William G. Grant, born at Glenlivet in 1873, went to South Africa in 1904 and was Professor of Gynaecology in Witwatersrand University from 1921 to 1938; and Arthur W. Falconer, born in Stonehaven in 1880, went to South Africa in 1920 and became first of all Professor of Medicine and later Vice-Chancellor and Principal of the University of Cape Town.

It was a Scottish immigrant, George Greig, who was the first private printer in South Africa, and, as editor and proprietor as well as printer, produced the first independent South African newspaper, the *South African Commercial Advertiser*, as early as 1824. Soon he was joined by two compatriots, Thomas Pringle, the poet, who had previously edited *Blackwood's Magazine*, and John Fairbairn. Like many Scots elsewhere, they were critical of the government, and had a five years' struggle, ultimately successful, to establish the freedom of the press. John Sanderson, who sailed from Glasgow in 1849, became at first a contributor to the *Times of Natal*, and later established and edited the *Natal Colonist*. He had, so it was remarked, 'the character of seldom agreeing with anybody about anything'.[1] Among later Scottish immigrants who made their mark on South African journalism were Charles D. Don, born in Bridge of Allan in 1874, who became editor of the *Times of Natal*, the *Rhodesia Herald* and the *Star* (Johannesburg); Bryce Boyd, born in Greenock in 1863, who was a journalist at home before going to South Africa to serve the *Natal Advertiser*, the *Gold Fields Times*, the *Johannesburg Times* and other papers; and Robert Allister, a native of Dunfermline, who went to South Africa in 1902 and joined the staff of the *Cape Times*.

Then there were the civil engineers. Andrew Geddes Bain was born at Thurso in 1797 and went out in 1816, presumably with Lieutenant-Colonel Geddes, a relative of his mother, when Geddes was returning to the Cape, where his regiment had been stationed since 1811. Bain became a noted road-builder, and died in 1864.[2] John Milne, a civil engineer in Edinburgh, went out to Natal at the age of fifty and in 1851 began to improve Port Natal. His work was abandoned after a time, but it was later continued by two other Scots, Edward Innes and Cathcart William Methven. The latter, born in Edinburgh in 1849, was Engineer in Chief to the Natal Harbour Works from 1888 to 1895 and was also consulted by Cape Colony and by the Portuguese government. If Scots thus contributed to the roads and the harbours of South Africa, they played a great part in the development of its railways as well, as railway managers and locomotive designers. They were also conspicuous as builders and contractors: Alexander C. Bell, who was born in Glasgow in 1860 and went to Natal in 1876, is only one example among many.

Several Scots became successful farmers, sometimes after earlier experience elsewhere. John Shedden Dobie had one of the more remarkable careers. He was born in 1819 at Beith, in Ayrshire, and sailed from Leith for Melbourne in 1839. There he entered into partnership with John Hunter Kerr in the establishment of a sheep-run, but returned home for the period 1844–50. In 1851 he was attracted to California by the goldfields, but took to trading in the Pacific and then made his way to the gold-workings in Victoria in 1852. Ten years later he settled in Natal, where he pioneered sheep-

[1] Alan F. Hattersley, *The British Settlement of Natal*, 184.
[2] Bain's *Journals* were edited by M. H. Lister for the Van Riebeck Society in 1949.

raising. George Shearer Armstrong was born in Victoria in 1855, but at the age of six his parents moved to Natal, where he became a farmer.

John L. Bisset, born at Pitarrow, Kincardineshire, in 1872, emigrated at the age of eleven, became a farmer and finished up as director of a creamery and owner of a cheese factory and a cattle ranch in Rhodesia. Others, like John S. Clark, who emigrated in 1914 at the age of eight, dealt in land as estate agents. One of the many lines of business in which Scots were active was shipping: Alexander Burness, born at Montrose in 1846, was a master mariner who settled in Natal in 1890 and became Deputy Shipping Master at Durban; Alexander McCulloch Campbell, born at Greenock in 1879, went in 1903 to South Africa, where he joined the staff of the Union Castle Company and was ultimately their chief agent in South and East Africa. But business of all kinds seems to have been a fruitful field for the type of Scot who went to South Africa, and an examination of a South African *Who's Who* discloses a very large number of successful Scottish business men and an astounding number of company directorships in Scottish hands.

There were also, as ever, professional men who took their skill from Scotland. South Africa seems to have been a happy hunting-ground for solicitors in particular, perhaps because Roman-Dutch law has close affinities with the Scottish system: examples are William M. Cameron, who was born at Fochabers in 1864 and went to Natal in 1889; John Gordon, born at Dumfries in 1869, who went to Natal in 1904; John Duthie, born in Aberdeenshire in 1881, who emigrated in 1904 and ultimately became a senator in South Africa; and John Fraser, an Edinburgh graduate in law, who settled in Natal in 1889. The allied fields of insurance and banking also provided careers for a great many Scots: Archibald C. Duff, born at Burntisland in 1865, is an example of a banker and P. A. Anderson, who was born in Perthshire in 1878 and emigrated to Natal in 1904, was one of the many who were in the insurance business. A less common form of work was taken up by David Hamilton, who was born in Ayrshire in 1847 and went out to Natal in 1877, and his son William, born in Durban in 1879; they were both hotel managers in Durban. Other Scots showed their ability in minor, but profitable, kinds of trading: W. M. Anderson, who was born in Perthshire in 1875 and was taken to Natal at the age of seven, and Richard Hall, who was born at Rutherglen in 1896 and went to South Africa in 1926, were examples of chemists; and James McLaren, born at

Blairgowrie in 1880, emigrated when he was twenty-three to Johannesburg, where he set up a hardware business.

Scots played a far less prominent part in political affairs and government in South Africa than in the other Dominions where they settled. But one notes Sir William Arbuckle, who was born at Larbert in 1839 and emigrated in 1849 and became agent general for Natal, and Thomas Hyslop, born in Ayrshire in 1859, who was Treasurer of Natal in 1903. Some Scots gave very useful service in local government. Angus McLeod, for instance, who was born at Tain in 1866 and emigrated in 1893, was a town councillor in Somerset West for thirty-six years. Robert Jameson was a town councillor of Durban for thirty years and mayor from 1895 to 1897. An unusual example of the transfer of experience in local government from the home country to a colony is to be found in the career of David Walker. Born at Cupar in 1868, he was Deputy County Clerk of Fife before emigrating to Natal in 1897; in his new home he became Town Clerk of Port Elizabeth (1902) and of Maritzburg (1905).

Reference was made at the beginning of this chapter to Scottish missionary effort in the Nyasaland area and to the foundation of the African Lakes Company. In the course of time the missionaries asked for British protection, partly as a precaution against the possible assertion of Portuguese sovereignty, and a British protectorate was declared in 1891, so that here, as in New Zealand, the flag followed the Bible. But it was also, of course, following trade, and in 1893 the African Lakes Company, which had done a certain amount to introduce river and lake navigation and to create roads but had been incompetently managed, was replaced by the much more businesslike African Lakes Corporation. In East Africa, too, the flag followed trade, and the territories developed by the British East Africa Company became ultimately the colonies of Kenya and Uganda.

The British South Africa Company was chartered in 1889 to operate in what became Rhodesia. Leander Starr Jameson, born at Edinburgh in 1835, was a friend of Rhodes and became managing director for the Company in Mashonaland and administrator of Matabeleland. Jameson's famous 'Raid', in 1895, was intended to overthrow the Boer government of the Transvaal in the interests of the British settlers there. In 1923 Southern Rhodesia was annexed to the crown and responsible government was introduced; and in 1924 Northern Rhodesia became a protectorate like Nyasaland.

Southern Rhodesia had gold, which attracted many of the 13,000 settlers who were there by 1898. In the course of time other minerals, and agriculture, including the cultivation of tobacco, broadened the economy, but in 1914 the total number of white settlers was still only 34,000. In Northern Rhodesia, where the white population was only 3,634 in 1921, copper was a source of wealth which in time led to considerable development, and in 1951 there were 37,221 Europeans. The entire white population of Nyasaland even in 1945 was barely 2,000. These areas are clearly of negligible importance as outlets for Scottish emigrants.

13

EMIGRATION SINCE THE FIRST WORLD WAR

THE vast movement of people outwards from Scotland, throughout many generations and to many parts of the world, has been traced in the preceding chapters down to the period of the First World War. Since then the migration has shown no signs of being permanently arrested, though its volume has fluctuated considerably.

In the years just after the First World War, conditions were such as to stimulate emigration on an unprecedented scale. It may be that all that was wrong at the time was that a period of adjustment had to intervene before Scottish industry was adapted to the new pattern of the world's economy. Certainly some time was bound to elapse before Scotland could recover stability after the dislocation of war-time, when so many men had been withdrawn from industry and so many factories turned over to the making of munitions, and before she could re-enter markets which had perforce been given up when the whole economy of the country had been directed to the immediate needs of the campaigns. But the attitude of the depressed sections of the community, and especially of the unemployed, was one of bitter disappointment and resentment. During the war, support for the allied cause, whether in the field or in the factories, had been stimulated by idealistic slogans about 'a war to end war' and 'a war for democracy', and promises had been made that when peace came Britain would be 'a land fit for heroes to live in'. That conditions after 1918 fell far short of the expectations thus aroused would be a gross understatement. Consequently, there was no likelihood that people would listen to explanations or wait patiently for the situation to improve. This was the background to a new phase of emigration from Scotland, far exceeding anything known earlier. In ten years, 1921–31, nearly 400,000 people left the country. The figure was not far short of double the average number which had emigrated in previous decades, as the following statistics show:

1881–91	217,418
1891–1901	53,356
1901–11	254,042
1911–21	238,587
1921–31	391,903

Owing to the outbreak of the Second World War in 1939 there was no census in 1941, but all the indications are that between 1931 and 1939 the loss of population was undoubtedly smaller than in many previous decades, for the depression in the United States at the beginning of that period drove many Scots home again, and during the 1930s the economic situation in Scotland itself improved slowly but perceptibly. After the Second World War, there was not the disillusionment which had followed the First, because more realistic views prevailed, but the continuation for many years of rationing and controls, a sense of restriction, frustration and lack of opportunity, diminished the attraction of Britain as a homeland. The spectacular rise in the standard of living, which produced the 'affluent society' of recent years, and the humdrum security provided by the 'welfare state', did little—or, at any rate, not enough—to offset the attractions held out by other lands. The National Insurance provisions made in the United Kingdom have recently been a certain disincentive to emigration in the minds of the more prudent or cautious, whereas a few years ago the superior terms offered by New Zealand were a positive magnet. The net loss[1] between 1931 and 1951 was of the order of 200,000, and most of it took place in the years after 1945, when the average annual figure was about 24,000. This, added to the net loss for the period 1901–31, meant that the loss for the first half of the twentieth century exceeded 1,100,000.

'No country on the continent of Europe,' it has been said, 'has lost such a high proportion of her people as Scotland.'[2] The phrase is carefully chosen, for 'the continent of Europe' excludes Ireland, which suffered more heavily than Scotland in the nineteenth century; but even with this qualification the assertion is sufficiently striking.

[1] That is, the difference between the natural increase, or excess of births over deaths, and the recorded increase in the population from one census to the next.
[2] Kyd, *Scottish Population Statistics* (Scot. Hist. Soc.), xxii.

Within the island of Great Britain itself the contrast was a sharp one, as can be shown by setting down the net loss, as a percentage of the whole population, for England (with Wales) and Scotland:

	England	*Scotland*
1901–11	1·5	5·7
1911–21	1·7	5·0
1921–31	0·5	8·0

During the third of those decades Scotland's loss was no less than sixteen times that of England. The contrast is shown equally by two other facts. Between 1931 and 1951 England had a net gain of 1·8 per cent whereas Scotland again registered a net loss, this time of 4·5 per cent. The other fact is that in 1931 there were in England itself no less than 366,486 people who had been born in Scotland.

That last fact means, though it is barely credible, that in the half century or so before and after 1900, when such vast numbers of Scots had been finding their way overseas, a greater number had actually settled in England than even in the United States. For the United States the figure was 354,323. The United States were conspicuously the greatest overseas magnet in the 1920s, despite the check imposed by the quota system which the American government operated in virtue of measures passed in 1921 and 1924 and the complaints about the manner in which emigrants were held up on the threshold of the States, on Ellis Island. The bulk of the emigrants were, of course, from the industrial (and depressed) belt of central Scotland, but it is curious and significant that once again, as in the eighteenth and early nineteenth centuries, some emigrant ships were sailing direct from the outlying parts of the country. In 1964 a press report drew attention to the return from America of a native of Lewis who had left the island on the *Canada* for the States in 1924 and now, after forty years absence, was setting foot on the mainland of Scotland for the first time. In that peak decade of Scottish emigration, 1921–31, there were actually more Scots than English entering the United States, although the population of England was about eight times that of Scotland.

Since the Second World War, the numbers of Scots emigrating to the United States have been relatively small—a total of 22,471 from 1951 to 1957 and some 3,000 to 4,000 in each year since—but even at those figures the movement is not insignificant.

From Britain as a whole, the rate of emigration was conspicuously lower after the First World War than it had been before 1914, and the British Empire's share in the emigration was spectacularly lower: in 1913 the balance outward to the Empire had been 223,521, whereas in 1924 it was only 88,913 and in 1925 fell even lower, to 62,886. So far as Scotland was concerned, after the United States—and England—it was Canada which received the largest share of Scottish emigrants: in 1931 the number of people in Canada who had been born in Scotland was 279,765. To Canada, as to the States, there was direct shipment of emigrants from the western isles: in 1923, 300 persons left Stornoway on the *Metagama*, for Ontario, where each man was to have 160 acres of land. Migration to the western provinces of the Dominion, checked first of all by a deterioration in their prosperity in 1912–13 and then (like all emigration) by the First World War, resumed once the post-war depression in Canada was overcome, from about 1924 onwards. But all parts of Canada, and perhaps not least Ontario, have continued to attract Scots between the wars and since World War II.

Canada was one of the Dominions which participated in a scheme, after World War I, for providing free passages for ex-service men and women and for widows and dependents (under which, between 1919 and 1922, a total of 86,000 persons were sent to Australia, Canada, New Zealand and South Africa at a cost to the British government of £2,500,000), and also in the provisions of the Empire Settlement Act of 1922, as a result of which an overall total of about 300,000 Britons were assisted to emigrate to Canada, Australia and New Zealand. Under this Act, Canada undertook to provide free transportation for children emigrating under the auspices of a recognized Child Migration Society and to provide reduced fares for men who had farming experience or were nominated by friends or relatives in Canada for agricultural employment, and also for women with household experience. In 1924, moreover, the British and Canadian governments undertook to advance funds for the settlement of 3,000 British families on farms of their own in Canada, and in 1927 Canada called for 14,000 farm workers, about half of them experienced, to whom cheap travel rates were offered. British immigrants to Canada numbered from about 40,000 to over 70,000 each year from 1920 to 1929, and in a period when Scottish agriculture was seriously depressed after the boom conditions of war-time there were farm-workers available to take advantage of the Canadian offers. After 1930 the movement became negligible until after the Second World War.

Organized child-migration, especially to Canada, began in the last quarter of the nineteenth century and by 1925 nearly 80,000 children had been sent out, 29,000 of them by Barnardo's Homes. Under the Empire Settlement Act the Imperial and Dominion governments contributed to the costs incurred by the societies. Some of the Canadian provincial governments had schemes for training boys immigrating for farm work. Among the organizations concerned with the emigration of children, there were some specifically Scottish. There was the Craigielinn Boys' Training Farm, which could train 100 boys a year and test them with a view to their emigrating to Canada and Australia as farm workers. The Church of Scotland training farm at Cornton Vale, Stirling, could also deal with 100 each year. The Orphan Homes of Scotland at Bridge of Weir and the Aberlour Orphanage were also recognized as juvenile emigration societies and the former was arranging the emigration of over 100 children a year even before 1914.

Australia's interest was not radically different from Canada's. After the First World War the Australian government assisted persons interested in farm work and domestic service, and granted reduced fares to persons whose friends or relatives in Australia undertook to find employment and accommodation for them, but there was still a degree of suspicion towards artisans, lest they should 'dilute' the labour market in the Commonwealth, and in 1927 Australia's policy became less liberal. In 1925 the British and Australian governments had concluded a Migration and Settlement scheme to aid the settlement of a total of 450,000 emigrants from the United Kingdom. Under the Empire Settlement Act, Australia promised assisted passages to persons selected by the Department of Migration and Settlement or nominated by persons already resident in Australia. Australia was, if anything, even more interested in youthful immigrants than Canada was, with a view to settling them on the land, and the well-known Big Brother Scheme began in 1924. From 1924 to 1928 the British emigrants to Australia numbered from 30,000 to 40,000 annually, but the figure then dropped to 19,000, 8,000 and (from 1931 to 1938) an average of 4,000.

Even before the end of World War II, the Australian and British governments agreed to continue the schemes for assisted passages. The British government, indeed, was less enthusiastic than before, because the low birth-rates of the 1930s had caused a certain dearth of young workers to serve Britain itself; but the Australian government, on its side, was more anxious than before for British settlers, after its experience of the peril from Japan during the war. There was no lack of eagerness among the British people, for half a million of them soon applied for assisted passages, but the British government felt it had to impose certain restrictions, there was for some time a shortage of shipping, and Australia did not want a tidal wave of immigrants to overwhelm its standard of living. All in all, no more than about 40,000 to 50,000 British immigrants a year could be conveyed and accepted, and between 1949 and 1951 the number of assisted immigrants to Australia from the United Kingdom (120,000) was exceeded by the number of displaced persons entering Australia from the continent of Europe (157,000).

In New Zealand, schemes of assisted immigration had been in force since 1871, except between 1892 and 1903. After World War I provisions for assistance were similar to those provided by Australia; under the terms of the Empire Settlement Act, assisted passages were provided for persons selected by the High Commissioner or nominated by residents in New Zealand, but there were specially generous terms for boys under nineteen and single women under forty, both of which classes received free travel. To New Zealand there were in all about 37,000 immigrants in 1921-4, nearly all of them British, and about 40,000 in 1925-30, but after that, as elsewhere, the stream dried up. The total number of assisted immigrants to New Zealand, from the earliest times to 1924, was 195,208. So far as Scotland has been concerned, the appeal of New Zealand appears to have been especially strong since the Second World War.

In South Africa, the 1820 Memorial Settlers' Association was formed after the First World War, to settle British people in South Africa. Applicants had to possess at least £1,500 if single and £2,000 if married, unless they were fully trained farmers, who required to have only £600. The Association made advances to settlers to enable them to acquire land and stock and equipment, and also established training farms. Southern Rhodesia was included in the scope of its operations. South Africa decided not to operate the Empire Settlement Act, and stated more than once that 'the limited field for white labour in South Africa precludes co-operation by the Union Government on the lines contemplated by the other Dominions'. A land settlement scheme under the Empire Settlement Act was, however, operated in Southern Rhodesia, providing for the placing of settlers possessed of £500 to £1,000 capital, on farms, after training. However, as the Union of South Africa came to be more and more dominated by the descendants of the Boers, it became less attractive to

Britons, and, after the Second World War, when the South African government's policy towards the coloured peoples aroused widespread criticism and, in the end, caused South Africa to secede from the British Commonwealth, few Scots have found their homes in the Union. The numbers of Scots entering and leaving the Union as migrants were as follows:

	Immigrants intending permanent residence	*Residents departing permanently*
1952	1,121	259
1953	790	274
1954	623	355
1955	504	383
1956	586	357

And, of course, for Africa generally it is true that the attainment of independence by what were formerly colonies, and the proclamation of various African nationalisms, has led to a kind of flight from Africa on the part of white settlers.

14

SCOTLAND'S GREATEST EXPORT—MEN

DURING many centuries there has not been a decade when Scotland has not exported some of her people. They have gone from every part of the homeland, they have settled in all parts of the world. A movement so vast in scope, so prolonged in time and so complex in its nature will clearly not admit of a single or a simple explanation. Certain elements can be discerned easily enough, among them what can be described in one word as frustration, for many of the Scots who emigrated had in one way or another been frustrated at home and left Scotland almost as an act of protest. The frustration could take many forms: it might be ecclesiastical, as in the seventeenth-century settlements of Presbyterians in New Jersey and South Carolina and to some extent both in some of the emigration of the Highlanders in the late eighteenth century and in the emigration of members of the Free Church in the nineteenth; it might be social, as it was with the eighteenth-century tacksmen, and with the later artisans who sought a more egalitarian society than they had at home; or economic, with tenants who complained of high rents, weavers whose labour could no longer yield a living wage, and the unemployed of the 1920s; or political, with radicals in the 1790s and Chartists in the 1840s. But with many, from the earliest times onwards, the frustration was less specific and perhaps less articulate: the energetic Scot who felt that there was no outlet for his vitality at home had become a soldier of fortune on the continent of Europe in earlier times and was to become an eager and restless colonist later. The wanderlust which had affected medieval Scots and which caused many later emigrants to move from one settlement to another, from one continent to another, was one symptom of the super-abundant energy for which Scotland offered too little scope.

The Scots who have left their homes have not all done so with a view to settling down to a new life in some far country. All through the generations and centuries, Scots have continued to seek fortunes and careers abroad, as they did in the Middle Ages, without neces-sarily contemplating permanent settlement, and in the last two or three centuries many of them have made their mark in parts of the world which have not been areas for white settlement or colonization at all.

One of their great fields of activity was India, as long as that great sub-continent was subject to Britain. It is often believed that the employment of Scots in India dates largely from the time of the Scot Henry Dundas, who was a member of the Board of Control for India from 1784 to 1801 and who had the reputation of placing many of his fellow countrymen in lucrative positions. Sir Walter Scott referred to the India Board as 'the corn chest for Scotland, where we poor gentry must send our youngest sons, as we send our black cattle to the south'. But, although Dundas did appoint many Scots, the em-ployment of Scots in India went back before his time.

Among the many books which reflect the habitual Scottish pride of family there is a publication, *Records of Clan Campbell in the Military Service of the Honourable East India Company* (1925), con-taining over 250 names. The earliest biographical note in it is that of an Alexander Campbell, who was a sergeant in 1704 and an ensign in 1708; and there are at least four others before the middle of the eighteenth century—Donald Campbell, a second lieutenant in 1741, John, a captain in 1748, Charles, of Barbreck, a lieutenant in 1749, and Peter, an ensign in 1749. In the second half of the century, and leaving the many Campbells aside, we find Charles Grant, born in 1746. He made a large fortune in the service of the East India Com-pany, was a member of the board of trade at Calcutta in 1787 and chairman of the directors of the Company in 1805; characteristically for a Scot, he was much concerned for the building of churches and schools in India and also in the home country. Sir John Macpherson, Grant's junior by one year, was a writer in the service of the Com-pany at Madras from 1770 to 1776, a member of the council at Cal-cutta in 1782 and governor-general of India from 1785 to 1786. Jonathan Duncan (1756–1811) was resident and superintendent at Benares in 1788 and governor of Bombay from 1795 to 1811. There were Scots who made a fortune by commerce, like Sir Charles

Forbes (1774–1849), who was head of the first mercantile house in Bombay, and John Farquhar (1751–1826), who was ranked as a millionaire after a career which started as a cadet in the Bombay establishment. The military tradition, of service as soldiers in the pay of the Company, is illustrated not only in the volume on the Campbells already referred to, but also in the careers of Sir Hector Munro (1726–1805), who routed an alliance of Hindu princes at Buxar in 1764, ensured British sovereignty over Bengal, Behar and Orissa and captured Pondicherry in 1778; Sir Eyre Coote (1726–83), who became commander in chief in India in 1777 after long service there and in 1781 routed Hyder Ali; and Sir David Baird (1757–1829), who served in India for over twenty years and is best known for his successes against Tipu Sahib in 1798. Alongside the achievements of the military conquerors must be set the remarkable contribution to the extension of British power made by a Scot, Hugh Cleghorn, who was not by profession a military man at all but had been professor of Civil History at St. Andrews University. In a career worthy of a John Buchan novel, Cleghorn secured the defection from the Dutch of the mercenary troops who were holding Ceylon, and his astuteness led to the almost bloodless conquest of the island. As long as there was conquest or re-conquest to be done in India, Scots had a hand in it: Sir Charles Napier (1782–1853) was the conqueror of Sind in 1843, and Sir Colin Campbell, Lord Clyde (1792–1863), was mainly instrumental in suppressing the Indian Mutiny in 1857. Nor did the succession of prosperous Scottish merchants fail: an outstanding example in the twentieth century was Sir David Yule, who was reputed to be worth £20,000,000 when he died in 1928.

But the adventurous and profit-seeking Scot was ubiquitous, and turned up in much less likely places than India. George McGhee Murdoch, born at Greenock in 1857, was a sickly child, and at the age of twelve, on medical advice that a sea-voyage might do him good, he was sent as captain's boy in a barque sailing for New Zealand. As he was very badly treated, he deserted at Auckland and found a job on a barquentine trading to the Marshall and Gilbert Islands. In the Gilberts he was taken charge of by a store-keeper. He married a native girl and set up his own business, very successfully, in Abemama. As he had become very influential, he had much to do with the establishment of a British protectorate over the islands, and under it he ultimately became Resident Commissioner.[1]

---

[1] Arthur Grimble, *A Pattern of Islands*, chapter 9. Robert Louis Stevenson was not favourably impressed by Murdoch, as he makes clear in *From the South Seas*.

Almost everyone has heard of Sir James Brooke, who established a dynasty of 'white rajahs' in Sarawak. But his career was paralleled, on a smaller scale, by John Clunies Ross, an early nineteenth-century native of Shetland. At first he served as a seaman on a Greenland whaler, but after some years became a trader in the South Seas. There he entered into partnership with an Englishman, Alexander Hare, who had served with the East India Company, and together they decided in 1825 to take possession of the Cocos-Keeling Islands which at that time were a kind of no-man's-land. Ross was much more energetic than his colleague, who ultimately retired to Singapore, leaving Ross to develop the resources of the islands, which he did with great success: he grew crops, raised livestock, started a fishery and even went in, successfully, for boat-building. In 1829 he was described as 'a most intelligent, honest and well-informed British sailor, with a most hospitable wife and a fine family of children'.[1] Ross died in 1854, to be succeeded by his son, and when the islands were proclaimed British territory Ross the younger became official Governor. He married a native woman of royal blood, but had his six sons educated in Scotland and visited Scotland himself in a schooner which had been built in his own shipyard. His eldest son in turn succeeded, and died in 1910, worth £207,000 exclusive of his properties in the Cocos-Keeling Islands. The group of islands later came under the authority of the Governor of the Straits Settlements, but the ownership and local superintendentship remained with the family of the original 'king'.

On yet another island, less remote than the South Seas, a family of Scots left their mark and their name. William Reid, of a Kilmarnock family, was sent abroad with £5 in his pocket to look for a climate suited to his poor health, and eventually landed at Madeira, where in 1836 he started work as a baker. In a dozen years he had established his own hotel, and after his death his sons founded the world-famous Reid's Hotel.

The motives which shaped the careers of such adventurers obviously stimulated some of the emigrants too, but whereas these adventurers were individualists, emigrants very often were not. The sense of community among so many Scots, and the readiness of Highlanders at least, in earlier times, to accept, or submit to, leadership, contributed to the making of emigration the mass movement it became. The 'epidemic' character of emigration, the snowballing effect which is discernible from time to time, were fostered by the

[1] Quoted by W. Fordyce Clark, *The Shetland Sketch Book* (Edinburgh, 1930), 138.

cohesion of the family, of the kinship group, of the local community. Yet, by something of a paradox, the individuality and initiative which were acquired by lowland Scots earlier than by Highlanders contributed to their success as colonists, and the powers of individual judgment which had been fostered by the Scottish ecclesiastical situation undoubtedly helped to shape that individuality and initiative. Among other characteristics which contributed to the Scots' success was the capacity for hard work which had been the response to challenging conditions at home. Somewhat remarkable was the industry displayed by Highlanders when they had opportunities to work under less dispiriting weather conditions and a less relaxing climate than they had to endure at home. The contrast was noted by an observer of the way in which the pioneering life in Cape Breton seems to have brought out the best in the Highlanders: 'Their industry from the first was notable in a people whose whole past was a negation of it. The Highlander who had mostly watched his women-folk sow and reap his miserable crops, became an accomplished axeman when confronted with Nova Scotian forests, and an industrious tiller of the soil he had cleared.'[1] In 1803 the Lieutenant-Governor of Upper Canada was informed by the Secretary of State for the Colonies that the Glengarry Highlanders who now proposed to settle in Canada 'would no doubt prove as valuable settlers as their connections now residing in the District of Glengarry, of whose industry and general good conduct very favourable representations have been received here'.[2] Another testimonial to the success of the Highlanders in Canada was given in 1852 by 'an intelligent public officer who has lately returned after sixteen years service in Canada, where he was much brought into connection with the highland settlers'; he wrote: 'Of all the several classes of poor emigrants who have for years past settled in Canada, none have been more successful than the inhabitants of Scotland in placing themselves not to say above want, but absolutely in a state of independence which would not be credited by those who have seen them only in the contracted sphere of operations where they have been brought up.'[3]

It was also true—and again it is something of a paradox—that the Scot, angular and rugged as he may be in his individuality, was often remarkably adaptable and ready to assimilate himself and conform to a new community in which he settled. And, despite his heritage of

[1] A. G. Bradley, *The United Empire Loyalists* (London, 1932), 163.
[2] Quoted in S. J. Johnson, *Emigration from the United Kingdom to North America*, 7.
[3] Highlands and Islands Emigration Society, Letter Books, i (6th July 1852), in H.M. General Register House, Edinburgh.

bitter division on ecclesiastical and political issues at home, he could be remarkably tolerant of the ways of others. The egalitarianism of Scottish society helped Scots to accept peoples of various social backgrounds, and it has been suggested that the existence in Scotland itself of two races and two languages made Scots less sensitive than many Europeans to differences of race and colour and therefore readier to establish and maintain good relations with natives. It was certainly true that with their broader and less insular outlook than the English they had the advantage that they did not regard all ways of life other than their own as necessarily backward or barbarous.

All in all, the success of the Scots abroad was not exaggerated by Sir Charles Dilke when he wrote: 'In British settlements, from Canada to Ceylon, from Dunedin to Bombay, for every Englishman that you meet who has worked himself up to wealth from small beginnings without external aid, you find ten Scotchmen.'[1] He also observed that in South Australia 'as in America, it is found that the Scotch and Germans are the best of immigrants. The Scotch are not more successful in Adelaide than everywhere in the known world. Half the most prominent among the statesmen of the Canadian Confederation, of Victoria and of Queensland, are born Scots, and all the great merchants of India are of the same nation. . . . Wherever abroad you come across a Scotchman, you invariably find him prosperous and respected'.[2] And, when the record of success abroad is viewed in relation to the frustration at home which led the migrants overseas, one is bound to agree with Dilke's further comments: whereas the Irishman crosses the seas 'in sorrow and despair', the Scot does so 'in calculating contentment'; and, he concluded, 'The Scotch emigrant is a man who leaves Scotland because he wishes to rise faster and higher than he can at home'.[3] The suggestion here is that over-abundant vitality had a lot to do with the whole movement.

Enough has been said in the preceding chapters to indicate the pattern of the contribution of the Scots to the life of the countries in which they settled—in the church, in education, in politics, in journalism, in management, craftsmanship and farming—and it has emerged that the emigrants took overseas not only their strong arms, their capacity for application and their intelligence, but also a stock of acquired skill in both industrial and professional life. To that extent they have enriched the United States and the great Dominions.

[1] Sir Charles Dilke, *Greater Britain* (1888), 525.
[2] *Ibid.*, 365–6
[3] *Ibid.*

With all their successes, in so many walks of life, the impression the Scots have made on the new English-speaking nations overseas has been curiously limited. They exported their ecclesiastical institutions, mainly for themselves, and they have preserved, again mainly among themselves, many of the trappings of Scottish, and more particularly highland, ways of life. But the law and the civil institutions of nearly all the communities overseas are essentially English and are assuredly never Scottish. Here the Scots' capacity for assimilation comes in: when transplanted from his homeland he seems to find no difficulty in accustoming himself to unfamiliar terms and institutions: he lives in towns which have 'mayors' and conducts his affairs according to a legal system in which every proceeding in the work of solicitors and the work of the judicature is radically different from those known in Scotland.

Whatever impression exiled Scots made on the communities overseas of which they became members, it must be true that the great migration had many effects on the Scottish homeland. It is obvious that the steady drain of manpower, often of individuals possessed of initiative and skill, was a clear loss, and it must be kept in view in any attempt to assess the reasons for the failure of Scottish inventiveness and enterprise in the twentieth century to equal the standards of the nineteenth. Equally, the heavy loss of men of working age aggravated the imbalance of the population which the lower birth-rate of the twentieth century produced, and meant that a heavy burden of maintaining the aged fell on an inadequate number of persons in their prime. It has also been pointed out that in a society which lays out enormous sums on the education and care of young people, the money expended on the early years of those who emigrate is sheer financial loss; it has been calculated that the amount so spent in the case of any individual is in the region of £2,500 and that, consequently, the emigration of even 20,000 people in a year represents a loss of no less than £50,000,000.[1] In earlier generations, the cost of educating a Scottish child was, of course, much lower, but it does seem hard that Scottish taxpayers and ratepayers should have incurred such enormous expenditure to equip citizens for other lands.

There are few material gains to set against such conspicuous losses, though no doubt many emigrants have sent remittances home to their parents or other kinsfolk, while others, on their visits home, have spent in Scotland a small proportion of the money they have

[1] J. G. Kyd, in *The Scotsman*, 4th March 1957.

earned overseas. Not many of the exiles have ever returned permanently, though a goodly proportion have announced their intention of doing so. One forcible expression of the intention to return came from Dr. David Monro after he had been in New Zealand for seven years: 'I have never entertained the idea of making this country my permanent home—God forbid: I loathe the place';[1] but he stayed in the colony for life. Yet occasionally an emigrant, or the second or third generation descendant of an emigrant, has returned, either to work or to retire. Few seem to return permanently from the United States (where, of course, a change of nationality is involved) and not many from either Canada or Australia. South Africa has been in a different position, for many seem to have regarded it as a place in which to make money rather than a place in which to settle for life, and they have returned to Scotland, in much the same way as wealthy planters and merchants came back from the West Indies and India to acquire estates in Scotland in earlier times. It seems, too, that it has been relatively easy for descendants of settlers in New Zealand to return and seek their careers in Scotland, perhaps because the way of life in that Dominion is not so different from that at home. Not a few of them rediscovered their ancestral home when they came on service during the First World War, and did not settle in New Zealand again. An outstanding example was Major-General David Carmichael Monro, a grandson of Sir David Monro, the New Zealand doctor, sheepfarmer and politician. He served in the R.A.M.C. in France in the First War and finally settled in London, though he gave medical service in India from 1918 to 1928 and in the Middle East during the Second War.[2] But, although New Zealanders have found it specially easy to return to Britain, some of the most famous men who have returned have come from Canada. Andrew Bonar Law was born in Canada of Scottish parents and returned to Britain, where he became prime minister of the United Kingdom. And there has been a recent example of a Scottish Canadian's career which has a certain appropriateness in view of the Scottish emigrants' connection with the newpaper world in so many countries: Roy (now Lord) Thomson, the great-great-grandson of Archibald Thomson, who went out from Dumfriesshire to New York State in 1773 and settled in Ontario in the early years of the nineteenth century, has in recent years built up a remarkable press empire in his ancestral

---

[1] Rex E. Wright-St. Clair, *Doctors Monro* (London, 1964), 129.
[2] *Cf. Gallipoli to the Somme: recollections of a New Zealand infantryman;* the author, A. C. Aitken, became Professor of Mathematics at Edinburgh University.

country. In the previous generation, William Maxwell Aitken, son of a Scot who settled in New Brunswick, became a leading figure in British journalism as Lord Beaverbrook.

There have certainly been some non-material gains to Scotland. Standards of general knowledge have been raised, and the stay-at-home's outlook has been widened, by the constant familiarity of Scots with the doings of their kinsfolk in far-off lands. To some extent, the European and non-insular outlook of the medieval Scot is paralleled by a cosmopolitan and equally non-insular outlook in recent generations. When one reads that, of the twelve sons of a miner employed in a colliery in Kilmarnock in 1845, six had emigrated to Canada (where one was a shipping agent in Montreal) and six to Australia, one realizes something of the force of the links between Scotland and a wider world.

It would have been surprising if it had not become common for the descendants of Scottish emigrants to attempt to trace their ancestry. In earlier times, Europeans of Scottish descent not infrequently wrote home for evidence of noble or gentle origins, so that they could matriculate arms in the country of their residence, and in more recent generations colonists or their descendants have continued to show curiosity about their Scottish origins. Among the enormous amount of pedigree-hunting which has been conducted among the Scottish records by generations of searchers a very large proportion has been on behalf of clients overseas. Scottish historians often, with reason, bewail the dearth of Scottish record material, and it is true that the medieval records suffered severely both because of English invasions and because of inadequate provision for their care in peaceful times. Yet Scotland is by no means ill supplied with the kinds of records which are helpful in ancestry research. Under the care of the Keeper of the Records of Scotland in the (old) Register House there are the Records of Testaments, going back in many cases to the sixteenth century and often giving particulars of the marriage and children of Scots of all ranks; there are the Services of Heirs, which preserve the succession of families holding lands of the crown and of many other persons as well; there is the remarkable Register of Sasines, which records the history of all transactions in heritable property—not only land, but houses and flats as well—since 1617, and incidentally often contains material enabling the inquirer to trace relationships; and the equally remarkable Register of Deeds, which contains copies of innumerable legal documents of all kinds, concerning Scotsmen of all social classes, from the sixteenth century onwards. In the custody of the Registrar General for Scotland in the New Register House there are the Parochial Registers of Baptisms, Marriages and Burials going back in a few cases as far as the sixteenth century, and also the Registers of Births, Marriages and Deaths which have been compiled since 1855, and these records are perhaps the most popular, at least as a starting point, with pedigree-hunters. It is, however, right to warn any inquirer that there are many gaps in those records, and also that unless he can give fairly precise information about an ancestor in Scotland it may be impossible to commence a search on his behalf. Searching had been done by professional searchers for a great many years before the foundation, after the Second World War, of the Scots Ancestry Research Society, a non-profit-making organization, which has accumulated considerable expertise in its work and is being used more and more by the overseas descendants of Scots. Recently the Society has been receiving more than 1,000 inquiries in a year, and the number of inquiries from overseas is, on an average, about double the number received from people in the United Kingdom. Among the overseas inquirers, citizens of the United States lead by a wide margin and indeed substantially exceed the total from other countries overseas. Inquiries from Canada are slightly more numerous than those from Australia and New Zealand together, inquiries from Africa and elsewhere are very few. The figures naturally bear a certain relation to the distribution of Scottish emigrants, but on a close analysis the surprising fact might emerge that Scottish Canadians show less curiosity about their ancestors than do the descendants of Scots in Australia and New Zealand.

Possibly the most revealing source to illustrate the constant contacts of emigrant Scots or their descendants with the home country is to be found in the pages of Scottish local newspapers. One takes up a copy of the *Oban Times*, shall we say, at random, and finds paragraphs about a visit of John Thomson, who, after an exile of forty years, was welcomed on his arrival from New York by his brother, a former provost of Oban, and about a visit by Mr. and Mrs. Angus Currie, from Vancouver, who were seeing their homeland again after thirty-five years. Or one takes up two successive copies of the *Shetland Times* and finds items like the following. William Nicolson, formerly of Sandwick, who emigrated to New Zealand in 1938 with his wife, is now making his first visit home. In New Zealand he was at first in the merchant navy, and then started a painter's business, which has grown until he has a staff of sixteen. John W. Gilbertson, who emigrated to Canada forty-two years ago, is also paying his first return visit to his native islands. He was a car-driver in Shetland, and is still a taxi-driver, now in Vancouver. 'Scotty Brown', a native of Dunfermline, emigrated to the States in 1923. He was at first an interior decorator, but has latterly been proprietor of the Brae Loch Inn, in New York State, a restaurant with a Scottish flavour and with a gift shop which sells Shetland knitted goods among other things. Mr. F. W. Gordon, a native of Bressay, emigrated to New Zealand in 1936. He visited Shetland in 1953, and worked his passage back as a deck-hand; later he became a merchant navy officer. His son is now harbourmaster at Greymouth, New Zealand, a position in which he had been preceded by another Shetlander. Miss Jemima Taylor left Shetland with her brother Alexander in 1923 and has now returned from Pittsburgh for a visit. Her brother Alexander settled ultimately at Toronto, and other members of the family are in Los Angeles and New Zealand. Such news items are in themselves mere *personalia*, but it is significant that the newspapers consider it worth-while to record them. And it is the total of literally millions of such individual pieces of information which make up the vast history of Scottish emigration.

APPENDIX A

BIBLIOGRAPHY

It is odd that no previous attempt has been made to give a general
account of a subject so important in the history of the Scottish nation and
in the history of the English-speaking countries. Andrew Dewar Gibb's
Scottish Empire (London, 1937) is deceptively named, for it deals mainly
with the careers of individual Scots explorers, soldiers and administrators
in the British Empire but hardly touches on the mass movements which
did so much to make that Empire largely Scottish. Besides, many of the
substantial and standard histories of the British colonies and dominions
have little to say of immigration at all, and simply take for granted the
influx of people which formed the nations of which they write. The
Cambridge History of the British Empire, for example, is almost useless for
the study of emigration. Consequently, pending the completion of a vast
amount of original research, the history of Scottish emigration can be
gleaned in the main only from stray references in a large number of books
which are concerned principally with other subjects. Some of the more
highly specialized works which have yielded scraps of information are
referred to in the footnotes of this book, and those which can more
profitably be consulted at length are mentioned below.

Among the books which do deal specifically with emigration, the following are important: W. A. Carrothers, *Emigration from the British Isles*
(London, 1929)—a good general survey; Stanley C. Johnson, *Emigration
from the United Kingdom to North America* (London, 1913)—an important
and comprehensive study; Edwin C. Guillet, *The Great Migration*
(Toronto, 1937), which surveys 'the Atlantic crossing by sailing-ship since
1770' on a substantial scale and has many illustrations; and Helen I.
Cowan, *British Emigration to British North America* (Toronto, 1961),
which is especially strong on conditions on emigrant ships.

On the subject of Scots abroad in the period before colonization outside
Europe began, there is source material in *Papers illustrating the History of
the Scots Brigade in the service of the United Netherlands* (3 vols., Scottish

History Society) and *Papers relating to the Scots in Poland* (Scottish History Society). The subject of *The Scot Abroad* is surveyed generally but inadequately by J. H. Burton (Edinburgh, 1881), and there are the following special studies: Francisque Michel, *Les Ecossais en France, les Francais en Ecosse* (2 vols., London, 1862); W. Forbes-Leith, *The Scots Men-at-Arms and Life-guards in France* (2 vols., Edinburgh, 1882); T. A. Fischer, *The Scots in Eastern and Western Prussia and Hinterland* (Edinburgh, 1903), *The Scots in Germany* (Edinburgh, 1902) and *The Scots in Sweden* (Edinburgh, 1907). There is also a pamphlet by A. I. Dunlop on *Scots Abroad in the Fifteenth Century* (Hist. Ass.), and an important article by James Dow on '*Skotter* in Sixteenth-Century Scania', in *Scottish Historical Review*, xliv. Some information about Scots in England is collected by G. Donaldson, 'Foundations of Anglo-Scottish Union', in *Elizabethan Government and Society* (Ed. S. T. Bindoff *et al.*, London, 1961). The authorities on the Scots settlement in Ulster are George Hill, *The Plantation of Ulster* (Belfast, 1877), and John Harrison, *The Scot in Ulster* (Edinburgh, 1888).

On Scottish efforts to found a colony of their own in America, we are fortunate to have two authoritative works by George Pratt Insh, *Scottish Colonial Schemes* (Glasgow, 1922) and *The Company of Scotland* (London, 1932). On the compulsory emigration of indentured servants, some useful information is brought together by Abbot Emerson Smith, *Colonists in Bondage* (University of North Carolina Press, 1947). George S. Pryde has some interesting things to say in *The Scottish Universities and the Colleges of Colonial America* (Glasgow, 1957). An article by J. H. Soltow on 'Scottish traders in Virginia, 1750–75', in *Economic History Review*, 2nd ser., xii, 83, is important.

The best background reading for the causes of highland emigration is Malcolm Gray, *The Highland Economy* (Edinburgh, 1957), and the most recent account of Scottish economic developments in Highlands and Lowlands alike is R. H. Campbell, *Scotland since 1707* (Oxford, 1965). Some attention has been paid to the eighteenth-century emigrations from the Highlands, in Henry Hamilton, *Economic History of Scotland in the Eighteenth Century* (Oxford, 1963), but most recent writers owe a great deal to the articles by Margaret I. Adam in *The Scottish Historical Review* ('The Highland Emigration of 1770', in vol. xvi, and 'The Causes of the Highland Emigrations of 1783–1803', in vol. xvii). Duane Meyer, *The Highland Scots of North Carolina, 1732–66* (Oxford, 1961), broke new ground.

On Scottish settlement in the United States there is background material in W. S. Shepperson, *British Emigration to North America* (1957), which deals mainly with official policy, and reference should be made to Edith Abbott, *Historical Aspects of the Immigration Problem* (Chicago, 1926); Ian Charles C. Graham, *Colonists from Scotland* (Ithaca, 1956), deals with emigration to North America from 1707 to 1783. T. J. Wertenbaker's lecture on *Early Scottish Contributions to the United States* (Glasgow, 1945) is very slight. The 'Scotch-Irish' have been the subject of a good deal of writing: Charles A. Hanna, *The Scotch-Irish* (New York, 1902); James G. Leyburn, *The Scotch-Irish* (Chapel Hill, 1962), which deals with the settlement of Ulster as well as the migration to America, but is rather superficial; Charles K. Bolton, *Scotch-Irish pioneers in Ulster and America* (Boston, 1910), an account of the migration from Ulster to America; and Wayland F. Dunaway, *The Scotch-Irish of Colonial Pennsylvania* (Univ. of N. Carolina, 1941). Rowland T. Berthoff, *British Immigrants in Industrial America* (Harvard, 1953), works out the place of Scots in America's industrial economy in the nineteenth century and is a model of the kind of study which is much required for other countries and periods. Thomas D. Clark, *Frontier America* (New York, 1959), gives some information about Scots in the Middle West, and P. A. M. Taylor, *Expectations Westward* (Edinburgh, 1965), which deals with the Mormons, has some information about Scots. On American Scots who have achieved some distinction, George F. Black, *Scotland's Mark on America* (New York, 1921), is little more than an annotated list, but behind it lies the *Dictionary of American Biography*. Black had been anticipated to some extent by W. J. Rattray, *The Scot in British North America* (4 vols., 1880), which gives much information about Scots who made their mark on the colonies before the War of Independence and thereafter deals with Canada.

On Canada generally, the standard large-scale history is A. Shortt and A. G. Doughty, *Canada and its Provinces* (23 vols., Toronto, 1913–17), from which a good deal can be gleaned about Scottish settlement. The best general account of the migration from the United States to Canada after the American War of Independence is A. G. Bradley, *The United Empire Loyalists* (London, 1932). Norman MacDonald, *Canada, 1763–1841: Immigration and Settlement* (London, 1939) is concerned mainly with official policy and political issues. The account of the Highlanders of Cape Breton by Charles Dunn in *Highland Settler* (Toronto, 1953), is to be compared with the account of the Scots on Lake Erie by John K. Galbraith, *Made to Last* (London, 1964). Gerald M. Craig, *Upper Canada* (Oxford, 1963), a well-told and well-illustrated narrative, and Edwin C. Guillet, *Early Life in Upper Canada* (Toronto, 1964), a lengthy and detailed work, deal generally with a province in which Scots were very important. The best book on Lord Selkirk is John M. Gray, *Lord Selkirk of Red River* (London, 1963). W. L. Morton, *Manitoba: a History* (Toronto, 1957), gives some information about the part played by Scots in the development of that province. For biographical studies of prominent Canadian Scots there is W. L. Grant, *Makers of Canada* (12 vols., revised edn., Oxford, 1926); vol. 12, which developed out of an index to the whole work, forms the *Oxford Encyclopaedia of Canadian History.* James H. Walker, *A Scotsman in Canada* (London, 1935), is an autobiography of an emigrant of 1923 who came back to Scotland in disillusion. James A. Roy, *The Scot and Canada* (Toronto, 1947), is an essay on the Scottish background rather than a contribution to the history of Scottish settlers in the Dominion.

For Australia, R. C. Mills, *The Colonization of Australia: the Wakefield Experiment in Empire Building* (London, 1915), is the most authoritative account of the Wakefield system. Stephen H. Roberts, *The Squatting Age in Australia,* 1835–47 (Melbourne, 1935, 2nd edn. 1965), deals with the many Scots who pioneered the expansion of New South Wales into the western lands, and T. M. Perry, *Australia's First Frontier* (London, 1964), is a more geographical account of the same movement. Frank Clune, *The Saga of Sydney* (Sydney, 1962), is helpful on Scots in Sydney. An outstanding book is Margaret Kiddle, *Men of Yesterday* (Melbourne, 1961), a detailed account of the early Scottish settlers in Victoria, their way of life and their influence on the colony. *Annabella Boswell's Journal* (ed. Morton Herman, Sydney, 1965) describes the life of Scottish settlers in New South Wales in the 1830s and 1840s, and David S. Macmillan wrote on 'The Scottish Australian Company' in *Scottish Historical Review,* xxxix, 16–30. *The Dictionary of Australian Biography* was edited by Percival Serle in 2 volumes (Sydney, 1949).

J. S. Marais, *The Colonization of New Zealand* (Oxford, 1927), is concerned only with the early period. A. H. McLintock, *The History of Otago* (Dunedin, 1949), and A. H. Reed, *The Story of Early Dunedin* (Wellington, 1956), are indispensable, the latter for its graphic account of the voyages to Dunedin as well as of the settlement. The story of the final settlement of Norman MacLeod's people in New Zealand is told by N. R. McKenzie, *The Gael fares Forth* (Wellington, 1935). G. H. Scholefield. *A Dictionary of New Zealand Biography* (2 vols., Wellington, 1940), is the standard work for biographies.

Colon T. Campbell, *British South Africa* (1897), deals in detail with the 1820 settlers. Alan F. Hattersley, *The British Settlement of Natal* (Cambridge, 1950), has a very good chapter on 'Scotland and Emigration to Natal'. John Bond, *They were South Africans* (Oxford, 1956), is an examination of the British contribution to the growth and development of the Union and refers to many Scots.

On emigration after the First World War, much useful information is collected in John Marriott, *Empire Settlement* (London, 1927), and R. S. Walshaw, *Migration to and from the British Isles* (London, 1941).

SOME MANUSCRIPT SOURCES

A BRIEF account was given in chapter 14 of those Scottish official records which are especially of value for descendants of Scottish emigrants who wish to trace their ancestry. There is also in the Register House a considerable amount of material relating to emigration and to Scottish interests overseas, and the Curator of Historical Records has provided me with the following information. Further details are available in duplicated Lists of Manuscripts relating to the United States and Canada, Africa, Australia and New Zealand.

Among the voluminous Unextracted Processes of the Court of Session there are thirty-four account books relating to the management of plantations in Virginia and Maryland, 1750–1817, and four letters in which Sandeman, an emigrant to the U.S.A., described his experiences in 1882. Far more conspicuous in this archive group are papers relating to Scottish investments in America, Australia and New Zealand, in connection with the following companies: Arizona Copper Company, Dominion of Canada Mortgage Company, Dominion Bank of Toronto, Bank of London in Canada, Matador Land and Cattle Company, New York Central and Hudson River Railway Company, Prairie Cattle Company, Scottish American Investment Company, Scottish American Mortgage Company, Scottish Manitoba and N.W. Real Estate Company, Scottish Mortgage and Land Investment Company of New Mexico, Scottish Ontario and Manitoba Land Company, Scottish Pacific Coast Mining Company, Swan Land and Cattle Company, Texas Land and Cattle Company, Western Ranches Ltd., Australian Mortgage Company, Mortgage Company of South Australia, New Zealand and Australian Land Company, New Zealand Meat Preserving Company, Scottish West Australian Land Syndicate, Scottish and New Zealand Investment Company. Further investigation in this vast accumulation of papers would undoubtedly reveal more material of this nature.

The 'Register House Series' includes a Report on the Australian Company of Edinburgh, 1845.

The Forfeited Estates Papers relating to the Lochiel estate forfeited after the 1715 rebellion contain papers relating to an estate in New Jersey claimed to have belonged to Cameron of Lochiel, 1713–25.

As already mentioned in chapter 5, the books of the Highlands and Islands Emigration Society are in the Register House, and include a list of the emigrants sent out under the Society's auspices.

The Church of Scotland Records contain several references, particularly in the eighteenth century, to the Scottish Presbyterian Congregation of New York, and Minutes of various African presbyteries are also included in this series.

Apart from the official records which owe their origin to government departments and similar bodies, the Register House now contains a great many collections of private papers which have been deposited by their owners and which are open to historical searchers in the same way as official records. The various collections which contain material relating to emigration are listed below in alphabetical order, with Scottish Record Office references attached.

Society of Antiquaries (GD. 103). Papers relating to the shipping of Highlanders to America after the Forty-five. They were indentured to Samuel Smith, merchant in London, who assigned them to John Hanbury for shipment to the American colonies to serve him for seven years and on discharge to remain in America. There are the signatures of 125 Highlanders.

Aitchison (GD. 1/92). Letters regarding the emigration to Canada of James Aitchison, son of William Aitchison, brewer in Edinburgh, and his life there and in the United States, 1834–8.

Barclay Allardyce (GD. 3). Account of the family and descendants in America of John Barclay, born 1702.

Bertram of Nisbet (GD. 5). Letter from George Bertram at Philadelphia asking for copy of family coat of arms and giving information about his birth and career, 1 March 1760.

Breadalbane (GD. 112). Petitions from inhabitants of North East Hope (Huron Tract, Upper Canada), township of Osgood (Ottawa District) and Reach (Canada West), asking, as former tenants of Lord Breadalbane's estates, for donations towards the erection of churches, 1835–6, 1848. Copy 'Great encouragement to Plowmen to go to America', 1802. Memorandum by William Young concerning the services of his father and himself in Nova Scotia, 1857. Letters relating to government policy in Australia, 1841, and New Zealand, 1845.

Broughton and Cally (GD. 10). Letters regarding emigration to America, early eighteenth century.

Buchanan of Leny. Memorandum on New Zealand as a suitable place for British settlement, *c.* 1815–23.

Bught (GD. 23). Five letters from Alexander Macrae concerning his journey to Virginia, 1804–5. Letter from George Ramsay, Albany, New York State, recounting his career since arriving in New York in 1794, 12th May 1810.

Campbell of Jura (GD. 64). Papers relating to emigration, 1853. Papers relating to William Cadell, late of New South Wales, 1840–42. Letters from Victoria, Australia, 1835–61.

Clanranald. Letters relating to emigration from Clanranald lands, including Benbecula, 25th February 1827.

Clerk of Penicuik (GD. 18). Nine letters from Savannah in Georgia, relating to trade with and emigration to the colony, 1727–48 (5360). Letters from Alexander Gordon, secretary to the Governor of South Carolina, 1741–7 (5023). Letter from John Campbell to Sir George Clerk of Penicuik relating to a memorial from the Glasgow magistrates on emigration, 11th February 1840 (3392). Rules issued by the Colonial Land and Emigration Commissioners, with despatches to the governors of Jamaica and Trinidad and memorandum on immigration into the West Indies, 18th May 1846 (3825). Letters relating to the settlement in Australia and Canada of sons of Sir George Clerk of Penicuik, 1844–60 (5591–5608).

Cuninghame of Thorntoun (GD. 21). Letters from George Wrey describing travels in America and elsewhere, his orange groves in Florida, plans to cultivate vines in California, sheep farming in New Zealand, 1876–83. Letters from Christian Cuninghame, on life in Australia, 1846–54.

Dalguise (GD. 38). Journal of a voyage from Leith to Cape of Good Hope, 1829.

Dalhousie (GD. 45), including papers of James Glen, Governor of South Carolina, and the papers of the 9th Earl of Dalhousie as Lieutenant Governor of Nova Scotia and Governor-in-Chief of Canada. Three volumes of plans of townships in Upper and Lower Canada, 1824 and n.d. (8). List of land grants in Nova Scotia passed between 1st January 1819 and 1st January 1820 (45). Memorandum on proposed new settlements in the district of Gaspé, May 1821 (68). Two letters from Robert Lamond, in Glasgow, on the subject of emigration, 15th June and 27th August 1821 (71). Ten letters from Lieutenant-Colonel William Marshall, mostly from Perth, Upper Canada, with lists of families in Huntly, Ramsay, Lanark, Packenham and Goulbourne in 1828 and papers concerning a public library for Dalhousie, 1824–8 (140). Letter from Donald McGregor in St. Andrews, seeking a place in Canada to settle twenty or thirty families of Highlanders, 5th November 1826 (169). Five letters from John Galt in Quebec, Guelph and London concerning schemes of colonization, 1828 and 1833 (226). Letter from John D. McConnell, in Gaspé, concerning a machine, invented by John McKay, a blacksmith in Pictou, for extracting stumps of trees from the ground, 26th October 1826 (449). Five letters from Robert Burns in Paisley, secretary of the society for promoting the moral and religious interests of the Scottish settlers in British North America, 1825–30 (481). Two letters from Dr. Andrew Brown, in Edinburgh, concerning education in Nova Scotia, in particular the proposed Dalhousie College and parish schools, 24th June and 3rd August 1818 (498). Letter from George Robertson at the General Register House concerning the flags, banners and insignia being made for the St. Andrew Society of Montreal, 1st October 1835 (606).

Dunlop, James (GD. 1/151). Letters from Canada to his family in Glasgow, 1773–1815, concerning material on trade with the U.S.A. and the war of 1812.

Forglen. Letters from James Abercrombie, an Episcopalian clergyman in America, regarding his ancestors in Dundee and his family in America, 1852.

Fullarton of Kilmichael (GD. 1/19). Papers regarding the claim of James Fullarton, Manchester, New Hampshire, to succeed to Kilmichael estate, 1889.

Inglis (GD. 1/46). Papers of John Inglis, sutler and merchant in New York, 1777–87.

Irvine-Robertson. Two certificates relating to Robert Stewart, a prisoner taken at Preston and sent to America, 17th October 1716 and 3rd May 1717.

Kinross House (G.D. 29). Letters from John Kennewie, clerk of Culross, referring to provision of women to be shipped to America, 1669.

Leven and Melville (GD. 26). Petition by Francis Makemie, minister in Virginia, 1689.

Lindsay. Letters and papers relating to John Lindsay (*d.* 1751), his land near Albany in New York State, his appointment as Lieutenant-Governor of Oswego and the efforts of his kinsfolk in Scotland to gain possession of his lands in America.

Logan Home of Edrom. Letters from Charles Home, merchant in New York, 1730–39. Letter from Patrick Home in Virginia regarding his proposed sale of Rappahannock Forge, 1796.

John MacGregor Collection (GD. 50). Instructions for James Campbell from Lord Neil Campbell and Robert Blackwood, elder, for the sale of property in East New Jersey, *c.* 1690. Three letters from James McGowan, Richmond, Virginia, relating to costs of carts, ploughs, etc., his work and wages and Scottish friends there, 1818–19.

Melville Castle (GD. 51). This collection includes papers of Henry Dundas, Viscount Melville, who held several offices of state at the end of the eighteenth century and the beginning of the nineteenth and had such complete control of government business and patronage in Scotland that suggestions and applications of every kind were apt to reach him. Letters relating to the colony of New South Wales, 1792, 1793 (1/479, 1/481/1–4). Memorial relating to a proposed settlement on the coast of Africa, 1793 (1/485). Letter relating to colony of Cape of Good Hope, 1795 (1/505/1–2).

Letter on emigration to America, 1795 (1/492). Applications for employment, referring to emigration to Canada, the West Indies and New South Wales, 1792–1828 (6/972, 6/1157, 6/1395, 6/2284). Requests for passports for intended emigration to America by Thomas Walker, saddler in Dalkeith, and Alexander Young, formerly a builder in Edinburgh, 1795 (1/492, 495).

Monro of Allan (GD. 71). Letters from Frank McKenzie, woollen manufacturer, Woodstock, U.S.A., regarding his wish to import sheep and cattle into America and the possibility of his relations joining him, 1875–1882.

Murray of Lintrose (GD. 68). Letters and papers relating to land in the Murray district, Western Australia, 1837–70, and to the settlement there of several members of the Murray family.

Riddell. Papers relating to Drummond Riddell, member of the Executive Council of New South Wales, 1848–54.

Seaforth (GD. 46). Letters on emigration to the Cape, 1819 (17/vols. 51, 53). Letters relating to highland emigration, 180 (17/vol. 23). Letters relating to recruiting by Hudson's Bay Company in Stornoway and emigration from Lewis, 1828–35 (1/530). Papers relating to emigration from Highlands and Islands to North America and Australia, with printed pamphlets published by the Commissioner for Emigration and forms of application, 1831–47 (13/184, 197, 206). Letter from the Duke of Hamilton requesting investigation of injustice done to Highlanders in Canada, 1834 (11/5). Memorial regarding the religious state of highland emigrants in Cape Breton, 1834, with correspondence relating to the establishment of Presbyterian ministers in the island, 1834–5 (11/7–9). Papers relating to emigration to America from Seaforth estates, 1835–6 (1/391). Letters relating to emigration from the Highlands and Lewis, 1837–41 (9/6).

Yule (GD. 90). Marriage contract of John Greenlees, merchant in Virginia, 1753.

INDEX